Penned from the Heart

Volume XX

Compiled and Edited by
Marilyn Nutter

Son-Rise Publications and Distributing, Inc.
51 Greenfield Road
New Wilmington, PA 16142

A Word from our Publisher

This 2014 Edition of Penned from the Heart features thoughts, spiritual insights, and Godly devotionals by people from all walks of life, all ages, and from all over the world. Not all of our writers are professionals, but everything written here has been sincerely "penned from each loving heart" to the glory of God. A list of our authors and the location of their devotions is found at the end of the book.

It is our prayer that all who read this book will find the way to eternal life with Him in Heaven, and abundant life while here on earth.

Florence W. Biros

Scripture references are from the following versions of the Holy Bible: King James Version (KJV), New King James Version (NKJV), New American Standard Bible (NASB), The Living Bible (TLB), New International Version (NIV), Revised Standard Version (RSV), New Revised Standard Version (NRSV), The Message, Jerusalem Bible, James Moffatt Translation, Amplified Bible, New Century Version (NCV), English Standard Version (ESV), Holman Christian Standard Bible (HCSB), New Living Translation (NLT), New English Bible (NEB), Today's English Version (Good News Bible) (TEV/GNB), Berkeley Version, New American Bible (NAB). The Holy Bible, New King James Version ©1982 by Thomas Nelson. New American Standard Bible ©1977 by The Lockman Foundation. The Living Bible ©1971 by Tyndale House Publishers. New International Version ©1987 by New York International Bible Society. Revised Standard Version ©1952 and New Revised Standard Version ©1989 by Division of Christian Education of the National Council of Churches of Christ in USA. The Message ©2002 by NavPress Publishing Group. Jerusalem Bible ©1968 by Doubleday & Company, Inc. James Moffatt Translation ©1994 by Kregel Publications. New Century Version ©2006 by Thomas Nelson, Inc. English Standard Version ©2005 by Crossway Bibles. Holman Christian Standard Bible ©2003 by Holman Bible Publishers. New Living Translation ©2004 by Tyndale House Publishers. New English Bible ©1970 by Oxford University Press & Cambridge University Press. Good News Bible (Today's English Version) ©1976 by American Bible Society. Amplified Bible ©1965 by The Lockman Foundation. New American Bible ©1969 Catholic Biblical Association.

Son-Rise Publications
51 Greenfield Road
New Wilmington, PA 16142
© 2014 Son-Rise Publications
All rights reserved
Printed in the United States of American
ISBN: 978-0-936369-52-5

Cover photo by Randy Nutter,
courtesy of Marilyn Nutter

A note from the heart of the editor…

When Florence Biros asked me to serve as editor for the 20th edition of *Penned from the Heart*, I was humbled at her invitation. She included the words, "I know you are supposed to do it. I think you need it." I was puzzled by the comment that I "needed" it, but as the months followed, it was obvious that I did.

In December, 2011 my husband Randy went to be with the Lord after suffering a fatal heart attack. After 42 years and 4 months of marriage, being alone is a major life adjustment. As I look back ten years, I see God's preparation for these days and His provision of *Penned* to encourage me.

Each day devotions were delivered to my inbox. To consider 366 for this edition meant that I read far more than that—perhaps as many as 500. The devotions ministered to me in countless ways--always the Bible verses, often the devotion itself or reflecting personally on the theme. *Jehovah-jireh*, one of God's names, means "The Lord will provide." He knows what we need and when we need it, and has provided ahead of time for it. In 2003, I left my teaching career at my husband's encouragement, to pursue my passions for writing and teaching Bible studies. Now ten years later, as a widow, when I needed to be saturated in God's Word, editing *Penned* has been one of the ways He supplied and provided. Thank you, Florence, for listening to the Spirit's prompting and for trusting me with this opportunity.

Thanks to the writers for their submissions, notes of encouragement and prayers. I especially thank Jana Carman and Pan Sankey for their prayers and proofreading; Jana, as former editor, for her mentoring; Kate Walker for her assistance; and my family and friends for their prayers and encouragement.

Finally, the cover photo was taken by my husband, and I honor him by using it. It's a reminder that the beautiful flowers which we enjoyed together, pale in comparison to what he sees now. May you be blessed by God's Word and its applications as you read each day, and know that not only has the writing come from the heart of the writer, but from God's heart to yours as well.

Blessings,
Marilyn
Marilyn Nutter

Dear Friends,

The flowers on the front cover are from God's exquisite creation. It was taken by our editor Marilyn's husband.

Poems, anecdotes and homilies in this volume are the result of many of God's children working together to create a beautiful bouquet of devotions.

Marilyn willingly took over the huge job of editing, but Jana Carmen and her sister, Pan Sankey, still contributed their time, talents and love to proofread that which Marilyn had arranged so beautifully. This book is Penned from so many Hearts.

It is with gratitude I mention not only Marilyn Nutter, but Gloria Clover (Peterman) and Frannie Pratt who have helped us reach the point of having put out 20 annual editions!

Special thanks goes to my dear dedicated Debby Schall who takes great pains to deliver your communiqués and books.

Also Jim Jackson's expertise in pagination and his cover designs are spectacular.

Thank you all,
Thank you, Jesus,

Florence W. Biros

January

FRESH STARTS FOR A NEW DAY

Marilyn Nutter   January 1

This is the day that the Lord has made;
let us rejoice and be glad in it. Psalm 118:24 ESV

On January 1st, people often begin resolutions. These might be losing weight, learning a new skill, going to a gym or focus on other self-improvement goals. The common denominator is a fresh start and an opportunity to change. Often by February, we break resolutions and become discouraged. Perhaps they were too big to tackle or unrealistic.

Instead of goals for the year, let's prayerfully consider daily changes to become the people God wants us to be. On a daily basis with God's help, I will

- ❖ make wise decisions instead of impulsive ones.
- ❖ speak with kindness, not smart remarks.
- ❖ lean on God's promises, not fall for discouragement.
- ❖ pray about my daily schedule, not jump in.
- ❖ take time to stop and be thankful.
- ❖ tell someone I love them, instead of assuming they know.
- ❖ capture joy, not chase happiness.
- ❖ listen instead of monopolizing a conversation.
- ❖ make an effort at friendship instead of waiting for someone else to initiate.

Each day offers a fresh start. Perhaps instead of *doing* on a grand scale, we can focus on daily *becoming* and like the psalmist, rejoice in the gift of our day.

CHOICES

Jana Carman   January 2

...Choose you this day whom ye will serve... Joshua 24:15 KJV

We agonize over choices: What school (or church) should I go to? What kind of work should I prepare for? Whom should I marry?

But the decision that will affect every moment of your life for now and forever, is: "What will I do with Jesus?"

In the Easter account that fateful choice is placed before each of Jesus' disciples. His disciples slept when they should have prayed, and fled when they should have stayed. (Matthew 26:56 NASV) Peter followed —at a distance—but when the test came, Peter denied Jesus, not once, not twice, but three times.

> Will you, like Peter, your Lord deny? Or will you scorn from His foes to fly? Daring for Jesus to live or die? What will you do with Jesus?*

The decisions of some were irrevocable. Two thousand years later, we still speak of the chief priests and Caiaphas, of Herod and Pilate, the two thieves and the centurion, and even late-blooming Joseph of Arimathea.

> What will you do with Jesus? Neutral you cannot be;
> Some day your heart will be asking, "What will He do with me?" *   *Hymn words by A .B. Simpson

SERVING BOLDLY

Veronica Young   January 3

While watching a basketball game I noticed my two-year old niece had left my sister's side. I looked around and spotted her walking up a flight of bleacher stairs. She handed her favorite Mickey Mouse doll to a stranger and attempted to climb on the seat next to her. I could see my niece chatting with the young lady. Her smile showed that she was clearly enthralled by my niece's boldness.

What if we approached serving God with that same kind of boldness and fearlessness? King David did. As a shepherd boy, he heard that Goliath, a pagan Philistine, was threatening the people of Israel. Defeating Goliath was no small feat, but David boldly accepted the challenge to fight him. David was called ridiculous and dismissed as a naive little boy. He responded, *"The Lord who rescued me from the claws of the lion and the bear will rescue me from this Philistine!"* (1 Samuel 17:37 NLT) Saul consented and said, *"All right, go ahead... may the Lord be with you!"* (1 Samuel 17:38 NLT)

The Lord *was* with David, and with his simple slingshot and stones and the power of God, the giant was killed.

What if we approached ministry in the same way--with bold teaching and bold ideas, knowing God's power is with us? David teaches us about the value of God's power over our weakness. This is the kind of boldness the kingdom needs!

COUNTING OUR DAYS

Eunice Porter   January 4

Teach us to realize the brevity of life,
so that we may grow in wisdom. Psalm 90:12 (NLT)

When I lived in Portland, Oregon, each morning, as I walked to the bus stop, I glanced into the lit windows of two large apartment complexes. I often saw older persons enjoying a leisurely breakfast. I envied them; the whole day was theirs to do whatever they wanted. It seemed light years away before I would join their ranks.

With a move and a change in jobs, the years seemed to move faster than I wanted. Before long, I retired too. Where did the time go? What did I accomplish? What is in store for me now? These are certainly golden years and I often reflect how much each day matters and how each year is important because life itself is so fleeting. It may appear to be attractive to leisurely spend a day doing what *we* want, but in my remaining years, I pray that God will give me His "heart of wisdom" to guide me so that what I do has significance. May He help me to make the most of every day and to glorify Him in all that I do.

LIVING WITH PURPOSE

Martin Wiles   January 5

But my life is worth nothing to me unless I use it for finishing the work assigned me by the Lord Jesus--the work of telling others the Good News about the wonderful grace of God. Acts 20:24 NLT

I had heard it's an exhilarating experience, but on February 21, 2013, I found out first hand, when Levi Andrew Wiles entered our family and I entered the "Grandpa world."

Within a few hours, Levi guzzled his first breath of air, wallowed in his first bath, underwent a thorough inspection by medical staff, gulped his first sip of mother's milk. And…I got to hold him.

As wonderful as it is to cast my eyes on this beautiful baby, being a "Pee Paw" isn't my life's purpose. Paul tells how every believer can live with purpose—completing God's assigned work and sharing His grace.

Living with purpose entails setting goals that align with what He's called me to accomplish, including those beyond my personal ability. Goals that when met, give God credit. Living with purpose involves sharing my faith just as I shared the news of Levi's birth with everyone important in my life. Good news...the best news... should be shared.

If you're wandering aimlessly through life, let God show you how to live with purpose and in finish life well.

Thank You, Father, for giving us purpose and the gifts to complete Your plans. When it appears we're floundering with little or no direction, re-birth Your goals in our hearts and minds.

WELCOMING THE NEW YEAR

Pamela Heemskerk   January 6
Show me the right path, O Lord; point out the road for me to follow.
Psalm 25:4 NLT

Early each year, I take stock of what activities I'm going to participate in. Just because I was in the embroidery group or played tennis last year, doesn't mean I'll just blindly continue this year. I reconsider each year because I want to be in the place that God wants me: the job He wants me in, the church He wants me in, and contributing to the community in the way that best honours Him.

I used to worry about this a bit wondering how to decide. Will I hear Him direct me? How will I know? What if I make the 'wrong' choice? What I kept forgetting, was God wants me there even more than I want to be there. And He won't hide this information from me. I just need to take time to listen.

Father, thank You that You speak to us about our lives, and are concerned enough to show us the place where You want us. Thank You that You are not restricted by our 'mistakes' and Your grace works through anyone who is open to serving You, no matter where they are. Amen.

DON'T SKIP THE BEGATS

Connie Alexander Huddleston   January 7

Skipping over the lists of begats in the Bible is tempting. The names are difficult to pronounce and the repetition of so-and-so begat so-and-so is so-o-o boring. But tucked in with the names are a number of intriguing one–sentence biographies. Some notorious characters like Achar, **brought trouble on Israel by violating the ban on taking devoted things** (*1 Chronicles 2:7 NIV*). Others identify heroes; **Enoch walked with God** (Genesis 5:24 NIV). Sheerah, who must have been the first woman architect, **built Lower and Upper Beth Horon as well as Uzzen Sheerah** (1 Chronicles 7:24 NIV). Sentence sagas tell us that Asher and his sons were **brave warriors and outstanding leaders** (*1 Chronicles 7:40)*. Jabez' short begat biography (1 Chronicles 4:10) inspired the best seller, **The Prayer of Jabez** by Bruce Wilkinson.

As I contemplated those concise life accounts, questions came to mind: If someone wrote a one sentence biography about me, what would it say? What would I want it to say? What am I doing to make that a reality?

What about you? What do you want your one sentence biography to say?

Dear Lord, as my own life story unfolds, may it be a biography that glorifies You. Amen.

ALWAYS WITH ME

Evelyn Heinz   January 8
And surely I am with you always... Matthew 28:20b NIV

The Lord has revealed much to me in my seventy-four years on earth. It is remarkable to think that He knew me before I was conceived in my mother's womb and formed my body (Psalm 139). He has known me each day of my life.

He has shown me there is good and evil on my path. He taught me to do His will and follow Him in His way. As an eager child of God, I have searched and stumbled. There are times I fell. I still do, but He picks me up and shows His mercy.

He has always been with me… to this very day.

LOOKING FORWARD

Monica Andermann   January 9
But his wife looked back from behind him, and she became a pillar of salt. Genesis19:26 KJV

When I was learning to drive a car, the instructor told me to "just glance" in the rear-view mirror. "No one can move forward safely while staring at the road behind them," he stressed.

I recently learned this lesson in another way. I had been ruminating over some past hurts. While looking back did not turn me into a pillar of salt like Lot's wife, it was seriously hindering me from going ahead to receive God's best future.

Pillars are stationery. When we are immobilized by reliving past experiences and hurts, they act as pillars. We're stuck, and we can't walk on the path God has for us.

Sometimes it's hard to put past hurts behind us; perhaps because it can be difficult to understand why God allowed those unfortunate circumstances into our lives. Often, the reason is not for us to know. In Proverbs 25:2 (NLT) we're told, *"It is God's privilege to conceal things."* He asks that we trust Him, not look back, but move forward in faith to receive His blessings.

Dear Lord, thank You for the past experiences that help to shape my life. Today and every day help me to move forward in faith with You. Amen.

NOT ALL THAT GLITTERS IS GOLD

Robert Gutierrez   January 10
And Lot lifted his eyes and saw all of the plain of the Jordan, that it was well watered... Then Lot chose for himself all the plain of the Jordan, and Lot journeyed east. Genesis 13:10-11 NKJV

We can't escape life's forks in the road. When tough decisions confront us we tend to opt for what appears most attractive. However, looks can be deceiving--what you see isn't always what you gain. You may even get the opposite of what you wanted.

In Genesis 13, Lot arrived at his fork in the road. He and Abraham had to separate because the land could no longer sustain both families and herds. Abraham offered Lot first choice of the land. Lot chose the land that looked good to his eyes.

This didn't bring him what he anticipated. Lot hoped for prosperity; he got tragedy instead. His journey east took him to Sodom. God later destroyed Sodom in judgment for its wickedness and only he and his two daughters survived.

Things which appear good aren't always good, and quick decisions can have grave consequences. Prayer is the best tool when decisions must be made. Seeking God's counsel can be life's greatest time-saver and pain saver.

Lord, help me to not make quick, rash decisions based on what I see, but to seek Your guidance in every decision. Amen.

THE TATTERED SHIRT

Donna J. Howard   January 11

When pride comes, then comes disgrace, but with humility comes wisdom. Proverbs 11:2, NIV

I cringed with embarrassment as my husband got out of the RV to secure a campsite for the night. That sloppy, tattered shirt! It looked so awful. Why does he have to wear that? What will she think of us?

I watched as he talked with the lady assigning lots. She asked him a few questions and they laughed together. She didn't even notice his torn shirt.

I had judged my husband's appearance, but soon cringed at the tattered condition of my heart. My awful, ugly pride. I talked to Jesus and repented of my sin. I felt His love and I sensed His forgiveness.

Father, by the power of Your Spirit, keep me from judging others. By that same power, remind me of the condition of my heart, that I may display Your love—not criticism. Amen.

BEND IN THE ROAD

Laurel Shaler   January 12

I was meeting friends for lunch. I thought I knew where the restaurant was, so I didn't take directions, but when I arrived, I realized it was the wrong restaurant. I kept driving until I came to a bend in the road. I couldn't see ahead, but I *knew* for sure I had gone too far. So, I turned around. I drove quite a way back when I decided to call for directions. It turns out I had not gone far enough the first time. When I came to the bend in the road again, I kept going, and as soon as I turned the corner, I could see the restaurant clearly.

Bends in the road are similar to twists and turns in life. We *think* we know what's ahead, but we don't really. Instead of trusting, we become afraid. *And we retreat.*

Proverbs 3:5-6 (NIV) says: ***Trust in the Lord with all your heart and lean not on your own understanding; in all your ways acknowledge him and he will make your paths straight.***

Regardless of what my human mind imagines I don't have a clue of what's really ahead. But God does. He has gone before me—and you. If we let Him take the reins by fully placing our trust in Him, *He* will lead us in the right direction, make our paths straight and get us to our destination.

COMMITMENT

Dr. K   January 13
***Commit thy way unto the Lord; trust also in him;
and he shall bring it to pass.*** Psalm 37:5 KJV

Have you ever heard anything like the following statements?
➢General to troops: We'll make history today, weather permitting.
➢Boy to girlfriend: I'll be over to take you to dinner Friday, if it doesn't rain.
➢Member to pastor: I'll be at Christmas Eve service, if I'm not too tired from shopping.
➢ Worker to boss: I'll be at work on time, if it's not a good beach day.
➢Seeker to Jesus: Let me wait till my father dies and I bury him, however long that takes, then I'll follow you.

Here's the kind of commitment we should have: Lord, with your help I'll walk with You, I'll be there for You, I will honor You, I will glorify You: in the rain, on a sunny day, when it's pleasant or inconvenient; now and forever.

*Savior of my soul, I want to be faithful in my commitment to You.
Please give me the strength to do it. Amen.*

I CANNOT, GOD CAN

Marion Gorman   January 14
I can do all things through Christ who strengthens me.
Philippians 4:13 NKJV

"I can't write a book. I don't want to write a book. I didn't study how to write books," I said to God and anyone who would listen.

I had asked a retired missionary if I could write an article sharing his testimony and how he was presently serving the Lord. At the time, his granddaughter was considering the mission field. "There will be a century of Smiths in missions," he enthused. "A book would be perfect." My pleas to explain I did not write books fell on deaf ears. Soon I was buried in researching his life.

Except for the leading of the Lord, I would not have made this commitment. I knew I could not write a book. I was out of my realm and comfort zone.

I learned the need to completely depend on the Lord, not only with this writing project, but also with my life. I had no choice but to step out in faith to allow the Lord to accomplish His will through me.

The book is in manuscript form after nearly a decade. How many times was I ready to give up? Countless. The Lord faithfully enabled me to share a life lived for His glory. What we cannot accomplish, God can.

Lord, give me the faith to depend on You. Amen.

FULL OF SURPRISES

Debbie Carpenter   January 15
So is my word that goes out from my mouth. It will not return to me empty, but will accomplish what I desire and achieve the purpose for which I sent it. Isaiah 55:11 NIV

I ordered 10 New Testaments and prayed that I would be able to hand them out as the Lord led, whether it was to friends or complete strangers. I slipped one of the Testaments into my purse and headed off to my exercise club.

While working out, I heard a woman say that this would be her last day at our club. Immediately I realized that I may never see her again; it was now or never. She completed her work-out and began chatting with another club member. I approached her, Bible in hand, feeling certain God was directing me to offer her the book. To my surprise, she was not interested, but the woman she had been talking with was looking with interest at the small Testament, so I offered it to her. She was pleased, said it was lovely, and she would read it.

God has wonderful ways of leading us and often surprises us. By approaching the woman that I knew, He directed me to give the Bible to the stranger. It was no surprise to Him. Now His Word can work in her heart.

JARS OF CLAY

Virginia Blackburn   January 16

Read 2 Corinthians 4:7-11 NIV

We are hard-pressed on every side,
And yet we are not crushed.
Perplexed by life's e're-changing tide,
But overcome, we must.

Not we, but Christ, is Victor now,
When we are in distress.
His life embraced in us will show
His Lordship we confess.

His passion, love, and faith we show
Christ's all-surpassing power we pray,
To meet the conflict, for we know
His treasure's wrapped in jars of clay.

A DIFFERENCE IN PLANS

Jamie Britt   January 17

"For My thoughts are not your thoughts, nor are your ways My ways," says the Lord. Isaiah 55:8 NKJV

The tears streamed down my face in a steady deluge of frustration and pain. "Lord, why? Why again?" I had just received notification that for the second year in a row, I didn't receive a scholarship to a conference. Questions surfaced. "Was I not good enough? Lord, what's going on?"

Later that day, I was notified I had received a scholarship to take a mission trip. God had another plan for me.

Have you ever had a plan only to discover something totally different was in the works? Let me encourage you to wait on God when things don't appear to be working out as you thought. You'll be amazed at what you find.

MY LOST COIN

Evelyn Minshull   January 18
Read Luke 15:8-10

I listened to Him speak this afternoon
and recognized a tale I'd told myself beside the well
       of how I'd lost a coin (one of my ten)
       and counted time and time again,
       hoping to find that I had erred. I searched
the house from sill to hearthstone,
           spilled out the earthen pots,
           turned out the bedding,
           swept clean the floor--even sifted
           all my store of flour through a loose-woven cloth
           on the slim hope that I had dropped it there.
I made my family frantic those few days—
even my slumber troubled
while mourning that lost coin
as though the one were many, the many one—
       until I shook it from a shawl I'd laid for mending.
       I roused the house, the street, the town to celebration!
          What had been lost was found!
I listened to Him speak this afternoon,
and smiled to hear that God seeks us with equal passion
       and Heaven itself reverberates with joy
       when one lost soul is "found."

Lord, thank You for seeking us with such patience and passion.
Amen.

MERCY

Laura Neary   January 19
*Because of the L*ORD*'s great love we are not consumed,*
for his compassions never fail. They are new every morning;
great is your faithfulness. Lamentations 3: 22-24 NIV

> **M**ay the Lord who loves you
> **E**ver hold you in the hollow of His hand
> **R**ighteousness, undeserved, imputed unto you
> **C**aptivated by God's matchless grace
> **Y**our life, your heart, secure in Christ.

IDOL THOUGHTS

Renae Adelsberger   January 20
Do not make an idol for yourself, whether in the shape of anything
in the heavens above or on the earth below or in the waters under the
earth. You must not bow down to them or worship them;
for I, the LORD your God, am a jealous God ... Exodus 20:4-5 HCSB

When I lived in Singapore, I met Joshua and Esther who had founded a church for first generation believers. By proclaiming faith in Christ, Joshua and Esther had been disowned by their Buddhist families. Esther's mother eventually converted to Christianity, but Esther says, "My dad believes in himself."

I know people who aren't Buddhists, but who believe in themselves rather than in God. We may think of idols as carved statues and golden calves, but by definition, an idol is anything we value more than we value God. When I trust my opinion more than God's wisdom, I make my knowledge an idol. When I rely on my own strength rather than ask God to empower me, I turn my pride into an idol.

Father, I don't want to be an idol worshipper. I want to put You first and be a light shining brightly for You.

FROM WHERE I SIT

Linda McCutcheon   January 21
Let us then approach the throne of grace with confidence,
so that we may receive mercy and find grace to help us
in our time of need. Hebrews 4:16 NIV

Do you have a familiar spot in your home where you sit and
ponder life issues? Perhaps one where you held your newborn,
watched family celebrations, or read an inspiring book. Maybe a
place where you stared into space because you lost your job, or
your heart broke because your husband told you he was leaving,
or your child was diagnosed with a serious illness.

As we sit in our chair, we ponder expectations and
disappointments. That chair will eventually become ratty and torn.
What then? There is always a chair waiting for us. Jesus is on His
throne and His throne is unmovable and everlasting. Psalm 103:19
tells us, *The Lord has established his throne in heaven, and his*
kingdom rules over all. (NIV)

Jesus' throne is a place to find healing, peace and refreshment
24/7. It never wears out. Jesus sits on His throne not only to
oversee His universe, but He wants you to go there to find rest and
guidance.

As you sit in your chair today, understand He is waiting for
you. You are not alone, dear one; He sits on the throne and meets
you where you are.

BREAD INTO STONE

Pollyanna Sedziol   January 22
"...command that these stones be made bread." Matthew 4:3 NKJV

As the pastor led us through the temptations of our Lord in the
wilderness, my thoughts did a dyslexic turn on the Scripture and I
began to think about *bread* being turned into *stone.*

I thought of how often my morning prayer time is rushed as I
am thinking more about what the day ahead holds than the people
for whom I am praying.

I considered how my Scripture reading is diluted by other
thoughts, rather than faithful attending to the passage and its
meaning.

I realized ruefully that even now this thinking was interfering with my attention to the message our pastor had for us! Prayer rose up in me to remember the goodness of real bread, and I resolved to return my focus this moment to the Bread of Life.

I've kept the idea alive, striving to stay with each moment—in prayer, in reading the Word, in performing a task—so that the living doesn't yield to distraction, becoming stone.

Holy Spirit of God, remind me to be faithful in prayer, in Scripture, in all the things of life that You put before me, so that each may be of Jesus Christ, heaven's Bread.

THE WRONG GOAL

Linda Bonney Olin   January 23
Therefore, since we are surrounded by so great a cloud of witnesses, let us also lay aside every weight and the sin that clings so closely, and let us run with perseverance the race that is set before us, looking to Jesus the pioneer and perfecter of our faith, ... Hebrews 12:1-2a NRSV

The young football player grabbed the ball and ran down the field with all his might. The excited crowd screamed and stood to their feet. His coach and teammates waved their arms wildly. He crossed the goal line and collapsed, exhausted but exultant—in the wrong end zone!

His team, who had tried to get his attention and turn him around, earned zero points for his hard work. His mistake handed two points to his jeering opponents. The boy's anguish and the onlookers' pity couldn't change the final score.

I don't want to end up like that boy when I finish my life's run. How bitter it would be to discover that the effort I devoted to "good" goals has taken me away from God's plans and priorities!

Almighty God, point me toward the right goal–the one You've set for me. Thank You for providing the Holy Bible as my playbook, the Holy Spirit as my coach, those faithful witnesses who cheer me on and offer correction when I head in the wrong direction, and for Jesus Christ, who blocks the opposition and leads the way to final victory. Amen.

ENDURANCE

Rachelle Moon   January 24

Therefore, since we are surrounded by such a huge crowd of witnesses to the life of faith, let us strip off every weight that slows us down, especially the sin that so easily trips us up. And let us run with endurance the race God has set before us. Hebrews 12:1 NLT

In high school, running track was torture for me. When I hit my mid-thirties, I began running as a way to relieve stress and spend time in prayer and worship. Running didn't become easier, I just grew determined to cherish that time with the Lord.

Last year I completed my second 5K Fun Run with a goal of beating my old time. I accomplished my goal. One of the track girls commented to me, "I hope I'll still be running when I'm your age!" To me this was the highest compliment I could receive as a runner.

In our day-to-day lives, it's easy to forget that we are running a race. Challenges don't become easier, but with perseverance and faith, we can finish well, cheered on by those who have run and finished the race before us.

TIRED EARS

Renae Adelsberger   January 25

"Nae, Mommy's ears are tired," she gently admonished.

I took a deep breath, swallowed, and chattered on. Not only was I a little girl who liked to talk, I had severe speech impediments and struggled. As I grew up, I had to learn to have patience with my mommy's ears. I could rattle on about any subject without realizing that there was no point to my story.

While praying the other day, I wondered, *Do God's ears get tired, too?* Then I read Romans 8:26 (HCSB): *In the same way the Spirit also joins to help in our weakness, because we do not know what to pray for as we should, but the Spirit Himself intercedes for us with unspoken groanings.*

My heavenly Father has ears to hear and understand everyone. That does not mean an automatic positive response to all our requests. But it does mean that when I'm really struggling, when not even I can find the words to vocalize my prayers, the Holy Spirit is praying on my behalf. Take comfort today in the fact that even if the world doesn't understand your pain and your struggles, God does, and He is always listening. His ears never get tired.

"WHO DO YOU THINK YOU ARE?"

Anjanette Barr   January 26

So if the Son sets you free, you will be free indeed. John 8:36 NIV

As a new Christian, I was cut deeply by the magnitude of my sins. Sick with guilt, I felt I had offended God in shocking ways for my young age. I poured out my lamentations to my best friend, saying, "I know God has forgiven me, but I don't know if I can forgive myself."

My friend's expression abruptly changed.

"Who do you think you are? Do you think you know better than the Creator of the universe? You're telling me that God sees fit to forgive you, but you still think you know better and should punish yourself? How prideful!"

Prideful? I was pouring out my heart in what I thought was humility, but my friend was right. Deep down, I hadn't accepted that God's word in my life was final. He said I was free, but I continued to submit myself as a slave to sin – not by sinning, but by picking up the chains that lay broken at my feet, wrapping them around my wrists, and refusing to step out into freedom that Christ had given me.

Yes, my friend's expression had changed, but so did my life with her words of truth. God has forgiven, forgotten and set me free.

CAREFUL COMMENTS

Monica A. Andermann   January 27

Likewise the tongue is a small part of the body, but it makes great boasts. Consider what a great forest is set on fire by a small spark. James 3:5 NIV

It was just a small joke, spoken between two cousins about another. Nothing bad intended. Surely a comment so innocently stated could bring about no harm.

Yet it did. The poorly chosen words sparked a flame that flashed through a family leaving ashes of hurt feelings. The result: a show-down between the commenter and her target. A heartfelt apology and generous forgiveness followed.

Our words have great power to either help or harm.

Psalm 34:13 instructs us to *"keep your tongue from evil and your lips from speaking lies."* Sometimes this seems difficult to do, yet so much regret and harm can be avoided by following this very wise directive.

The tongue is small and powerful. Just one small comment can start a fire in a family. Lord, help me to remember to choose words wisely and speak in the spirit of truth and love. Amen.

A GRADUAL CONQUEST

Robert Gutierrez																																	January 28
... being confident of this, that he who began a good work in you will carry it on to completion until the day of Christ Jesus.
Philippians 1:6 NIV

The Christian life is more of a marathon than a 100 yard dash, yet many new believers expect an immediate life transformation once they accept Christ as Savior. Early in my walk with God I discovered that old habits die hard. When I didn't arrive at spiritual perfection within a few months, I became discouraged. I couldn't overcome all my faults, failures, and sins. I regularly told myself I was wasting my time, that I was never going to change.

I learned it would take time for God to flush out the 27 years of junk I had accumulated in my heart. I realized that a renewed mind doesn't emerge overnight, but after months and years of perseverance with God's help.

We will never completely conquer our flesh and reach perfection in this earthly life. But gradually, little by little, as we persevere and are faithful, God is faithful to complete the work He began. His promises will accompany our walk and He will drive out the strongholds in our lives.

ORDINARY WOMEN--OR NOT?

Judy Dippel																																	January 29
...love one another deeply, from the heart. 1 Peter 1:22 b NIV

I value an annual get-together to reconnect with friends from my old neighborhood. Nearly all of us have moved to new cities or states. We raised our "little darlings" together. We're like family, and we know "friends are the family we choose."

With age, we haven't mellowed, at all! We're a high energy group of women. Busier than ever, with creativity and talents galore, when we're all together we could be a recipe for disaster. Instead, each encourages and appreciates the other's talents and successes. I've had enough life experience, and a few hurtful episodes with close friends, to know that unconditional appreciation and love isn't always the case.

What will friends say when one or more of us is gone?
- She showed me how to overcome real-life obstacles with living courage.
- Her enthusiasm to learn was infectious.
- Such an adventurous spirit—always trying something new.
- The outdoors was her playground. Didn't we have fun?
- Such tenacity to complete a project. Wow!
- Her faith showed the reality of God.
- How she made us laugh!

It's not about success as the world sees. It's much deeper and quite the opposite. The list of human legacies we leave is long—choices and actions that still flicker when we're gone. No, these women are not ordinary! Extraordinary? Absolutely, yes! And we love each other deeply…from the heart.

INSTRUMENTS

Diane Sillaman   January 30
Therefore do not let sin reign in your mortal body so that you obey its evil desires. Do not offer any part of yourself to sin, as an instrument of wickedness, but rather offer yourself to God as those who have been brought from death to life; and offer every part of yourself to him as an instrument of righteousness. For sin shall no longer be your master, because you are not under the law, but under grace. Romans 6:12-14 NIV

In the hands of a talented flautist, a flute produces music. I have heard beautiful classical and delightful Celtic music from this instrument that lifted my soul.

When a performance is completed, the artist receives standing applause. His name may become famous. He is renowned for his talent, but he couldn't have done it without the flute. As a master, he takes good care of his flute. It is precious and valuable. It is worth a great deal of money, but more than that, it is his chosen instrument.

The flute rests in his hands. His fingers move the valves. His very breath blows through; the flute yields to the master's touch. Music flows.

We are like the flute. He is the Master. Let our music flow.

A MESSY COOKBOOK

Gloria Doty   January 31

All Scripture is God-breathed and is useful for teaching, rebuking, correcting and training in righteousness, 2Timothy 3:16 NIV

My daughter borrowed my favorite cookbook. When she returned it, she told me I definitely needed a new one. I insisted I did not; I liked the one I had.

"But, Mom," she protested, "Look at some of these pages. They have notes written on them and coffee stains and they are coming loose from the binding."

She was right. My cookbook was certainly looking "used". I insisted I liked it that way; I could easily find my favorite recipes by the most tattered and stained pages.

When I read my Bible the next morning, I smiled. My Bible looked almost as bad as my cookbook. I have marked favorite passages, some of the pages are loose and there are many smudges on it.

I'm not suggesting we ruin a Bible or a cookbook or never purchase a new one. What I am suggesting is we need to *use* our Bibles, not preserve them in pristine condition. We can't find the right recipe for our dessert if we don't open and read the cookbook. We can't find the recipe for life and salvation if we don't open and read our Bible.

Father, help us make good use of the words You have given us.
Amen.

February

THE LOVE OF MY LORD

Joan Clayton   February 1

One thing have I desired of the LORD, that will I seek after; that I may
dwell in the house of the LORD all the days of my life, to behold the
beauty of the LORD to inquire in his temple. Psalm 27:4 KJV

In the stillness of the night I find Him waiting in my secret place.
He receives me with gladness.
I am precious in His sight.

He tells me of His everlasting love.
My innermost being knows this is true.

I hear His gentle whisper,
"I will always be there…
In the sunshine, in the rain
In the storms and in the pain."

The heavens and the stars reflect His glory, but
He has time for me.
I am sheltered by His love.

The breaking of dawn finds me in His embrace.
I hear the still small voice,
"I will never leave you."

THERAPY

Angela L. Davis   February 2

The heartfelt counsel of a friend is as sweet as perfume and incense.
Proverbs 27:9 NLT

I have been seeing the same therapist for more years than
I can remember. She is available anytime, day or night, seven
days a week. She doesn't have a fancy office. Nor do I need
an appointment to speak with her. She prescribes only two
medications—coffee and chocolate. My therapist's name is Lisa.
Whenever I need a therapy session, Lisa meets me at a
favorite restaurant. We share food, fellowship, and fun. There is

nothing I cannot share with her. As any good therapist, Lisa is a good listener. She offers support, encouragement, and prayer. I can also count on her to offer words of caution if she feels I am heading down a wrong path. Conversation is relaxed and easy. Her therapy is not only helpful, but completely affordable!

We should always take our concerns to God, but He brings the right friends into our life. They offer the support and encouragement we need to get through our tough times and share our good times. Lisa is my therapist, my cheerleader, and my friend. By the way, therapy always includes dessert!

Heavenly Father, thank You for surrounding me with special friends. Help me to be that kind of friend. Amen.

PRUNING THE HEART

Jean L. Croyle   February 3

Watching my elderly neighbor pull weeds and trim winter's harshness off his beloved berry bushes was akin to seeing a painting emerge from mere brush strokes. He was meticulous. Each snip was careful and upon completion, the bush looked full and lively again. The perennial grasses were resplendent once more. He gathered all the dead pieces and wheeled them away, giving a rejuvenated newness to the yard.

God does this in our hearts and spirits when sin and unbelief wash over us. He instructs us: ***"Break up your fallow ground, for it is time to seek the Lord, Till He comes and rains righteousness on you."*** (Hosea 10:12b NKJV) He wants to bring us back to intimate fellowship with Him. When we yield to His beckoning and submit our cold heart to Him, we are revitalized and energized in the spring of His love once again.

God, break up my sins and let me turn away from them. May I find Your spirit and revel in its newness, again.

HOW DO I LOVE YOU, LORD?

Margaret Steinacker   February 4

*"Love the Lord your God with all your heart and with all your soul
and with all your strength and with all your mind; and, Love your
neighbor as yourself".* Luke 10:27 NIV

How do I love you, Lord? In countless ways.
I love You more each day, in solitary quietness,
In joyous songs of praise on piano and organ keys,
in Psalms of peace, in quiet affirmations
You send through mundane tasks of life.
I love You when you feel close,
when notes of Your abundance overflow
from the fullness of my heart next to Yours,
I burst into song.

Even when I feel alone, by faith and trust in Your Word,
I love you – in spite of…
I love You passionately, but strive to increase such passion.
I love You when you bless me with answers to prayer.
And when You choose to say "wait," I love You still,
Knowing that in time, all will be well.

I love You with every breath You give me.
I love You with indescribable joy as Your spirit dwells in me.
Joys, sorrows, each moment of my life.
And, if God choose,
I shall but love You better, praise You unceasingly,
and revel in Your glory after death.

IN THE TWINKLING OF AN EYE

Marcia Schwartz   February 5

*Listen, I tell you a mystery: We will not all sleep, but we will all be
changed—in a flash, in the twinkling of an eye, at the last trumpet.
For the trumpet will sound, the dead will be raised imperishable, and
we will be changed.* 1 Corinthians 15:51 NIV

A nasty virus was ravaging my body. I managed to get out
of bed and, slowly descending the stairs, made my way to the
kitchen. I prepared a glass of Alka-Seltzer Plus to try to ease
my discomfort. My last conscious memory was mixing the drink,

flipping off the light over the sink before turning to imbibe the remedy in the living room. In a nanosecond, in the twinkling of an eye, I must have fallen, for I awoke later on the cold kitchen floor, the refrigerator at my right, and a table leg on my left. I had narrowly escaped hitting my head. My feet were wet and sticky from the spilled Alka- Seltzer.

After I assessed where I was and how I had gotten there, I heaved a prayer: *Thank You, Lord that I landed safely!* My head avoided a gash, no bones were broken. In the blink of an eye—without warning—it had all happened!

One day, in a flash, in a twinkling of an eye, Jesus will come for us. At the sound of the trumpet, we will wake up, not on a hard, cold floor, but land safely in the warm embrace of heaven.

THE PURSUIT OF HAPPINESS

Andrea Roe   February 6
"...I have loved you with an everlasting love;
I have drawn you with unfailing kindness." Jeremiah 31:3 NIV

From the pit You took me
And placed me on Your lap like a little girl welcomed home
No longer am I lost.
You found me and called me Yours.
In ashes I was covered
As depression and self-hatred were my shield
No one could come near
But
You
Who desires me above all other things,
Ran after me.
You would not leave me alone.
You kept pushing.
You would not give up on me.
Even in the darkest of times You were there.
I thank You for Your faithfulness in my life.
Your love that never fails.
Your tender whispers revealed Your heart.
Only You have satisfied my soul.
You are now my everything.
And I will never let go.
I will never let go.

AMAZING LOVE

Donna J. Howard   February 7

***For God so loved the world that He gave His only Son
that whoever believes in Him would not perish,
but have everlasting life.*** John 3:16, NKJV

My daughter Nancy bought me a sweatshirt. On the front, each of the letters in the word GRANDMA is enclosed in colorful little boxes. A photo of a computer mouse along with the words www.grandkids.love is under the boxes.

A teenager stopped my husband and me while I was wearing the shirt and asked, "Is that really a website?" Quickly, my husband answered, "No, she just likes to show her love for her grandchildren." I smiled, thinking, *That's right, that's what fathers and mothers and grandparents do.*

Then I thought about our Heavenly Father. Everyday He shows His love for His children in many ways every day. Many years ago, He showed His love for us in an amazing way. He sent His son Jesus to die for us and take our sins upon Himself so we could go to heaven someday.

I love my children and grandchildren very much, but my love for them is a tiny spark alongside of God's amazing love for us.

Thank You, Heavenly Father, for Your amazing love. Thank You for sending Jesus to die for us so we can spend eternity with You. In Jesus' name. Amen.

LOOONG LOVE

Jo Ann Walczak   February 8

. . . I have loved you with an everlasting love . . . Jeremiah 31:3 NIV

A fire blazed, our only light on a mid-winter night. Wyatt and Mack, my grandsons, sat on a tablecloth with me before the fireplace as we ate popcorn and talked about their lives. What funny thing happened in Wyatt's class? What did daddy do that made Mack giggle? Their eyes glistened.

"I think this is the best night of my life!" Wyatt whispered.

"Boys, I love the two of you so much!" I said, my heart overflowing with these quiet admissions.

"Oh, I know you love us." Wyatt shook his head like this was old news. "You've loved us for . . . 63 years!"

"I'm 63 now. How could I have loved you that long?"

"You know . . . you've loved us . . . *forever*!" Wyatt exclaimed, certain that I had loved them from the beginning of time.

That's how you love us, Lord . . . from the beginning of forever. Before we were even born, You knew us and loved us. "Forever" we have had a place in Your heart. Your love is everlasting.

When the cold winter's night of life tries to freeze you, draw near to the flame of His love. Remember His promises. Warm your heart with His forever love.

WINTER PRAYER

Bill Batcher   February 9
**The Lord is close to the brokenhearted and saves those
who are crushed in spirit.** Psalm 34:18 NIV

Winter's days are cold and short, its nights long and dark.
We want to hole up, snuggle deep beneath covers
(praying its winds cannot penetrate), remain isolated,
and distance ourselves from others, even from ourselves.
But as surely as snowflakes race each other from the sky,
and moons wax and wane, You assure us
that spring will come, days will warm,
and darkness will shrink its hold.
Lord, sit with us in the night, lie with us under our covers,
wait with us for the dawn. Amen.

SECURE IN HIS LOVE

Pamela Heemskerk   February 10
**Let them give thanks to the Lord for his unfailing love
and his wonderful deeds for mankind ...** Psalm 107:8 NIV

I've been a Christian for almost 40 years and sometimes wonder what my life would have been like without Jesus.

As a young person, I was acutely self-conscious— insecure, awkward, lacking any confidence. I often wondered if people were laughing at me. Looking back, I realise I was probably too hard on myself. Over the years, I have become aware of the deep abiding love that God has for me; a totally unconditional love where we are completely and utterly loved by Him, no matter what we think of ourselves.

Explaining this to a friend has helped me to comprehend it much more. When I talk to her about how God loves her, it reinforces how valuable I am to Him as well.

I understand now why the Bible describes God's love as 'jealous.' He loves us with intensity and commitment despite our shortcomings. When I glimpse the constancy and depth of passion He has for us, I feel secure in this love: I no longer focus on who I am, but rather on who He is.

LOVE TO DIE FOR

Linda Bonney Olin   February 11
...perhaps for a good person someone might actually dare to die. But God proves his love for us in that while we still were sinners Christ died for us. Romans 5:7-8 NRSV

I watch TV reports in awe, as emergency workers enter burning buildings or plunge into raging floodwaters to rescue total strangers. Soldiers and peace officers, too, brave injury and death to protect people they've never met.

Would I risk death to save anyone? My spouse, my children, my parents? Yes, because I love them dearly. I'm not so sure I'd risk my neck for other family and friends, let alone strangers. I definitely would not accept certain death to save some guy whose own despicable acts got him in a jam. Take a convicted criminal's place in the electric chair, so he can waltz away free? Ridiculous!

Yet that's what Jesus did for me. He submitted to scourging and mockery, then trudged to Calvary, carrying the cross on which He would die. He knew, even as he suffered, that His sinless life was being sacrificed to give eternal life to a multitude of guilty sinners.

Selfless Savior, let me never take Your loving sacrifice for granted. Help me extend a loving hand to anyone in need of rescue. Amen.

WILL YOU LOVE JESUS?

Donna Morse   February 12
Jesus said to him, "I am the way, the truth, and the life.
No one comes to the Father except through Me. John 14:6 NKJV

Fourteen of us sat around a large square table in the small meeting room at a Bible College one warm August day. We were touring the school to help our high school seniors decide if this was the place to attend following graduation.

We joined a group of missionary kids there for the same reason. The tour guide asked the students to introduce themselves, those who had accompanied them, and tell where they were from. Their introductions revealed impressive credentials and experiences. We were the last introduced. We had no credentials. I wondered how my granddaughter Emily would handle the introduction.

"This is my Mom, and my Grandma, and I'm Emily," she said. "We're from Olympia, Washington, and I just love Jesus."

That was it. She was finished. Her only credential…Jesus Himself. My heart leaped. She had said it all…she loved Jesus. He was her motive, her passion, and her focal point.

When it comes down to it, God requires only one credential from any of us…Jesus. Only our relationship with Him counts for eternity.

In February, a month of "love", Jesus lovingly welcomes all who will come to Him. Will you just love Jesus?

JOY!

Pollyanna Sedziol   February 13
"…unto God my exceeding joy…" Psalm 43:4 KJV

Several years ago I was asked to teach the 3rd grade Sunday school class one morning to relieve the regular teacher. With such short notice, I thought quickly, said yes, then spent a pleasant hour with several eager children. We completed an art project, then talked about JOY: Jesus – His only begotten Son (John 3:16); Others – bearing one another's burdens (Galatians 6:2); You -- whatever you do, do all to the glory of God (I Corinthians 10:31). The children responded with enthusiasm as they shared what each of those meant.

Years later, the memory of teaching on short notice, but putting Jesus first, others second and serving Him the best I could, was joy for me and still is. Whenever I come upon an unexpected situation, I recall those third graders and use them as my joy-filled guide.

EYES OF LOVE

Darlene Rose (Bustamante)   February 14
Inspired by the Gospel of John 8:1-12 NKJV

He stooped down to write
An angry crowd – all around
Nothing could be heard
Not one voice – not one sound

Thrust in – my sin exposed
I've nowhere to hide
As He raised Himself up
My eyes – opened wide
Then He spoke – gentle tones
This One – Who could He be?
This Man – neither condemns
Nor accuses – sinful me

Gently spoken, "Sin no more."
With eyes of love – filled with grace
Before me stands – the Light of the world
Jesus, the Christ – face to face!

THE PURPOSE OF LIFE

Geanna Steinmetz   February 15

Many Christians go through life without discovering their God-given purpose. Some even serve in ministry yet have no idea why God created them. Others have identified and used their talents, skills and spiritual gifts, but don't fully understand their purpose. Most Christians would say their purpose is "to spread the Gospel," or "to love God." These are good answers, but the real answer is found in 1 Peter 2:9 NIV: *But you are a chosen people, a royal priesthood, a holy nation, God's special possession, that you may declare the praises of him who called you out of darkness into his wonderful light.*

We were hand-picked to "declare the praises of him who called you." Everything we do should reflect His glory and give Him praise. When we choose to honor God in all that we do, think and say, we begin to be effective Christians. Our primary purpose as Christians is to praise God. We do that by spreading the Gospel and loving God, but these are a means to the end—praising Him!

YOU LOVED ME FIRST

Linda Bonney Olin   February 16
We love him, because he first loved us. 1 John 4:19 KJV

You are Alpha and Omega, the beginning and the end.
You created earth and heaven, all of nature, all of men.
You're the kingdom and the glory, mighty Lord of all you see.
Yet you care for lowly creatures, and the lowliest is me.

You're the Author of Salvation, the Redeemer of the lost.
You were spit upon and tortured, then you died upon a cross.
Thus, in love you ransomed sinners, paid the price to set them free.
Even then, you knew that one of those lost sinners would be me.

Like an unexpected shower prompting buried seeds to sprout
or the gentle sunshine coaxing flower buds to blossom out,
your abundant love came freely, never asked for, never earned.
Now in gratitude I humbly offer my love in return.

(You are invited to listen to the melody of this song at www. LindaBonneyOlin.com/audio)

PRAYER ON PRESIDENTS' DAY

Marilyn Nutter   February 17
I urge, then, first of all, that petitions, prayers, intercession and thanksgiving be made for all people—for kings and all those in authority, that we may live peaceful and quiet lives in all godliness and holiness. (1Timothy 2:1-3 NIV)

February 22 was originally established in 1885 as a national holiday to celebrate George Washington's birthday. In 1971, a Uniform Monday Holiday Act was passed to create more three-day weekends for our nation's workers. The third Monday in February is now viewed to honor all past and present US presidents.

For you, this may be a day off from work or school, a time to shop Presidents' Day sales, or a free day to tackle a project or meet friends for lunch, but let's take time to pray for leaders in our local, regional and national government.

This is how The Message translates 1Timothy 2:1-3: *The first thing I want you to do is pray. Pray every way you know how, for everyone you know. Pray especially for rulers and their governments to rule well so we can be quietly about our business of living simply, in humble contemplation. This is the way our Savior God wants us to live.*

Let us *pray*.

THE FAITH OF A CHILD

Debbie Carpenter   February 18
'...Assuredly I say to you, whoever does not receive the kingdom of God as a little child will by no means enter it.' Mark 10:15 NKJV

My six-year-old granddaughter Jannah looked up at me with eyes that asked for my complete attention. "Nanni, when I am singing strong and singing praise songs, it makes little tears in my eyes."

I thought of the times *I* stood in church singing praises, but my thoughts raced in different directions. How tender was this young heart who carefully thought of the words as she sang and was touched by them. Is this what Jesus meant when He said we should come to Him as little children? The faith of children is sincere. They trust Jesus with their whole heart. They believe the stories in the Bible are true. They want to be like the heroes in these stories.

The faith of a child: believing, trusting and following.

Heavenly Father, give me a childlike heart. Help me to trust completely, follow steadfastly, and grow in grace and character. May tears come to my eyes. Amen.

OUR ETERNAL GLORY

Liwen Y. Ho   February 19

For our light and momentary troubles are achieving for us an
eternal glory that far outweighs them all. So we fix our eyes not
on what is seen, but on what is unseen, since what is seen is
temporary, but what is unseen is eternal. 2 Corinthians 4:17-18 NIV

I worked at a Christian counseling center where the employees
met weekly for prayer. During one meeting, when my colleague
Marty asked for my prayer requests, I said, "Please pray for
my brother-in-law's health and my father-in-law's salvation. My
brother-in-law struggles with mental health issues and has trouble
caring for himself and keeping a job." The sorrow and concern in
Marty's blue eyes touched me. "I know his situation is not good,
but he is still better off than my father-in-law."

Marty's eyes widened in surprise.

"My brother-in-law believes in God and has eternal life," I
explained. "My father-in-law, even though he is healthy, doesn't
know God."

Scripture reminds us that our lives are temporary and so are
the troubles we face. Though our struggles, whether they involve
health or finances, are real and difficult, we still have hope in God.
We can face each day with the assurance that there is more to
this life. As God's children, we know everything on earth pales in
comparison to the spiritual abundance we will have in eternity.

A GENTLE WHISPER

Liwen Y. Ho   February 20

The Lord said, "Go out and stand on the mountain in the presence of
the Lord, for the Lord is about to pass by." Then a great and powerful
wind tore the mountains apart and shattered the rocks before the
Lord, but the Lord was not in the wind. After the wind there was
an earthquake, but the Lord was not in the earthquake. After the
earthquake came a fire, but the Lord was not in the fire. And after the
fire came a gentle whisper. When Elijah heard it, he pulled his cloak
over his face and went out and stood at the mouth of the cave.
1 Kings 19:11-13a NIV

I learn to wait
in stillness and quiet,
heart laid open,

eyes and ears closed to the world.

For the Lord appeared to Elijah
not in the great wind
that tore apart the mountains of old,
not in the mighty earthquake
that grumbled deep beneath the sea,
nor in the awesome fire
that burned red in the sky,
but in a whisper so gentle
that he knew the Lord had come
close enough
for his heart to hold.

APPOINTMENTS FOR A NEW NORMAL

Patsy Sanders   February 21
My times are in your hands. Psalm 31:15a NIV

Life changes, doesn't it? Variety. No two days are ever the same. Remember Forrest Gump's comment in the movie: "Life is like a box of chocolates; you never know what you're gonna get"? Without warning, life presents unwelcomed detours.

Recently, listening to a panel of women share testimonies of their unexpected 'new normal', I was reminded of the unpredictability of life. Circumstances ranged from becoming widows at an early age, losing children, financial crisis, divorce, and devastating heartache. Expectations sorrowfully dissolved, as disappointment and heartache overshadowed each one.

Though difficult to comprehend, nothing happens to God's child unless filtered first through His mighty hands. It may be difficult to face disappointment as God's appointment, but learning to access grace and courage and live out His purposes for us, is far greater than any personal expectations we may have.

Are you in a new normal? Know that you are in God's appointment slot on His calendar for you. His grace is sufficient, His strength is made perfect in weakness, and He is sovereign. He doesn't owe us explanations, but we owe Him our willingness to glorify Him, even in our 'new normal.'

MY FAVORITE BOOK

Tommie Lenox   February 22
This is the day the Lord has made, let us rejoice in it and be glad.
Psalm 118:24 NKJV

When I was little, each morning my mother and I read from the Bible and I learned about God's promises. I memorized verses that told me of His love and words of thanksgiving and praise.

After my father died, books became my dearest friends. Reading helped me escape from the realities of Pearl Harbor, rationing and blackouts. My favorite story was Pollyanna, about a little girl who smiled through the worst of times. Her father showed her that in the Bible God often commands His people to rejoice. Those words comforted her after her parents' death. When an accident crippled her, despair took hold, but not for long.

I related to that little girl. I missed my father. Mother now cared for foster children at home and I had to share my room and my mom with four other kids. At a time when despair could have defeated me, I found solace in the book with a happy ending.

Now as an adult, when tragedy strikes, I am blessed with verses that have sustained me all my life. Nothing can equal the truth of the Word of God.

Your word is a lamp to my feet and a light to my path.
Psalm 119: 105 NKJV

TRAPPED?

Stacy Williams   February 23
The thief comes only to steal and kill and destroy; I have come that they may have life, and have it to the full. John 10:10 NIV

I have lived with severe chronic pain for nineteen years. I'm a prisoner in a body that doesn't work the way it's supposed to. It prevents me from doing things that I need to do and often want to.

As I look around, I know others are imprisoned too. Some are trapped in sin, addiction, debt, low self-esteem and difficult relationships. Their traps also keep them from living life fully. They often feel stuck and without hope.

God's Word reminds us living fully is found in Him, apart from our circumstances. Today, if you find yourself feeling trapped, cry out to Him. He will strengthen you, and give wisdom and direction. He desires that you find hope and a full life in Him.

GOD'S TRACK RECORD

Jana Carman   February 24
By faith Abraham, even though he was past age—and Sarah herself was barren—was enabled to become a father because he considered him faithful who had made the promise. Hebrews 11:11 NIV

My father phoned to tell me, "I'm bringing you a set of antique chairs the next time I come to New Jersey."

"Oh, thank you!" I replied.

I didn't receive the chairs for several weeks, but I thanked him for what I had not yet received because I knew my father, and his promise would be carried out. I had faith in the one who promised.

When Jesus promises something, we, just like Abraham, can have perfect faith that His promise will come to pass. Hebrews 11:1 (NIV) describes faith as being sure of what we hope for and certain of what we do not see. We can have confidence—perfect faith— because we know His track record.

Hebrews 10:35-37 (NIV) advises: So do not throw away your confidence; it will be richly rewarded. You need to persevere so that when you have done the will of God, you will receive what he has promised. For in just a very little while, "He who is coming will come and will not delay."

That is only one of God's promises! Make a list of God's promises, and see what He has in store for you!

THE VALUABLE SECRET

Donna Morse   February 25
Draw near to God, and He will draw near to you. James 4:8 NKJV

I scooted to the edge of the pew, ready to listen. The missionary speaker promised to reveal the secret of the Christian life. I longed for a closer relationship with my Savior. This was my chance to learn.

"Here's the secret," he said, pausing. I waited, and then was stunned as he spoke with absolute confidence, "Read the Bible and pray!"

My mind repeated his words. *Read the Bible and pray?* Is *that* the secret…is that *all*? I already know that! But…am I doing it?

He went on to explain that it's not easy to make Bible reading and prayer a daily priority. Yet, that's what it takes to have a close abiding relationship with Christ. As we do this, we find that we not only learn about God, but we better understand His purposes. We sense His nearness. Our praying ceases to be a list of concerns and requesting shallow blessings. It becomes a conversation with a trusted friend.

"Lord," I prayed "help me to make my relationship with You a priority. I don't want to just know *about* You; I want to know you. Help me consistently read your Word and pray with an open heart."

GENERATION TO GENERATION

Jennifer Kanode   February 26
Charm is deceptive, and beauty is fleeting, but a woman
who fears the Lord is to be praised. Proverbs 31:30 NIV

I was excited when the Lord gave me a daughter. Now that Calea is getting older, I am giving her some things that I had kept while growing up. Recently, as I was getting jewelry and dolls from the attic, the Lord brought some other things to mind. While it is a blessing to share some of my girly things with her, there is something even more important I should share.

In our highly sexualized world, we need to teach our daughters to respect themselves. They see scantily dressed, skinny young girls on TV and believe that is acceptable.

May the Lord help those of us with young daughters to teach them that they are loved just the way they are. May we pass down to our girls the value of modesty and self-worth. With the Lord's help we can raise up a generation of godly women.

Dear Heavenly Father, I pray that You will help us raise up a generation of godly women who will have the courage to stand up and live for You. May they not conform to the world's standards but live holy and modest lives. Amen.

LITTLE BY LITTLE

Kelly Lyman   February 27
Being confident of this, that he who began a good work in you will
carry it on to completion until the day of Christ Jesus.
Philippians 1:6 NIV

During the past year, I'd spotted an old rundown farmhouse on a road I travel frequently. I often thought that I wish someone would take a wrecking ball to it. However, over the past few months, construction workers have been working on it, little by little. They tore down the old decayed wood and rebuilt parts of the frame. They have put up new windows, new doors, and new stone. The mud around the house has slowly begun to turn into grass. The house, which was once an eyesore, has begun to look like something new. Something inviting. And now, I comment on how much I would love to live there.

When I think of that old rundown house, I think of my life. My life is dirty, and sometimes it's quite an eyesore. Everyone has parts of their lives that are ugly and messy. But when we let Christ into our lives, into our hearts, so He can work in us, He takes that dirt, that decay, and cleans it, little by little. He takes what is old and He makes it new. He makes it beautiful.

BRINGING GLORY TO GOD

Janet R. Sady   February 28
..."Everyone is looking for you!" Jesus replied, "We must go to the
nearby towns, so that I can tell the good news to those people. This
is why I have come." Mark 1:37-38 CEV

We Christian writers have different styles, topics and motivations for writing, but one thing is certain: the glory belongs to Almighty God for anything we accomplish.

There is nothing inherently good in us. The only goodness we have comes from our salvation through Christ. When He becomes our Savior, God no longer sees our faults and weaknesses; He sees Christ's blood which has cleansed our hearts. His Spirit has given us gifts to use for God's purposes and glory. 2 Corinthians 3:5 (NIV) tells us, *Not that we are competent in ourselves to claim anything for ourselves, but our competence comes from God.*

The messages God gives us to write are meant to be shared

with others. We continue His work when we go and tell, and when we write His message to be read by the lost and to encourage Christians.

Father, thank You for trusting us with Your Gospel message. Lord, may we be faithful to write Your words to bring glory to You. Amen

THE MERCY RULE

Sherry Taylor Cummins   February 29
Therefore be merciful just as your Father also is merciful.
Luke 6:36 NKJV

In the movie Gone with the Wind, Scarlett O'Hara betrays her friend Melanie Wilkes. As Melanie hosts guests at her home, she overhears women speak unkindly about Scarlett. Melanie's display of mercy surprises everyone, especially undeserving Scarlett. She takes Scarlett by the arm, and lovingly speaks highly of her before the guests. This moving scene left an impression on my twelve-year-old heart that I have never forgotten.

While hanging on the cross, Jesus prayed words of mercy for the two criminals beside Him and for those who crucified Him. He pardons our sins and displays mercy to us, not giving us what we deserve.

The rule of mercy is to be merciful with others as the Father is merciful with you. When you are inconvenienced because the person ahead of you in the express lane at the grocery has 11, items instead of 10, can you show mercy? When someone speaks sharply to you and you don't deserve it, show mercy. There are countless interruptions in our day where we can selflessly show mercy.

Showing mercy leaves an indelible mark on another's heart. It also changes you and brings you closer to the Father.

March

ON EAGLE'S WINGS

Linda Bonney Olin   March 1

But those who hope in the LORD will renew their strength. They will soar on wings like eagles; they will run and not grow weary, they will walk and not be faint. Isaiah 40:31 NIV

Dead weight in dead air
I drift in doldrums
waiting for a saving breath of wind.

Help doesn't come from faithless men
or to them.
They weary of waiting.
They faint.
They die.
But I
I wait upon the Lord.

Ah, see! He rises
in all power from the grave!
His resurrection whirlwind
snatches up my spirit
lifts me with him
higher
ever higher to the heavens
as if borne aloft on eagles' wings!

FINDING SHALOM

Shirlee Abbott   March 2

You will keep in perfect peace [shalom] all who trust in you, all whose thoughts are fixed on you! Isaiah 26:3 NLT

Here's the trick for finding peace. Don't look for peace; look for God.

Dear God, so often I try to make peace a do-it-myself project and fail miserably. Forgive me for looking for shalom in all the wrong places. Thank You for Your gift of peace.

THE JOY OF SERVING

Elizabeth Rosian   March 3
Serve the Lord with gladness. Psalm 100:2

I had been sick all week with the flu. My house was a mess when friend, Doris, phoned and offered to do some ironing. I wasn't overly concerned about clothes when germs were dancing in the bathtub and tasteless meals were being thrown together. Doris was a great cook. Why hadn't she offered to create one of her delicious meals? *Well,* I thought, *at this point I'm grateful for any help I can get.* I wondered about it, until she arrived.

"I was going to cook dinner for you," she said brightly. "But I love to cook and that wouldn't be service. So I decided to iron, since that's the job I hate most."

I thought of my areas of Christian service. I sang in the choir. I taught a Sunday school class. I loved to do both. Was I missing something? Did it not count if I truly enjoyed the work?

Fortunately, this faulty thinking was soon evident when I read we are to serve Him with gladness. Helping others should be a joy, not drudgery. He gives us skills that we enjoy and use to serve others. Praise the Lord for that!

Thank you, Lord, for giving us commandments that can be a joy to obey. Amen.

DRIFTING

Gloria Doty   March 4
***I will instruct you and teach you in the way you should go;
I will counsel you with my eye upon you.*** Psalm 32:8 ESV

If you've lived in the northern states as I have, drifting has only one meaning: accumulated snow due to high wind. The first time I heard the term drifting, while talking about auto racing, I was confused.

This type of drifting, however, had nothing to do with weather. In this form of racing, the driver is constantly turning the steering wheel as tightly as possible in one direction while the rear of the car is actually drifting around the track almost sideways in the opposite direction. (Similar to driving on ice) I often live my life like that. I furiously try to steer my life my way instead of listening to God, and therefore, I am continuously sliding around the track of my life in the opposite direction. How much better it would be if I allowed God to steer and keep me from drifting off the path He has chosen for my life.

Heavenly Father, I want to stay by Your side as I travel around the track of life. Keep me from drifting. Amen

THE SILLY OSTRICH

Marcia Schwartz   March 5
He will cover you with his feathers, and under his wings you will find refuge. Psalm 91:4a NIV

When the ostrich is threatened by danger, he buries his head in the sand and lies as low as he can, thinking he is hiding from whatever threatens him. But his large bulbous body is hard to flatten so his tail feathers wave high in view.

We are often as silly as an ostrich. We think we can hide from God but we cannot. Instead of burying our heads in the sand, we need to run directly *to* Him for forgiveness of sins. Instead of fear and moving away, we can approach Him for rest and peace. In uncertainty, He is available for wisdom. No heads in the sand for us! God stands ready to protect and offer a refuge.

Dear Lord Protector Father, Forgive me when I bury my head in the sand, and give in to doubts, fears, and guilt. Cover me with Your grace and help me trust You for all things. Amen.

HOW DOES YOUR GARDEN GROW?

Angela L. Davis   March 6
Do not be deceived, God is not mocked; for whatever a man sows, that he will also reap. Galatians 6:7 NKJV

In the spring, after the threat of frost is gone, I plant seeds in pretty pots to add color to my front porch. I insert a small stake with the name of the flower I have planted. Weeks later, the seeds begin to sprout and eventually I have pots full of bright, colorful flowers. Where I planted marigold seeds, I find marigolds blooming. Where I planted petunias, petunias bloom. I am never surprised at what blooms in each pot. No surprises. No exceptions. I always reap that which I have sown.

Spiritual sowing and reaping follow the same process. If we sow anger, bitterness, and jealousy, we will reap a miserable life that bleeds into the lives of those around us. If we sow compassion, kindness, and love, we will reap a life of joy, contentment, and blessing. That too, spills over and affects others. We do indeed reap what we sow. No surprises. No exceptions.

Father, please help me plant my spiritual garden so that I will reap a harvest that is pleasing to You.

JUST BECAUSE

Patsy Sanders   March 7
Every good gift and every perfect gift is from above, and comes down from the Father of lights, James 1:17 NKJV

Whether given to special friends, secret sisters, outreach, or someone hurting, 'just because gifts' communicate volumes without saying a word. Ever receive one? I have; just the other day! Considering that someone thought of me, purchased a gift, and made sure I received it intensely impacted my heart.

We daily receive similar gifts from our heavenly Father—unexpected--the ones freely given solely because He loves us and desires to make us happy by encouraging our heart. His good and perfect gifts are all around – answered prayer, a faithful spouse, friendships, a home, great children, health, something on sale you needed, or even a parking place at the mall! His gifts are great or small, too many to count, and given because He longs to bless us!

Some gifts reflect a selfish motive while others indicate only the most expensive is acceptable. However, genuine gifts always seek to bless, not impress the other. A gift may brighten someone's day, place a smile on a saddened face, reach a soul for Christ, or encourage the forgotten, hurting person. By giving, you may be surprised to find you are the one blessed!

COMFORT FOOD

Monica Andermann   March 8
"I am the bread that came down from heaven." John 6:41 NIV

There I went again, reaching for another piece of chocolate. I've always had a tendency to be an "emotional eater," a person who seeks comfort in food during stressful or frustrating times. While chocolate may provide me with temporary satisfaction, the ill effects of its empty calories last much longer.

Some seek solace and reassurance in unfortunate places such as a medicine cabinet, the refrigerator, alcohol or an unhealthy relationship. However, our Lord offers us another option.

In John 6, Jesus says He is the bread of life. Throughout his ministry on earth, Jesus fed the lone sinner and the multitudes with His teaching and comfort. His words and works still feed us. When we partake of His bread, His nourishment fills us. Only in knowing God better can I find true and lasting comfort and wholeness.

Dear Lord: I turn from earthly temptations and instead choose to be fed by Your word. Amen.

POSITIONING MYSELF

Kimberly Henderson   March 9
O God, You are my God; Early will I seek You...
Psalm 63:1a, NKJV

I never expected the Lord to use the hound dogs next door to bless my life, but as I stared out my kitchen window one winter morning, I couldn't help but notice them huddled on my neighbor's back fence. The more I thought about it, I realized I had seen them on that fence for several mornings in a row-- curled up in the spot where the first warm rays of sun hit the yard.

I marveled at those silly, barky hounds. They knew exactly where to go for warmth. No one had to teach them. They just instinctively positioned themselves for survival first thing every morning.

The Lord reminded me of my need to position myself for survival. I know I can do nothing apart from Him, I know in His presence is the fullness of joy, and yet, how many mornings do I bulldoze forward into my day and my to-do list instead of sitting and soaking in time with the Lord?

I may not have noticed those dogs much before, but now they serve as a sweet reminder in my life--a reminder to be quick to bask in the warmth of time with the Son each and every day.

EVER NEAR

Beth Roose   March 10
... without faith it is impossible to please God, because anyone who comes to him must believe that he exists...
Hebrews 11:6 NIV

I awoke at 5am. When I pulled up the blind I noticed a luminous moon in a clear sky. One bright star hung above it. Suddenly silvery grey clouds enveloped both, and the brilliance was hidden from my sight. Soon the cloud moved; the moon shone brightly and the star reappeared.

The moon and the star were there all the time, but for a few brief minutes God's handiwork was obscured only by a cloud that hid the light from view.

Sometimes our circumstances blind us to the fact that God exists and we feel that He is hidden from us. Like the clouds, our circumstances obliterate our vision. Sadness and sorrow may overwhelm us.

Moses heard Him speak: *"I AM WHO I AM"* (Exodus 3:14 NIV). God is ever near--He *is*, and He exists. He is present all the time, even beyond the cloud that may obscure our vision.

OLD AGE

Bonnie Rose Hudson   March 11
Even to your old age and gray hairs, I am he, I am he who will sustain you. I have made you and I will carry you; I will sustain you and I will rescue you. Isaiah 46:4 NIV

What will I be when I am *old*? The thought hit me by surprise. Once it came, it lingered. What will life be like? Would I face crippling arthritis that would twist my hands and confine me first to a wheelchair, then to a bed, like my grandmother? Would I struggle to remember simple things? Would I awake each day with pain and end each day the same way? Will I be lonely?

"What will I be when I am *old*?" As the question echoed inside my heart, God answered my fears with one word.

"Mine."

Lord, help me rest in the peace that You know my tomorrows and will carry me through each of them, just as You have carried me through the past to this moment. Amen

DON'T THROW YOUR TOYS

Bonnie Rose Hudson   March 12

Because of the LORD'S great love we are not consumed, for his compassions never fail. They are new every morning; great is your faithfulness. Lamentations 3:22-23 NIV

God had led me through the same obstacles many times before, providing for all of my needs each step of the way. I felt foolish struggling with the same challenge to my faith again. How many times must God remind me to trust Him? How many times had He shown me that He was worthy of my trust?

I thought of the birthday party I had attended just the day before. The star of the day was Caleb, a beautiful two-year-old so full of energy that he can't help but do everything with gusto. How many times yesterday did I remind him, "Caleb, don't throw your toys."? But it's his nature, just like it's my human nature to struggle with fear and doubt.

I know Caleb has a lot of growing to do, and I know he'll need to be reminded again and again not to throw his toys. But he'll learn. God reminds me, "Trust me." I have growing to do and I will learn too.

Thank You, Father, for being so patient with me. Amen.

I LIFT MY EYES

Nola Passmore   March 13

During a short-term mission trip to Mexico, our team travelled a distance to perform Christian dramas for a youth group. I was distracted by the heat, tensions among our team members and homesickness for Australia. As I walked back to the change room after the performance, I suddenly felt a sharp pain on the bridge of my nose. I fell backwards onto the floor as if I had been punched. Stunned, I sat there in a daze before realizing I had walked into a glass door.

Years later, I bear a small mark on my nose as a reminder and the object lesson it continues to represent. If I had been looking up instead of at the ground, I would have seen the glass door and would have escaped a painful injury.

God has tremendous compassion on us when we're feeling sad and lonely, but He also wants us to look to Him and not be distracted by our circumstances. The Psalmist knew this when he said, *"I lift up my eyes to the hills—where does my help come from? My help comes from the LORD, the Maker of heaven and earth* (Psalm 121:1-2, NIV). Regardless of our troubles, let us remember to lift our eyes to the Lord and the comforter of our souls.

TUG-of-TIME

Sarah Lynn Phillips   March 14

"Could you go with Dad and Mom to her doctor's visit Monday?" My out-of-town sister's question created another tug-of-war in my mind. Mom's appointment fell on the same day our teenager would embark on her first missions' trip. Over and over, I needed to be two places at the same time. Husband, parents, children, friends . . . I wanted to support them all, but I found myself conflicted—and frustrated.

We're human. Limited. Unable to be everywhere for everyone at once. I'm learning to pray, seek God's wisdom, and try to prioritize well. I'm not indispensable; sometimes individuals need to take responsibility or others can take up the slack.

Unlike us, God is never limited by time and space. David pondered this truth: *"Where can I go from Your Spirit? Where can I flee from your presence?"* (Psalm 139:7, NIV). Jeremiah recorded (God speaking): *"Can anyone hide in secret places so that I cannot see him . . . . Do not I fill heaven and earth?* (Jeremiah 23:24, NIV).

I cannot be two places at once. But God can! He simultaneously accompanied my parents to the doctor and Elisabeth to Baltimore. Later, He escorted one daughter home from work while standing by her sister's side in a hospital operating room. There's no tug-of-time with Him. His omnipresence trumps our humanness every time!

A PLACE OF REFUGE

Margaret Steinacker   March 15
Keep me safe, my God, for in you I take refuge I say to the LORD, "You are my Lord apart from you I have no good thing."
Psalm 16: 1-2

I struggled with varying levels of depression for several years. I still played keyboards for the congregation and choir, went to work everyday, sang weekends in other churches with my family, and tried to keep things going at home. My husband realized the severity of my distress when I failed to pay the utilities bill. Twenty-five years later, my depression is minimal.

During my struggle, we spent two fishing vacations in a rustic cabin in northern Wisconsin. The time away from work and household duties gave me extra time to bask in nature, read the Bible, and pray. I sensed God's presence as a refuge in my time of trouble. Memories of the simplicity God provided in that pristine forest by a small lake, with abundant fish, loons, and blue herons, still comfort me.

God has proven to be my refuge many times before and since the depression. I thank Him for His protection.

Thank You, God for the refuge You offer freely when we seek Your face. Keep us tuned to Your ways. Show us how to overcome troubles. Amen.

TO AN AUDIENCE OF ONE

Joan Clayton   March 16
Worship the LORD with gladness; come before him with joyful songs. Psalm 100:2 NIV

The aged white haired gentleman sat on the front pew and stood as the song leader announced we would only sing the first two stanzas of a familiar hymn. Unaware that the congregation had stopped, the man continued on to the third stanza. The congregation listened with tears as he sang from his heart and praised God.

All through the Bible we read songs of thankfulness and praise. Moses and the Israelites sang for their great deliverance. David wrote and sang many songs and praise for his God.

Singing songs of praise is a good start to any day. God is always there and He will listen, even when we sing alone.

EACH DEED A SIGN

Debbie Carpenter   March 17

Then the chief priests and the Pharisees gathered a council and said, "What shall we do? For this Man works many signs. If we let Him alone like this, everyone will believe in Him...
John 11: 47, 48a NKJV

Dear Lord, You want all men to know
That when You lived so long ago,
Each deed You did was meant to show
Your full divinity.
You turned the water into wine
Each miracle became a "sign,"
That God Himself with man aligned
As You walked in Galilee.

You touched blind eyes and made them see,
You healed the lepers, set them free.
You spoke and calmed a troubled sea,
Yet You were called, "the Lamb."
You fed large crowds with little bread,
The demons looked at You with dread.
You had the strength to raise the dead.
You are the great "I Am."

A BLOWN OPPORTUNITY

Joseph Hopkins   March 18

*You shall receive power when the Holy Spirit has come upon you; and you shall be my witnesses....*Acts 1:8 RSV

It was 1966. I was traveling solo around the world, visiting mission stations and the Holy Land. At Katmandu, Nepal, I boarded a plane bound for Calcutta. A couple of American hippies walked down the aisle. The girl took the window seat beside me.

Her boyfriend's seatmate, judging from appearance, was a well-dressed American businessman. The aroma emanating from the girl indicated a long absence from soap and water. I asked if she would like me to trade seats with her friend. She politely thanked me. As I took my place beside the gentleman, I said, "I thought I would do us both a favor."

Forty-four years later, I have regretted my impulsive action.

God had given me a chance to share His love with this young woman, and I blew it.

Forgive me, Lord, for the many times I have failed to reach out to those in need of Your saving grace and power. Help me to be more sensitive and obedient to Your call to share the love of Jesus when You give me the opportunity. Amen.

HOLD ME!

Lydia E. Harris   March 19
How priceless is your unfailing love! Both high and low among men find refuge in the shadow of your wings. Psalm 36:7 NIV

While my husband and I babysat our two grandchildren, my husband played pretend games with two-year-old Clara while I rocked baby Owen. When their mom returned, I handed Owen to her. Clara immediately looked up at me and asked, "Do you want to hold me?"

I didn't hesitate. I scooped Clara into my arms, bounced her on my lap and hugged her. Clara had waited hours for my attention, and I was glad to assure her of my love.

In Psalm 36, David paints a picture of a God who knows our needs and delights in loving us, His children. When we come to God with our needs, we don't need to question his love and ask, "Do you want to hold me?" God's Word assures us of His limitless, steadfast, precious love that extends far beyond anything we can ever comprehend. And we know God holds us: ***"The eternal God is your refuge, and underneath are the everlasting arms"*** (Deuteronomy 33:27 NIV)).

O Lord, how precious to me is Your unfailing love! Thank You for always providing a refuge for me under the shadow of Your wings.

PRAY AND BELIEVE

Carol J. Lee   March 20

Therefore I tell you, whatever you ask for in prayer, believe that you have received it, and it will be yours. Mark 11: 24 NIV

Our 9 year old grandson's mom took him to the ER when he turned a gray/blue color, got a rash and swollen face. While there, she called us to pray. Doctors diagnosed an allergic reaction to almonds. We were relieved and thankful to learn the reason for his symptoms. Treatment was timely and effective.

After they got home, the family gathered in the living room and our grandson came downstairs, stood in the middle of the room, looked from one family member to another and declared, "When you pray you gotta believe God can do it or it ain't going to happen!"

Wow! I was amazed at his spiritual wisdom. He had such belief when he prayed that God would be with him and help him. God was! I was humbled to hear his faith in action. It was a lesson for me to "...believe and not doubt..." (James 1:6) when I pray.

Lord, increase my faith so when I pray according to Your will, I too will believe and not doubt.

SERVICE WITH A SMILE

Elaine Given   March 21

How much more, then, will the blood of Christ, who through the eternal Spirit offered himself unblemished to God, cleanse our consciences from acts that lead to death, so that we may serve the living God! Hebrews 9:14 NIV

We know we cannot earn salvation but how often do we serve others in an attempt to gain a good conscience? With the advent of modern technology, we are overwhelmed with need. Attempts to salve our conscience often give us grief as we overload ourselves with good causes. We may only serve the living God with a smile when we know He has commissioned us.

What is God commissioning me to do today for Him? He will not ask me for more than He equips me to do, nor does He condemn me when I do less. It is important that I serve with a genuine smile rather than a gritted teeth grin. Genuine love from God will flow as I recognize His will for me today and I will have joy.

HELPING AT HOSPICE

Cindy Evans   March 22
A new command I give you: Love one another. As I have loved you, so you must love one another. John 13:34 NIV

I took my place behind the desk,
settling in the familiar chair,
the feeling of peace I'd come to expect
was gently evident there.

As people passed, they seemed sad,
yet thankful for this place,
and a cheery voice and flowers
and a smiling, friendly face.
Some walked by the pond,
some sat in the chapel in prayer,
some people slept in the rooms,
you could see how much they care.

A chaplain walked by
and gave a little wave.
One of the staff let me know
an ambulance was on the way.
I was taking it all in
and just blessed to be a part
of God's love in action
and sharing of His heart.

LISTEN

Adele Jones   March 23
Read John 10:1-18 (NIV)
... his sheep follow him because they know his voice.
John 10: 4b NIV

I'd spent a wakeful night explaining to God how I needed a job. As a young graduate, I moved back to live with my parents. Job options in my profession were few. My finances were low. The only positive was that I had plenty of time to spend in prayer and scripture.

"What should I do, Lord? I can't live with my parents forever."
Move to Toowoomba.

Was that a whisper? Did someone just tell me to move to that city two hours east of my family's farm? The words were so clear. I fell into a peaceful sleep.

The next day a friend called. "Hi! I'm moving to Toowoomba! Want to be my flatmate?"

I hadn't told anyone what I'd heard.

We moved. I reconnected with family and friends, including the man I ended up marrying. A job came up utilizing the skills for which I'd trained.

The Shepherd had spoken and I'd recognised His voice.

This verse doesn't say that the sheep follow the shepherd because they know what he looks like, but that they hear and know his voice. How encouraging to know whatever circumstance we're facing, when we cannot see a way forward, the Good Shepherd calls to us.

May we know His voice.

BE HAPPY FOR OTHERS

Dr. K   March 24
Rejoice with them that do rejoice, and weep with them that weep.
Romans 12:15 KJV

Two little girls were at our community pool today. One was somewhat timid. She enjoyed the water, but refused to leave the step. She splashed herself in the cold water and stood at the edge despite the urging of her grandma to go with her into the deeper part. As she watched her sister go into the middle of the pool with mom, she cheered "Yay!" She was happy for sis even though she herself was afraid to launch out into the deep.

I couldn't help but be struck by the Christian reality that that's the way we should feel about someone else's adventurous success. "Yay, good for you. I'm happy you made it."

Too often we resent another's success, happiness, confidence or faith. The success of my friends or family members can enrich my life if I am happy for them.

Dear God, help me to find joy in being happy for others. Amen.

REDEEMING THE TIME

Donna J. Howard   March 25

***"Sow for yourselves righteousness, reap the fruit of unfailing love,
and break up your unplowed ground; for it is time to seek the Lord."***
Hosea 10:12 NIV

I pulled into a parking space, switched off the engine and glanced at the clock on the dashboard. Fifteen minutes early.

You left home too early, I scolded myself. *You could have used this extra time at home.* I looked around and thought, *I should have brought the book I was reading. I could have read a couple of chapters while I wait.* Another glance at the clock showed that three minutes had passed. Drumming my thumbs on the steering wheel, I began to fume. "Waiting is such a waste of time," I grumbled.

Then the Lord spoke gently to my heart: "You could use this time to fellowship with Me."

Chagrined, I thanked the Lord for reminding me that He desires regular fellowship with me, that He is always available for prayer and praise, and that time with Him is never wasted. I began to pray. The time went so fast, I was nearly late for my doctor appointment.

Heavenly Father, help me to use my time wisely and may it include spending time with You. In Jesus' name. Amen.

AFTERMATH OF THE LANDSLIDE

Joseph Hopkins   March 26

After 24 hours of heavy rain, a large portion of the face of Mt. Mullange, Malawi's highest mountain, crumbled in a huge landslide. The rushing water, propelling mud and huge boulders, destroyed everything in its path, including entire villages. Five hundred people perished.

As missionary pastor and seminary teacher, I drove to the disaster site a few days later. I came to an isolated area where the torrent had divided a narrow strip of land, sparing several trees and thatched-roofed houses. The mournful, silent occupants were seated on the ground as I approached.

I spotted the tattered, mud-stained pages of a book written in the Chichewa language of the Malawian people. I picked them up, to find the final chapters of First Corinthians and the opening ones of Second Corinthians, I read Paul's great message of hope in the resurrection chapter (I Cor.15), but also these verses from 2 Corinthians 1:3,4: *Blessed be the ...God of all comfort, who comforts us in all our tribulation.*

As best as I could, I greeted the villagers in their native language. I offered a prayer thanking God for sparing them, asking Him to provide for their needs and to be their comfort and hope.

PEACE I GIVE YOU

Monica Andermann   March 27
"...the Lord turn his face toward you and give you peace."
Numbers 6:26 NIV

When I got the call to meet my brother Louis at the hospital, I knew it wouldn't be good. When I arrived at the emergency room, the situation was worse than I expected. My brother, the victim of a random beating, was battered and bloody from head to toe. Calling on the Lord for strength, I managed to remain calm, even cheerful, as I tried to encourage him.

After treatment, the attending physician handed Louis' discharge paperwork to me and allowed me to take him home. Before we left, the doctor said something that gave me pause. "You must be a very religious woman," he remarked. "Most other family members would have been crying through this."

There is a certain peace apparent in those who strive to know God. He gives a "peace which transcends all understanding" (Philippians 4:7). Keeping our Lord foremost in our lives allows us to trust with His peace.

Lord, life sometimes presents frightening circumstances. How good it is to know that during those times I need only call upon You to feel Your calming presence. Amen.

CONNECTED

Tabitha Abel March 28

***When the poor and needy seek water, and there is none, and their
tongue faileth for thirst, I the Lord will hear them, I the God of Israel
will not forsake them.*** Isaiah 41: 17 KJV

While my husband and I were walking our dogs the other day, I
talked non-stop. I paused and said, "Now it's your turn," but he had
nothing to say. Later he told me, "When you talk a lot, I don't hear
you. I tune you out." So that's how it works. Talk less and he will
hear me when I do talk.

I'm glad that God has a different take on this. The psalmist
says, ***"The Lord will hear when I call to Him."*** (Psalm 4:3b NKJV) He
hears anyone who calls Him, anytime. He doesn't tune us out, He
doesn't have call waiting. He is never too busy. He does not keep
9-5 hours.

Our lives are full of challenges. We can confidently face them
if we remember we have an open line to talk with the Lord, and He
"will hear us". We talk; and then listen to "His turn" in giving us wise
answers.

PACK FOR ADVENTURE

Barbara Major Bryden March 29

***You have made a wide path for my feet to keep them
from slipping.*** Psalm 18:36 NLT

My family and I enjoy back packing in Idaho's Sawtooth
Mountains and on the Pacific coast of Washington state. All of the
trips have been fun in spite of snow, lightning storms, steep trails,
slick rocks and fog. However, on our Washington trip, although
we'd planned ahead, the combination of hungry raccoons, lots
of adults, and young children created new problems. The sheer
number of people made it hard to keep our tents zipped shut.
Sleeping bags and one daypack disappeared down a trail,
accompanied by raccoons.

Sounds a bit like life. Personal trials, natural disasters, a tough
economy and world problems, can seem like starving raccoons
that steal our joy.

We can't avoid trials, but we can prepare for them if we:
   read our travel guide (Bible) daily.

listen for updates from our CEO (God).

submit needs and emergency to the head office in a timely manner (pray).

Thank God for his help when you climbed over that enormous tree (large problem) lying across your path.

praise God every day.

You're traveling with Jesus and He knows your path well. Anticipate a great adventure!

MY SOUL IS MAGENTA

Pauline Beck   March 30

"Make glad the soul of Your servant, For to You, O Lord, I lift up my soul." Psalm 86:4 NAB

My soul is magenta,
but I dress in browns and grays.
My soul sings and dances
while I plod away my days.

My soul spins and sparkles,
but no one here can see.
They're too concerned with how I look
to see this inner me.

My soul already knows the truth
that my mind still tries to find;
it plays among the heavens with God
and leaves me here. . .behind.

SONG OF ASCENT: A NEW PSALM, COME WORSHIP

S. Niggemeier   March 31

O come, let us sing for joy to the Lᴏʀᴅ, Let us shout joyfully to the rock of our salvation.
Psalm 95:1 NASB

Leave behind your loneliness, find fellowship and friendship.
Always put God first, come worship on Sundays.

Leave behind your fears, find strength.

Always put God first, come worship on Sundays.

Leave behind your hurtful ways, find concern for others.
Always put God first, come worship on Sundays.

Leave behind your soccer games, find a new way.
Always put God first, come worship on Sundays.

Leave behind your greediness, find sharing and generosity.
Always put God first, come worship on Sundays.

Leave behind your desperation, find hope for better ways.
Always put God first, come worship on Sundays.

Leave behind your guns, find protection.
Always put God first, come worship on Sundays.

Leave behind your cheating ways, find honesty.
Always put God first, come worship on Sundays.

Leave behind your intolerance, find acceptance.
Always put God first, come worship on Sundays.

Leave behind your impatience, find grace.
Always put God first, come worship on Sundays.

Leave everything behind to find peace and love,
Always put God first, come worship on Sundays

April

A FOOL'S LEGACY

Connie Ansong   April 1

The wise shall inherit glory,
But shame shall be the legacy of fools. Proverbs 3:35 *

Psalm 24:1 states: *The earth is the Lord's, and all its fullness,*
The world and those who dwell therein. This earth is precious to
the Lord and He designed an orderly and beautiful home for all
creatures. But we have "created" a world where evil is admired
and goodness is shunned. As the Psalmist wrote, *The fool has said*
in his heart, "There is no God." They are corrupt, They have done
abominable works, There is none who does good. The Lord looks
down from heaven upon the children of men, To see if there are any
who understand, who seek God. (Psalm 14:1-2 *)

Who is a fool? Anyone who lives his or her life without the
Lord's guidance. When we deny the Lord in our hearts as the true
Creator of our world and our lives, then we are indeed fools *(...fools*
despise wisdom and instruction Proverbs 1:7b*). But when we seek
for God and His wisdom in our lives, we begin to discern who He
is. *(The fear* of the Lord is the beginning of knowledge... Proverbs 1:7a)

Lord, help us to be wise, not fools, to be mindful of who You are,
and to live by Your word and will alone.
In Jesus' name we pray with thanksgiving. Amen and amen.
(* all quotes are from NKJV)

SMALL BIRD GREAT PRAISE

Kenda Turner   April 2
Because you are my help, I sing in the shadow of your wings. I cling
to you; your right hand upholds me. Psalm 63: 7-8 NIV

While on my walk one morning, I was startled by a loud string
of chirps and tweets--a boisterous tune that could only come from
a very large bird. Or so I thought. Instead I was surprised to see
a tiny feathered friend perched on the highest tip of a tree. Out
of its beak poured forth a song far more powerful than its size
suggested.

How could the wee creature sing so mightily--and joyfully--

while clinging to such a precarious perch?

The answer popped clear. Because of the Hands that upheld it.

Jesus' words in Matthew 6:26 (NIV) came to mind. ***Look at the birds of the air, they do not sow or reap or store away in barns, and yet your heavenly Father feeds them. Are you not much more valuable than they?***

Do not worry. If God upholds the birds of the air, won't He much more uphold us, even though life's branches shake and sway? Cling to Him. Then--like that small warbler high on the wind--our joyful praises will pour forth, too.

Lord, my heart is full of praise in the comfort of
Your unwavering love. Amen.

PINK---SOURCE OF MY TEENAGE BRAVADO

Evelyn Minshull   April 3
"On Christ the solid Rock I stand; all other ground is sinking sand..."
[from the hymn "My Hope is Built..."]

Pink. No other color need apply when I was due for a new dress to be made—or, less frequently, bought. Pink, as impertinent as wild honeysuckle, spoke false courage from within my crippling shell of teenage shyness.

One dress in particular glows in memory. I was fourteen, by then, increasingly insecure, a less than adequate second violinist in the school orchestra which was scheduled, one April evening, to perform. Only this twice-worn dress—crisp, frothy, confident, and blatantly pink—could be considered.

Mother said the grass stain should wash out easily. "You'll be fine for tonight," she assured me.

After school, she somberly presented a miniaturized dress—identical to mine in every detail, yet telescoped to doll-size.

"As soon as it touched the water, it melted in my hands." Mother hugged me. "I'm so sorry, honey."

Often, we depend on worldly promises, individuals or objects to embrace and protect us. Such props—as insubstantial as the bold bluster of the Wizard of Oz—rust, melt, wither, crumble, break, betray or fade away. Only in God can we discover stability, safety and genuine courage.

LORD, grant us wisdom to seek You, and courage to stand with You. AMEN

JESUS UNDERSTANDS

Pat Collins   April 4

Let us then approach God's throne of grace with confidence, so that we may receive mercy and find grace to help us in our time of need.
Hebrews 4:16 NIV

When others turn from us,
and they don't understand,
just reach up for Jesus,
hold fast to His hand.

Jesus is no stranger,
to heartache and pain,
one who knew sorrow,
suffering and shame.

He knows when you're hurting
your whole world looks dim,
That's when He brings comfort,
and heals from within.

WATCH, WAIT, WISH

Doris Richardson   April 5

My friend Kerry has two Chihuahuas. When they think it is time for a treat, they sit at her feet, *watching* every move she makes, cocking their heads to the side, ears pricked up, eyes following all her movements. Not impatient, barking or distracted by anything else going on, they *wait* expectantly for her to give them a treat. They simply *wait*. It's obvious they are *wishing* for a treat.

I believe God wants us to have the same traits in relation to Christ's return. We should be *watching, waiting*, and *wishing* for Him to come. In **2 Timothy 4:8** (KJV), He offers a crown of righteousness to all those who **"love His appearing."**

He tells us to **"watch"** because we don't know when He will come (Matthew 5:13). We are to **"wait for His Son from Heaven, whom He raised from the dead, even Jesus, which delivered us from the wrath to come"** (1 Thessalonians 1:10 KJV). We are to **"hope to the end for the grace that is to be brought unto you at the revelation of Jesus Christ"** (1 Peter 1:13 KJV).

When Jesus comes, may He find us *watching, waiting, and wishing,* because we love His appearing.

BACKYARD THEOPHANY

Bill Batcher   April 6
Lord,
Help me listen to the sounds of spring:
birds at the feeder, chirping,
chasing squirrels,
buzzing wasps,
fluttering new budding leaves,
and may I recognize these as Your voice.

Attune me to the smells of spring:
lily, amaryllis, wild onion, skunk cabbage,
gardens redug,
farm fields dressed,
sea breezes,
and may I recognize these as Your fragrance.

And when my face feels sun warm,
my bare arms cool,
when I feel potting soil between my fingers,
or a hose nozzle leaking on my wrist,
remind me I've been touched by God.

THE LORD MY HELPER

Elouise H. Hults   April 7
God is our refuge and strength, a very present help in trouble.
Psalm 46:1 KJV

When I needed extra income, I advertised for house-cleaning jobs. Calls came, and I accepted two.

At job #1 the layout of the house seemed to be a maze. I hardly knew where to start. "Lord, help," I prayed. He showed me a routine that worked best and the tasks flowed smoothly.

Job #2 presented a different problem. I needed to clean the side-by-side refrigerator, but, because of its location, I couldn't open the doors completely. I tried every angle, only to fail.

Frustrated and nearly in tears, I prayed again, "Lord, help me."
In that instant, I felt the Lord guide my hands. Removing and
replacing glass shelves and vegetable drawers—in that non-
flexible refrigerator—solved the puzzle.

The Lord brought answers to my prayers: when I needed jobs,
they came; when I needed direction, I received it; when I needed
immediate hands-on help, God was there.

No problem is too small for us to pray about. No dilemma is too
big for Him to answer.

Thank You, God, that You are personally interested in me.

LIFE'S MESSES—GOD'S MINISTRY

Patsy Sanders   April 8
I can do all things through Christ, who strengthens me.
Philippians 4:13 NKJV

It was one of those days; the kind when nothing seemed
to go right and everything seemed to go wrong - one big mess!
Has that happened to you? You feel discouraged, stressed, and
overwhelmed--questioning why the unexpected seem to create an
impossible life?

Isn't it ironic that God's classroom requires participation? His
children must discover that managing life requires dependence on
a power much greater than our own. Undoubtedly, every 'mess' in
life is a glorious opportunity for ministry.

What are you facing today? A financial setback, job loss,
wayward child, health issues? Maybe it is a broken marriage or
shattered relationship. Whatever it is, God knows, understands
and cares. He invites dependence on Him.

One of Satan's effective tools is discouragement. In the middle
of the word *discouragement* is *courage*. To live victoriously, God's
children must pray for and utilize God's power. His empowerment
provides an opportunity to shine brilliantly in the bleakest of times.
No wonder it has been said that trials don't necessarily *make*
someone, they *reveal* him. Use your messy day to shine for Christ
as He strengthens you.

NATHANAEL

Pollyanna Sedziol April 9

"How do you know me?" Nathanael asked. Jesus answered, *"I saw you while you were still under the fig tree before Philip called you."* John 1:48 NIV

If Christ saw me there,
and He says that he did
then I know why
the struggle was so fierce.
I did not want to make
the decision that I made.
It is at once a frightening
and an inspiring thing
to ask God for His will.

He might answer
as He did me
when I struggled in prayer
by a fig tree.
It comes to me now,
that if it is frightening
and if it is inspiring
it is also comforting
to know that He knows of it all.

*… Your will be done, on earth as it is in heaven…*Matthew 6:10b NIV

FORGOTTEN?

Elouise H. Hults April 10

They may forget yet will I not forget thee. Isaiah 49:15 KJV

Nothing was in my mailbox. My email was empty. My answering machine silent. Caller I.D. displayed no missed calls. My family had forgotten to remember me on my special day.

I was disappointed. I reminded myself that people are busy. Activities fill their calendars. Schedules leave little opening for those outside of the immediate demands of the week. People go from one rush-hurry-up-running-out-of-time to another. My loved ones are no exception. I know that they didn't mean to overlook me. They were simply caught up in the busyness of their own lives.

I settled back in the comfort of my recliner with a soothing cup of hot tea. I remembered that I am loved and secure in the everlasting arms of God my Father. (Deuteronomy 33:27) He will take care of my family, as He takes care of me. I am blessed and I am loved.

Thank You, Lord, that You have not forgotten me.
Your Word forever settles this truth in my heart. Amen.

GLIMMER OF LIGHT

Joy Bradford   April 11

When Jesus spoke again to the people, he said, ***"I am the light of the world. Whoever follows me will never walk in darkness, but will have the light of life."*** John 8:12 NIV

My neighborhood is very dark at night, so I decided to buy inexpensive individual solar lights for my front yard. I thought it would be fun to stake them in several flower pots. Now as I look out at the sinister nighttime, I see light, and it's a comfort to me.

A theme from start to finish in the Bible is the contrast between darkness and light. The apostle John reminds us, ***"In him was life, and that life was the light of all mankind. The light shines in the darkness, and the darkness has not overcome it."*** John 1: 4-5 NIV

Light is connected to Christ over and over again. He is the "light of the world." Our world looks so dark at times, yet, Jesus' light and truth shines brightly. We can have hope in circumstances, even when we do not understand. As we look out, His light is a comfort.

Lord, the world looks so dark at times. We thank You for giving us light. We acknowledge Your power and because of that power, we have hope. Amen

FAST FOOD CHRISTIANITY

Michelle S. Lazurek   April 12
"I am the vine; you are the branches. If you remain in me and I in you,
you will bear much fruit; apart from me you can do nothing."
John 15:5 NIV

After a busy day, I stopped at McDonalds for dinner. When I
opened the bag of food, I reached for a french fry. Cold and soggy,
it bent under the weight of the grease. I unwrapped the hamburger
to find a stale bun, wilted pickles and cold, burned meat.

Disappointed, I made a decision--I ate it anyway. And it was
terrible. I regretted my decision to settle for mediocre fast food
instead of a nutritious meal.

In my Christian journey, I often do the same. I settle for the
mediocrity of life rather than the vibrant relationship Christ has to
offer. Instead of enriching my life each day by spending time in His
Word and prayer, I settle for a quick Bible verse on my calendar or
listening to Christian music in the car.

Fast food or nutrition for good health? It seems like a clear
choice whether I am feeding my body or my soul.

Dear Lord, help me not to settle for the convenience of mediocrity,
but to dive into the Word to provide my soul with the nutrition it
needs.

PARADES, DONKEYS AND OBEDIENCE

Lydia E. Harris   April 13
Read Matthew 21: 1-11

I love a parade with its colorful uniforms, waving flags, and
lively music. It's fun to watch bands and drill teams march in
synchronized steps. Often hometown celebrities wave from shiny
convertibles and decorated floats.

But I recall parades where I wasn't merely a spectator. As the
drum major's shrill whistle blew, I marched forward with my high
school band. I watched from the corner of my eye, keeping in
step with other trumpet players. I wanted our band to win another
trophy.

Perhaps you could call Palm Sunday a parade. Waving palm
branches, shouts of "Hosanna in the highest," and an honored

celebrity were part of the procession. The atmosphere was jubilant as King Jesus rode into Jerusalem, not on a fancy float but on the foal of a donkey. Crowds honored him with cheers and spread cloaks before him.

When I reread the story, Matthew 21:6 (NIV) stood out: *"The disciples went and did as Jesus had instructed them."* They didn't argue, "We can't walk up to a stranger's barn and take his animals." They simply did as Jesus asked.

Just as my band followed instructions to gain approval from parade officials and earn a fading award, even more so, may we obey God's Word and reap eternal rewards from our heavenly Judge.

PASSION WEEK

Marilyn Nutter   April 14
For God so loved the world that he gave his one and only Son, that whoever believes in him shall not perish but have eternal life. For God did not send his Son into the world to condemn the world, but to save the world through him. John 3: 16-17 NIV

Passion week, sometimes also referred to as Holy Week, is the time from Palm Sunday through Easter Sunday. It is named because of the passion with which Jesus willingly went to the cross, suffered and paid for our sins. The events of Passion week are described in the Gospels: *Matthew 21-27, Mark 11-15, Luke 19-23,* and *John 12-19.*

This week, perhaps you can choose one of the Gospel accounts to read each day and reflect on the passionate love Jesus has for us.

JESUS PRAYS FOR US

Donna J. Howard   April 15
Read John 17:6-26 NIV

Moments before Jesus and His disciples went to the olive grove where Judas would betray Him and Jesus would be arrested, Jesus bestowed a special honor on His disciples. He prayed for them! He asked God to bind them together, "… that they may be one . . ." (vs. 11); that they might have His joy (vs. 13); that God would "protect them from the evil one" (vs. 15); and that He would set them apart to do God's will (vs.17).

Jesus' prayer was not only for His disciples. *"My prayer is not for them alone. I pray also for those who will believe in me through their (the disciples') message."* (John 17:20) Jesus was praying for future generations, so His prayer was for US! He still prays for us. I John 2:1 (NIV) says: *My dear children, I write this to you so that you will not sin. But if anybody does sin, we have an advocate with the Father—Jesus Christ, the Righteous One."* What a wonderful Savior we have!

Dear Lord, I can hardly take in the depths of Your love for me. May I never take it for granted. Amen.

IF I COULD

Bonnie Rose Hudson   April 16

When Pilate saw that he could prevail nothing…*Then released Barabbas unto them: and when he had scourged Jesus, he delivered him to be crucified.* Matthew 27:24a, 26 KJV

When I think of the whip striking your back, Lord, curling around your side and tearing your skin, I want to cry, "Stop!" Please, if only I could do something. If only I could take just one blow from the burden You are bearing in my place.

But I can't.

When You looked at me, You saw the sin burdening my back and curling around my heart, strangling the life from today and the hope from tomorrow. You saw my desperate need for You, Lord. You saw the sin I could not pay for myself.

So You did.

Lord, thank You for bearing the weight of my sin and doing for me what I could never do. Amen.

ECHOES OF THE PASSION: BETRAYAL

Jana Carman   April 17

[Jesus] said, "I tell you, one of you will betray me." They were very sad and began to say to him one after the other "Surely not I, Lord?"
Matthew 26:21,22 NIV

The disciples knew their weaknesses, so each one wondered

if he might accidentally betray Jesus. To them it was inconceivable that one of them might deliberately betray their beloved Master. But each of the gospel accounts makes it clear that Judas' betrayal was both deliberate (Matthew 26:14,15) and Satan-orchestrated (Luke 22:3).

Judas' action rouses disgust in us. We find ourselves saying, "Surely not I, Lord?" Yet, like Peter, we join unbelievers around their "fire" (or water cooler?) and hide our allegiance to Christ. Or we betray by keeping quiet when people misuse our dear Savior's name.

Peter, who was guilty of his own brand of betrayal, wrote later out of his bitter experience, *Live such good lives among the pagans that, though they accuse you of doing wrong, they may see your good deeds and glorify God on the day he visits us* (1 Peter 2:12 NIV).

Dear Lord, if (or when) I betray you out of cowardice, offer to me as You did to Peter, forgiveness and reinstatement, because: "Lord, you know all things; you know that I love you." (John 21:17b NIV)

ECHOES OF THE PASSION: NEEDS

Jana Carman   April 18
... you will find a tethered colt on which no one has yet ridden. Untie it, and bring it here. If anybody asks you, "Why are you doing this?" just say, "The Lord needs it..." Mark 11:2, 3 Phillips

The Master needed a young unbroken donkey to ride into Jerusalem. To ride a donkey was the historic symbol of a king coming in peace, not war. Zechariah prophesied, *Rejoice greatly, O Daughter of Zion! ... See, your king comes to you, righteous and having salvation, gentle and riding on a donkey, on a colt, the foal of a donkey* (Zechariah 9:9 NIV).

That day Jesus rode a donkey into Jerusalem in peace, bringing salvation. But in Revelation 19:11-16, Jesus, riding a white war horse, will bring justice and a war to end all wars.

That day 2000 years ago, other than an unbroken colt, what else did the Master need? He needed listeners as He taught in the Temple, friends to eat with, disciples to stay awake and pray, strength and fortitude to endure taunts and beatings. How great were His human needs!

When we feel our human needs are overwhelming, the

promise in Philippians4:19 NIV reassures us: *And my God will meet all your needs ...*

Thank You, Lord, for meeting my needs so superabundantly —"according to [your] glorious riches"! Amen.

REDEEMED

Virginia Blackburn April 19
For meditation: Philippians 3:7-11 NIV

Not by deeds that I have done
Nor even honors I have won,
Can I attain His saving grace
And meet my Savior face to face.

It was the Father's grace that won
When He gave His only Son,
Purchased salvation full and free,
Died in agony on the tree.

He rose again! Death could not stay.
His resurrection paved the way
For my redemption, for His glory
The world must hear salvation's story.

JESUS

Earl Kugle April 20
The angel said to the women, "Do not be afraid, for I know that you are looking for Jesus, who was crucified. He is not here; he has risen, just as he said. Come and see the place where he lay. Then go quickly and tell his disciples: 'He has risen from the dead and is going ahead of you into Galilee. There you will see him.' Now I have told you." Matthew 28:5-7 (NIV)

He is risen,
Hallelujah!
He is risen,
Praise the Lord!
He has taken away sin's prison;
Give Him praise in one accord.

We will sing of hope and gladness,
He is the everlasting Lord.
He is the Lord of all creation
And He is God's Holy Son,
So give Him laud and honor
'til our work on earth is done.
Forever we will praise Him,
For our salvation He has won!

SPECIAL SECURITY

Evelyn Heinz   April 21

Now that I'm older I collect Social Security. But beyond that earthly Social Security we have a "Special Security" in knowing Christ.

That security lasts forever!

"Stand at the crossroads and look; ask for the ancient paths, ask where the good way is, and walk in it, and you will find rest for your soul." Jeremiah 6:16 NIV

SERVICE OF LIGHT

Tommie Lenox   April 22

Jesus spoke to the people once more and said, "I am the light of the world. If you follow me, you won't have to walk in darkness, because you will have the light that leads to life." John 8:12 NLT

One of my favorite joys at the Easter season is the service of light held on Saturday night before Resurrection Day. The air is cold, the wind whips through the trees as we stand around a fire, holding unlit candles, waiting for the light. We hear the liturgy as the priest dips the Easter candle into the fire until the wick blazes to light. He lights the candle held closest to him, a light that is then shared throughout the gathering crowd.

Aflame with the spirit,
candles dispel the darkness.
One by one the light is given
To each one the gift of Heaven

A mighty wind chills the night air.
The breath of God?
Hands shelter each faltering flame

Eyes focus, mesmerized
Keep the light burning! Never let it fade

The wind of the Spirit brings us to the light.
Focused on Christ, with unwavering faith
We will keep His Light alive.
One by one, the light is given.
To each one, the light of Heaven.

FINCH OR SERPENT?

Debra L. Butterfield   April 23

A sharp-shinned hawk perched in the locust bean tree that grows fifteen feet from my apartment patio. The usual morning songbirds were conspicuously absent. They knew enough to stay away from this ruffian. But one tiny finch fluttered nearby. The hawk showed no apparent interest—motionless as a statue. Soon the finch came closer, and in a strike quicker than my eye could perceive, the hawk captured the little bird in its claws.

As the hawk flew off to enjoy his breakfast, a thought struck me: How often am I like that innocent little finch, ignorant of danger lurking nearby? Sin, like that hawk, looks beautiful and harmless, disinterested in us. We often think we can get close without becoming its prey. But before we realize it, sin has clutched us and taken us captive.

Matthew 10:16, (NKJV), says, *"Behold, I send you out as sheep in the midst of wolves. Therefore be wise as serpents and harmless as doves."* I gain that wisdom by reading the Bible and asking for God's help. With His Word and wisdom I'll recognize sin when it perches next to me and flee before I'm caught.

BEAUTY SPEAKS IN EVERY PLACE

Keren Threlfall   April 24
The heavens declare the glory of God; the skies proclaim the work of his hands, Psalm 19:1 NIV

Beauty speaks from every place
From tender shoot, to granite face.
Shy, mournful glance from dimming eyes,

Pink glories stroked across the skies.

Beauty speaks on bloodstained cross,
First glance, appeared as heaven's loss.
The beauty of this Life laid down,
No greater love was ever shown.

The horror that the cross was mine,
But borne by Man who is Divine.
Beauty streams forth from paradox,
"He is the King!" cry out the rocks.

Beauty's tale, it is not done,
Nothing new beneath the sun,
The stories new, and yet the same,
All beauty serves to praise His name.

RESURRECTION

Evelyn Minshull   April 25
There was a violent earthquake, for an angel of the Lord came down
from heaven, and, going to the tomb, rolled back the stone and sat
on it. His appearance was like lightning, and his clothes were white
as snow. Matthew 28:2-3 NIV

Resurrection.
For me, the term implies no gentle, quiet translation,
no body eased from stillness—no placid reclamation
of relative or friend.

Rather, the word denotes raw energy—
explosive, cosmic, rending—
stark contradiction to the codicil contending:
Death is the ultimate, the universal ending.
LORD, You ruptured the roof of Hell…for us.
You defied and defeated Death…for us.
Once and for all, You signaled Satan that He lacks the power
to hold what is Yours…and we are Yours, LORD.
Hallelujah! AMEN.

FINDING THE ANSWER

Shirley S. Stevens   April 26
Then some of our companions went to the tomb and found it just as the women had said, but him they did not see. Luke 24:24 KJV

A riddle relating to Grant's Tomb, asks "Who is buried in Grant's Tomb?" Of course, the answer is Grant.

When Mary Magdalene and Mary the mother of James went to the tomb after Jesus' crucifixion to anoint His body with spices, they found no body in the tomb. Although they told the disciples what they had found, Peter and John had to go and see for themselves.

Christians know the answer to the question, "Who is buried in Jesus' tomb?" No sealed tomb holds the Son of God. Jesus is not there. He was buried, but is now alive.

Thank You, Father, for giving us Your son, a risen Savior, who is in the world today. Amen.

JUST DON'T DO IT

Dr. K   April 27
When the LORD HAS DONE ALL HE PROMISED AND HAS MADE YOU LEADER OF ISRAEL, don't let this be a blemish on your record. Then your conscience won't have to bear the staggering burden of needless bloodshed and vengeance. 1 Samuel 25:30-31a NLT

David was furious. Nabal had disrespected him and he was on his way to kill Nabal when Abigail, Nabal's wife appears. She brought a magnificent feast with her: hearth baked bread, rich red wine, roast lamb, corn, and, for dessert, raisins and fig cakes. She brought this gift to David, and urged him not to take revenge on Nabal. Her reasoning was wise. When God does good things for you in the future, you don't want this incident to be a pain in your heart, remembering that you let your anger get the best of you.

Isn't she right? I know I can look back on some things I have done in the past, and though they're forgiven by God, when I think about them I'm embarrassed and grieved. I wish, even many years later, I had been wise enough not to commit the sin.

Why carry such hurt in our hearts? Just don't do it!
Oh God, give me wisdom to keep me from doing things I will remember with shame. Amen.

MEMORY BENEFITS

Carol J. Lee   April 28
One generation commends your works to another; they tell of your mighty acts. Psalm 145:4 NIV

One day I opened a memory door to a room of the past. There on shelves, neatly stacked and labeled, were examples of God's works in my life. I reached for a memory of the time my husband was out of work and I had a part-time job. Our savings account was slowly diminishing. Covering basic needs was stressful. I recalled how God provided in ways we could not have imagined. Friends gave us two grocery store gift cards. What a treat to be able to buy staples and a few extra items.

In that difficult time, I learned to focus on God not the circumstances. I grew to trust Him more rather than relying on my solution.

There were more memories on the shelves, but my soul found peace recalling that one. Now when my faith is weak, I am learning to remember that I can trust Him. He cares and is in control.

Thank You, Lord, for the gift of memories of what You have done. Show me opportunities to share your faithfulness with others. Amen

THINGS THAT GO AND COME BACK

Cherie Brooks Reilly   April 29
Do to others as you would have them do to you. Luke 6:31 NIV

A ball on a paddle
  A child on a trampoline
  Leaves on a tree
  A bee from a hive
  A boat from the shore
  A random act of kindness

The truth in the last line of this poem became crystal clear as I stood in the check-out line at the supermarket. I had a full basket of groceries and when a young man lined up behind me, I noticed he only had one item so I told him to go ahead of me.

"Thank you," he said. "When I was at the donut shop this

morning, I bought a cup of coffee for an old man who was fumbling for his wallet. Thank you, I hope that works out for you."

I was puzzled at the time, but now I know what he meant. As he stepped in front of me, he asked, "By the way, may I help you put your items on the conveyor belt?"

Never have I had a random act a kindness return so quickly!

Dear Lord, make me ever mindful to treat other people the way I want to be treated. Amen.

DRIVING ON EMPTY

Marilyn Nutter   April 30
Seek the LORD and his strength; seek his presence continually!
Psalm 105:4 ESV

Driving down I-85, the sound of a ding distracted me from the music on my favorite CD. A bright orange light appeared on the dash near "E" on the gas gauge. I had just passed a gas station and the next one wouldn't be available for several miles. As I approached the exit, I couldn't get into the lane so I passed it and waited for the next. The needle had gone to the left of "E". How many miles could I go before I would come to a halt? My pleasant drive had turned into stress because of my negligence.

What about us? Have we spent days distracted by a "To Do" list, frustrated by working in our own strength or trying to figure things out independently of prayer? We don't have to run on empty. Scripture says seek His face, look to Him for strength, and know the sufficiency of His grace. God promises to supply our needs.

Father, You have promised to supply my needs. Help me to re-member to consult You before I run on empty. Amen.

May

May 1 is the National Day of Prayer
NO ONE ELSE

Diane Sillaman   May 1

Then Asa called to the LORD his God, and said, "LORD, there is no one besides You to help in the battle between the powerful and those who have no strength; so help us, O LORD our God, for we trust in You and in Your name have come against this multitude. O LORD, You are our God; let not man prevail against You".
2 Chronicles 14:11 NASV

One of the characteristics of severe trial is that it causes us to lift our eyes off of our helplessness to one who is in a position to help. Very often we are in circumstances from which no policeman, fireman, president, or pastor can deliver.

The fires in Colorado, my state of residence, in June of 2012 and 2013 were just such events. Although we had hundreds of firefighters and terrific air support, the fires would still be burning and destroying had God not intervened. He caused the temperatures and winds to drop. He caused the afternoon rains. Only He could have done that. Many called out to Him on behalf of our state, and He heard. He rescued.

Our nation also needs God's help in many areas. Let us seek our mighty God and pray.

MY CRY REACHED HIS EARS

Margaret Steinacker   May 2

But in my distress I cried out to the LORD; yes, I prayed to my God for help. He heard me from his sanctuary; my cry to him reached his ears. Psalm 18:6 NLT

The medications given after surgery often blur thinking. After my back surgery, I knew God was there, yet my usual communication with Him seemed far away. When I closed my eyes to meditate on His goodness, everything seemed black. Eventually, my cry progressed to sobbing. I wasn't sure what was wrong – too much medication or not enough, depression made worse by pain, or missing family. However, my cry to God reached His ears. In the meantime, the prayers of God's people and the uplifting cards sent served as a connection from God to me.

Sometimes outside influences seem to block our path to God. Yet, in the midst of agonizing pain, God is there, even when we feel distressed, discouraged, or depressed. He promised never to leave us or forsake us.

God, help us to remember to cry out to You, knowing that You sit in Your sanctuary and hear us. Use any means possible to communicate to our hearts, that You are still there, even when all we feel is darkness. We know You bring light.

BRAVO!

Bill Batcher   May 3
And he said to him, "Well done, good servant." Luke 19:17a NKJV

The boy knew where his parents were sitting, as well as his aunt and uncle, his piano teacher, and his fellow students. There were also dozens of strangers in the audience waiting to hear his performance. He was nervous, but he resolved to do his best.

A mere three minutes later he played the final measure, took his hands off the keyboard, smiled, and took a deep breath. Everyone applauded and a few shouted the traditional "Bravo!" His audience was pleased. And so was he.

When Majid Mohiuddin published a collection of devotional poems in 2001, he titled it *An Audience of One.* He knew that in our walk through life there is only One whose approval we should seek.

However, as we gather each week in our churches—where the chancel is often called the stage, where the seats are arranged in rows like a theater, or where the congregation may applaud after the choir or soloist sings, it is easy to forget Who our real audience is.

As we try our best to serve the Master, wouldn't it be great to hear Him calling "Bravo!" to us?

GOD'S UNCHANGING LOVE

Donna J. Howard   May 4
Give thanks to the Lord, for he is good. His love endures forever.
Psalm 136:1 NIV

Our grandson's baseball game went into extra innings and
we left the ball field later than usual. As my husband and I drove
home, the sun was setting. Brilliant orange splashed across the
sky. It was beautiful and I felt at peace.

Without warning, the sun's beauty was marred by dark clouds.
My countenance darkened along with it.

Sometimes my life is like that. When things are going well, I'm
at peace, but when a problem or sadness comes into my life, I'm
troubled.

My feelings change with circumstances but God's love doesn't.
When we focus on His constant love, peace is renewed.

*Dear God, thank You for assuring me that Your love continues
forever. In Jesus' name, Amen.*

NOT REMEMBERING

Carol J. Lee   May 5
*For I will forgive their wickedness and will remember their sins no
more.* Hebrews 8:12 NIV
*...as far as the east is from the west, so far has he removed our
transgressions from us.* Psalm 103:12 NIV

While thinking about my relationship with my mom, there was
an incident for which I felt I needed to ask forgiveness. When
I mentioned it to her, she paused a moment, then said, "I don't
remember." I was taken aback, as I had remembered the incident
clearly. But I felt relief that it was no longer an issue between us.

I realized that episode is similar to my relationship with my
Heavenly Father. 1 John 1:9 tells us, *If we confess our sins, he
is faithful and just and will forgive us our sins and purify us from
all unrighteousness.* (NIV) My asking for forgiveness of my sins
and His not remembering them anymore, reconciles me again in
fellowship with my Father God. My part is to confess, accept His
forgiveness and believe He is not remembering.

*Thank You for forgiving me and not remembering my sins. Help me
to forgive others and not remember.*

VIEWPOINT

Pollyanna Sedziol   May 6
*...take up your cross daily, and follow Me... Luke 9:23b KJV,
...what woman having ten pieces of silver, if she lose one piece, doth
not light a candle, and sweep the house, and seek diligently till she
find it? Luke 15:8 KJV*

"I haven't done a thing today!"
my neighbor said to me;
but I had seen her on the porch
chatting with her children –
I saw her stop to watch
the white clouds nod their heads –
I had watched her listening
to what the robins had to say –
and in the early afternoon
she read a book by her favorite tree.

I had scrubbed and swept and dusted,
I could say my house was clean,
"You've lived a good day," I responded
And so have I, I thought.

Jesus challenged the disciples with the idea of the cross being
a daily life style. For the Christian, the things that fill our daily lives
are the paths along which we follow our Lord. It is in our daily
tasks that we live as we believe. Both the neighbor enjoying her
children and her world, and the housewife observing her, are living
their daily faith. By including the parable of the housewife as He
spoke of the Kingdom, Jesus honored our ordinary lives.

*Lord Jesus, for each new day to live, to enjoy my life, for You...
Thank You.*

MY IDENTITY IN PSALM 23

Read Psalm 23

Carol Cleal   May 7

The Lord is my rock.
He provides all things.
He gives me rest and peace.

He gives me strength.
He directs my steps so I might live according to His Word.

Even in times of trial, I have peace because He is with me.
He provides for me regardless of the circumstances.
He fills my life with blessings.
Everywhere I turn, I see God's love,

And I know that I will live with Him for eternity.

Father, Thank You for being my Rock, for giving me peace, and for Your great love. Amen

THE SKY IS FALLING

Sonya Lee Thompson   May 8
The way of fools seems right to them, but the wise listen to advice.
Proverbs 12:15 NIV

In the English fairy tale "Henny Penny," a hen by that name is hit on the head by an acorn. She assumes the sky is falling and decides it's her job to warn the king. The rest of this delightfully rhyming story goes on to show how she influences other farm animals. Soon she has enlisted a whole slew of cutely named creatures to go with her and warn the king about the falling sky. In the end Foxy Loxy, a sly fox that convinces them the king's lair is on the other side of his cave, outwits them. You can probably guess what their fate was.

Henny Penny had no authority to declare the sky was falling. She misinterpreted the unusual events around her. Had she stopped to ask advice from an Owl, perhaps she would have realized how preposterous this theory was.

If you are in an unknown situation, be careful not to make

assumptions or rely on someone's opinion. Seeking godly counsel and looking for principles in God's Word can make the difference between prospering and being lured into Foxy Loxy's cave. Who will you listen to today?

BE SPIRITUALLY SAFE

Dr. K   May 9
So, if you think you are standing firm, be careful that you don't fall!
1 Corinthians 10:12 NIV

While on vacation I watched from the fifth floor balcony as a number of birds took temporary roost on the peaks of other buildings nearby. Smart! Up high they escaped the dangers of dogs, cats, and other earthbound threats. But even in that position of apparent safety they must remain on the alert. As safe they are from house cats, there are predators that can get just as high or higher: hawks, eagles, falcons.

Bird or Christian, it is always good to get to a high safe place. Bird or Christian, we need to keep an eye out for unexpected dangers. We don't want to fall prey to that which can destroy or ruin our lives spiritually or physically.

What is a high place of faith? A place where a person reads his Bible, talks to God in prayer, attends worship, avoids sin, loves his family and his neighbor, and depends upon God for protection.

Have a good roost.

Oh Lord, help me, to see You high and lifted up. Help me to "roost" in a high spiritual place so that You can help me be all that you want me to be, day by day. Amen.

GOD WAITS!

Kathleen Bradley   May 10
For the eyes of the LORD run to and fro throughout the whole earth, to show Himself strong on behalf of those whose heart is loyal to Him. 2 Chronicles 16:9a NKJV

Sometimes I meet myself coming and going. Busyness seems to pervade every waking moment. By the end of the day, I wonder what I actually accomplished with my time. I quickly read a few verses from my Bible before falling into an exhausted sleep without ever giving God praise or thanksgiving.

God waits for us in our quiet times, even when we do not show up! This set apart time means as much to God as it does to us. He longs for a relationship with us. He desires that we not use Him as an Aladdin's lamp to grant our wishes, but instead to rely on Him as our best friend whom we cannot live without.

Spending time with God has great advantages for us. He leads us into all truth, encourages us, and gives us peace and strength. As we face daily challenges and run in the race of life, He renews our strength. He speaks and we listen. He acts and we follow. He is our only hope of fulfillment in life.

Mother's Day is celebrated each year in the US on the second Sunday in May.

MOTHER'S DAY

Dr. K   May 11
Her children arise and call her blessed; her husband also, and he praises her*: Proverbs 31:28 NIV*

Immediately after the monster tornado that devastated Oklahoma City in May 2013, one memorable photo showed a mother carrying her rescued daughter out of the destruction. That photo appeared on television and in news magazines all over the country and possibly the world. That photo is symbolic of all that moms do. They are there for their kids through physical, emotional, or spiritual devastation. They carry their kids because they birthed them or adopted them, because they love them more than they love themselves, because their loving embrace comforts the child and illustrates God's love.

That's why her children rise up and call her blessed. God bless you, mom!

O Lord, thank You for these special people, mothers, who, like You, are always looking out for us. Amen.
In the US, National Nurses' Week begins each year on May 6, and ends on May 12, Florence Nightingale's birthday.

MINISTERS OF LIGHT

Parise Arakelian   May 12
*Let your light shine before men in such a way that they may see
your good works, and glorify your Father who is in heaven.*
Matthew 5:16 NASB

As the candle was lit, the students recited in unison,

> "I will do all in my power to maintain and elevate the standard of
> my profession and will hold in confidence all personal matters
> committed to my keeping and family affairs coming to my knowl-
> edge in the practice of my calling."

Each student received her cap and a miniature likeness of the
lamp that Florence Nightingale carried as she made her nightly
rounds tending wounded soldiers during the Crimean War of 1853-
1856. Florence became famous as "The Lady with the Lamp" and
is recognized as the mother of modern nursing. As a student nurse
ready for clinical duty, I began my forty-year career as a registered
nurse.

Florence made her way through darkened wards, her lamp
bringing hope to her patients. We can be faithful witnesses by
spreading peace, encouraging faith, loving others, and offering
hope to those with whom we come in contact. The psalmist
proclaimed, *Your word is a lamp for my feet, a light on my path.*
(Psalm 119: 105 NIV) Guided by His Word, we can lead those around
us who are in darkness to paths of light.

WHEN SORROW IS ALL WE FEEL

Judith "Cookie" White   May 13
*We are hard pressed on every side, but not crushed; perplexed, but
not in despair; persecuted, but not abandoned; struck down, but not
destroyed.* I Corinthians 4:8 NIV

Exhausted, she fell to her knees. She felt as unequipped to
handle the situation at hand as a small child does an oncoming
ocean's wave as it crashes onto the shore. This situation equaled
the strength and tenacity of Niagara Falls.

The words of Paul in I Corinthians echoed in her mind. She
felt that she was extremely close to being crushed, perplexed and

struck down.

"Refreshment is urgently needed, Lord, for this thirsty soul," she prayed. "My only resolve is to humbly come to the foot of the cross…not for answers, but to lay the abundance of my sorrow, tears and pain before You and request a shower of anointing strength. Then may the Holy Spirit enable me to take Your promises and rub them as comforting balm over the broken pieces of my heart."

Lord, may we come to You in the midst of all our human emotions and realize You are the holy balm that heals, comforts and restores. Help us to know that joy does come in the morning for all believers. Though surrounded by darkness, a new day will dawn and the Son of God will illuminate our path. Amen

REMEMBER

Carolyn Rice   May 14
Yet I am always with you; you hold me by my right hand.
Psalm 73:23 NIV

My husband and I enjoy hiking, but I have a fear of heights. Some of the walking trails are narrow and in a few places there is quite a drop over the edge. The most dangerous places have guardrails, but some don't. When only one of us can fit on the narrow trail, my husband, knowing my fear, reaches out and takes my hand or offers me the crook of his arm.

Isn't that how Jesus walks with us? At the narrow parts, where it gets hard, or we're fearful, He offers us His hand and supports us along the way. It seems as if He whispers, "It's okay, I'm with you."

The next time you're in a narrow spot in life, a spot where you may be fearful or it's hard to take the next step, remember Jesus is standing next to you, holding your right hand. He's walking with you through this part of the journey, and you are never ever alone.

THEY HAD A PLAN

Norma C. Mezoe   May 15

"For I know the plans I have for you," declares the Lord, *"*PLANS TO PROSPER YOU AND NOT TO HARM YOU, PLANS TO GIVE YOU HOPE AND A FUTURE.*"*
Jeremiah 29:11 NIV

Every time I passed the house, it seemed more paint had peeled from the shingles and the appearance was becoming more run-down. I knew the owners of the home; they were hard-working responsible people and not the type to neglect their property. I also knew the husband had health problems and I wondered if they were struggling financially. Each time I drove past their house, I prayed for their needs.

One day workers were busy constructing a new addition. Later, new siding, windows and other updates were added. While I had wondered about the deterioration of the house, the owners had a plan all along to bring about new and attractive alterations to their home.

As the owners had plans for the renewal of their house, so God has a plan for each Christian's life. While we may wonder and worry about our futures, God knows exactly what lies around the bends of our lives. He will bring about the construction that will be most helpful in building our lives according to His plans. He has worked in our past, works today and is already in our future. In each season, He works and builds for our good to guide in our lives.

Father God, help me to allow You to work the plan You have for each of our lives, knowing You have a perfect blueprint for me. Amen.

YES, LORD

Melanie Rigney   May 16

...the blind men came to him; and Jesus said to them, "Do you believe that I am able to do this?" They said to him, "Yes, Lord." Then he touched their eyes and said, "According to your faith let it be done to you." And their eyes were opened.
Matthew 9:28-30 RSV

Have you ever felt as if God wasn't listening to you, wasn't aware of just how desperate your situation was? Even people seemingly in total harmony with God, those who we admire greatly, have days like that. Or weeks. Or months. Or years.

Consider the persistence of those folks... or of the blind men in Matthew 9. We have no idea how long they had been blind, or how many times they had prayed for sight. But when Jesus asked them if they believed, they didn't say, "Well, sort of," "I guess so," or "Sure, why not, nothing else has worked." They said simply said, "Yes, Lord."

We never know the day or the time when our suffering may be alleviated or our prayers may be answered (or how, for that matter). But like the blind men we can continue to believe, regardless of how many roadblocks or temptations appear. We can say, "Yes, Lord, I believe You can do this," and we can keep our eyes open.

CLEANING UP MESSES

Gloria Doty   May 17

Read: 2 Corinthians 5:16-19
If we confess our sins, he is faithful and just and will forgive us our sins and purify us from all unrighteousness. 1 John 1:9 NIV

You've probably seen a commercial for paper towels where a dog shakes mud and dirt onto every kitchen surface, the blender has no lid and spews liquid everywhere, Dad spills his coffee and the spaghetti sauce is boils over onto the stove. Mom comes to the rescue with paper towels to clean up the mess and in minutes the kitchen is neat and clean.

This scenario is staged but there are days in our lives that look similar. We may not make messes in our kitchens, but we mess up our marriages, friendships, health, finances, and our relationship with God. There are often repercussions from our messes; some we aren't *able* to clean up and some we aren't *willing* to clean up.

The good news is: Jesus was willing to clean up our messes with his death on the cross. As we walk our Christian journey, we make messes and Jesus continues to forgive.

Jesus, thank You for dying for me and continuing to clean up the messes I create. Amen

HOLY GROUND

Dorsee Bernat   May 18

Do not come any closer," God said. "Take off your sandals, for the place where you are standing is holy ground." Exodus 3:5 NIV

A lonely, quiet desert
Rugged and steep
The mountains nearly barren,
But for a solitary bush.

A most unique bush, this...
Burning, yet not consumed
The shepherd now approaching
Is about to be changed forever.

"Moses, come no closer.
Take off your shoes,
For the Place upon which you
Stand is holy".

Lord God,
Your presence transforms
The commonplace
Into the sacred.

IMAGE, REPUTATION, OR INTEGRITY

Jana Carman   May 19

He that hath no rule over his own spirit is like a city that is broken down, and without walls. Proverbs 25:28 KJV

When a famous athlete presented his public 'apology' for his various 'misbehaviors' including adultery, a commentator remarked after his speech that he was either trying to rebuild his image or pick a fight with the media.

Rebuild his image? Hmm. A reputation, once destroyed, proves very difficult to restore. In this case, it became obvious that his reputation was merely an image, gold-plated over lead, not solid-gold integrity. If a reputation is not solidly built on truth, honor, and integrity, all attempts to "rebuild"—i.e. cover with "gold" once again —will still be liable to cracking off.

Reputation is what people think about you.

Image is the outward shell.

But honor and integrity go clear to the bone.

We need to examine ourselves, not only to avoid being exposed for what we really are underneath, but so we don't bring disgrace to the One whose Name we bear.

So, if you think you are standing firm, be careful that you don't fall.
1 Corinthians 10:12 NIV

CLEAR VIEW

Marilyn Nutter   May 20
Plans fail for lack of counsel, but with many advisers they succeed.
Proverbs 15:22 NIV

My friend Lanette and I walk in our neighborhood several times a week. Our conversations range from updates about our families, critiquing beautiful lawns, commenting on newly painted doors and the privilege of living near our spectacular lake. As we crossed a street I said, "I don't understand why they built that huge beautiful house on a bare corner."

She anticipated my next sentence and said, "Their patio and upper deck look at a street."

I know." I answered. "The crepe myrtles will take forever to grow. They should have planted faster growing trees or some hollies." Apparently our neighbors didn't seek advice, but chose trees that looked pretty, without thinking of the speed of their growth.

Proverbs reminds us to seek counsel when making plans. God provides principles and instruction in His Word. He also gives people knowledge, skills and experiences to help us. Whether we're making decisions about a career, vacation or landscaping, it makes sense to find people who have expertise to give us answers. Proverbs says that leads to success.

HOPE GROWS

Shirley S. Stevens   May 21

***There is surely a future hope for you, and your hope
will not be cut off.*** Proverbs 23:18 NIV

Valley Care, a local adult day-care center, uses horticultural therapy to encourage those who have Alzheimer's disease. The therapist, Lisa, built eight raised containers that include a mixed flower garden and a pizza garden. The latter includes basil, oregano, onions, tomatoes, and peppers. She also has a "flowers just for pressing" garden with cosmos, scented geraniums, and pansies. Before planting, the clients study a colorful display of the plants to be featured in each container. They talk about the season and share a poem or quotation about that season. Clients water the garden after the horticulturist weeds.

This green thumb activity improves their physical, psychological, and emotional well being. Clients use the flowers to decorate cards and stationery.

Lisa, a horticulturist, had been grieving for her father who died of pancreatic cancer. One night she dreamed about him. When she awakened, she had the name for her work: "Hope Grows". Lisa got a grant from the state's department of public welfare to start the gardening project at Valley Care.

*Dear Lord, help us to reach out to others. In doing so, we may
experience healing for ourselves. Amen.*

LIFE EDGED WITH GOLD

Marion Gorman   May 22

***You make known to me the path of life; you will fill me with joy in
your presence, with eternal pleasures at your right hand.***
Psalm 16:11 NIV

Life is like a prism
Ever changing, growing old,
Following the shimmering path
God has edged with gold.

Life is graced with riches
The world cannot behold.

Salvation is a ray of light
Jesus edged with gold.

Life seeks out the Kingdom
The path lit to the fold
With words to walk and live by,
The Spirit edged with gold.

BEHIND CLOSED EYES

Elizabeth Rosian   May 23
Let us fix our eyes on Jesus, the author and perfecter of our faith.
Hebrews 12:2 NIV

Soft organ music wafted through the sanctuary, reminding the congregation that it was time for worship, time to put aside the cares of the week and plans for the future. The room became quiet. In the spirit of reverence, I closed my eyes to concentrate on the presence of God, and prepare my heart in prayer. As soon as my eyes closed, there it was: the computer game grid! Etched on the inside of my eyelids were the colorful lines of Symbolic Link.

What we look at long enough becomes part of our thinking and makes a statement about us. It shows where we've been fixing our eyes. It burns into our vision screen.

What a blessing it would be, if we fixed our eyes on Christ and His Word so that is what we see when we close our eyes! Truly we would be hiding His word in our hearts and His image behind our eyelids.

Dear Jesus, give us a vision of You that will bring inspiration and purpose to our lives.

OUR SAVIOR'S ARMS

Dorsee Bernat   May 24
The eternal God is your refuge, and underneath are the everlasting arms... Deuteronomy 33:27 NIV

I was delighted to see Rebecca in the group being baptized. Her deep, unwavering faith despite many physical obstacles and trials is an inspiration to everyone who knows her.

When Rebecca's name was called, she slowly made her way

forward. As she approached, I thought, *How will she get in?* The baptismal has steps, and Rebecca uses a walker.

Our pastor picked up Rebecca in his arms and gently lowered her into the water. After immersing her, he lifted her out, not caring that his own clothes got soaked in the process. Rebecca rejoiced too take this step of obedience to Christ. What looked like an obstacle, became a scene of tender victory because someone had done for her what she couldn't do for herself.

Isn't that what Jesus does for each of us? We can't make ourselves right with God on our own. From the moment we call on Him for salvation, He picks us up, helps us to walk in obedience, and creates His likeness in us. He's not afraid to "get wet" for our sake, meeting us at our deepest points of need, identifying with our frailty. Because He loves us unconditionally, we can come to Him in total confidence. His arms are the safest place we can be.

PERCEIVING GOD

Vanessa Perez   May 25
Blessed are the pure in heart: for they shall see God.
Matthew 5:8 KJV

Several months ago I was in a waiting pattern and couldn't see or understand the Lord's plan for me. I felt as if my faith was shaking apart. I finally came to the place where I gave up my goals and plans. I released doubts and worries. Once I did, His direction started to become clear.

Understanding or seeing God's will can be difficult. We may be confused at what He is telling us to do. We may be too busy or impatient to hear His voice.

Scripture tells us to have a clean and pure heart so that we can know His heart. Releasing our will and plans unlocks the way to hear His voice and know His heart. He desires that we be single-minded. When we are, He shows us His way.

DO YOU KNOW YOUR SHEPHERD'S VOICE?

Michelle S. Lazurek   May 26

My husband, our eight-month old son and I took a trip to the mall. I proceeded to window shop, and my husband and son went off to do the same. I heard a loud, happy, unmistakable scream piercing through the crowd. I whipped my head around and, yes, I spotted my husband and son a distance away; my son waving happily and blowing me kisses. Among the thousands of other sounds filling the crowded mall that day, I distinguished the sound of my son's voice.

As I spend more time with Jesus, I am learning to distinguish His still small voice amidst the clamor of the world. John 10:27-28 says, *"'My sheep listen to my voice; I know them, and they follow me. I give them eternal life, and they shall never perish; no one will snatch them out of my hand.'"*

As sheep who belong to Jesus, we know our Shepherd's voice because of the care He invests in us and the time we spend with Him.

Do you know your Shepherd's voice? Is it being muffled by the sounds of the world?

Dear Lord, please call to us so we may know Your voice. Help us decipher Your voice over the mumbles of the world. Amen.

VALUABLE EXPERIENCES

Christy Fitzwater   May 27

For several years, I taught a small Bible study class of 10 third graders and I loved it. When our church began a new program, the attendance of children and teens on Wednesday nights increased from about 40 to over 200. I was asked to continue to teaching, but to about 70 kids and over a dozen adult leaders, a task not for the faint of heart.

In middle school and high school I had taken several speech classes. When others might have cowered at the thought of standing in front of 80 people and teaching, I was prepared, with the confidence of years of experience in public speaking behind me.

David's life experiences prepared him to face a giant. When facing Goliath, he told King Saul, *"Your servant has killed both the lion and the bear; this uncircumcised Philistine will be like one of them."* (1 Samuel 17: 36a NIV)

God uses our life experiences to prepare us for the good works He wants us to do. Thank Him for the experiences of your life, even the hard ones. You never know how they will be used in the future.

BACK AND FORTH PRAYER PLAN

Carol Weeks   May 28
The prayer of a righteous person is powerful and effective.
James 5: 16b NIV

I like to pray in the car as I'm out and about during my day. Many people do, but I have adopted a plan for my praying.

I start by praying for where I've just come from. Thinking about my home, my husband, and other things helps me focus on the many blessings God has poured out on me.

About half way through the drive, I switch the prayer to *focus on my destination.* As I make my way through the trip, I concentrate on who will be there and what I'll be doing, always remembering to include a prayer for those unexpected happenings that can crop up. This destination prayer reminds me that God is in control and his plans are waiting for me.

As I leave my first stop and drive on to the next, *I praise God for what happened,* asking him to bless everyone there and bring up needs that I have seen or any special circumstances that God has placed on my heart. *Heading to my next stop,* I switch to the destination prayer and repeat my requests and thanksgiving with different people in mind.

I encourage you to try my "Back and Forth Prayer Plan" the next time you're driving. The blessings will multiply throughout your day.

WHO Really Knows

Margaret Adams Birth   May 29
Praise be to the Lord, the God of Israel,
from everlasting to everlasting. 1 Chronicles 16:36 NIV

You think
You see
WHY
Things are the way they are.
You look.
You consider the world around you

WHERE
There is the whole of creation as you know it.
Yet, you are
WHAT
You are at the same time
I am . . .
I AM.

WEED AND FEED

Read: Matthew 13:1-9

Gloria Doty   May 30
So when the plants came up and bore grain, then the weeds appeared also. Matthew 13:26 ESV

We apply the "weed and feed" method to our lawns in early spring. The "weed" part is supposed to kill emerging weed seeds, while the "feed" element nurtures and enhances the grass. It's essential to do this early in the year when the weeds are still in the seed or pre-emergence stage before they have started growing.

We can use the weed and feed approach for our spiritual growth. We ask God to help us remove small behaviors and attitudes that can become sinful habits and large weeds. Next we can develop the habits of feeding ourselves with God's Word. Our spiritual life will have a better chance to survive and bloom if we do both.

Father, give us strength to recognize the weeds in our lives and remove them and give us the desire to be in Your Word to develop the habits which please You. Amen

MY LAST OPTION

Gloria Doty   May 31
Do not be anxious about anything, but in every situation, by prayer and petition, with thanksgiving, present your requests to God.
Philippians 4:6 NIV

When my grandson played baseball for his high school team, he often needed me to pick him up after practice. There was a day when I told him it would be difficult, but not impossible, for me to provide the ride. He assured me he would try to find someone else and only use me as his *last option*.

How often in our daily lives do we use God as our last option? We stew and worry about many situations in our lives, but nearly always try to find the solution ourselves or think of ways to fix problems using our own means and strength.

Too often, we fall on our knees and ask God for help only when all else fails and we are desperate. He is our last option.

Asking for God's guidance and wisdom should be our *first option*. Only then can we use the skills He gives us to find peace amidst our problems.

The next time a difficulty arises in your life, ask God first for guidance, before attempting to find a solution on your own.

Heavenly Father, help us to first seek Your help in times of turmoil.
Amen.

June

FAMILY REUNION

Norma C. Mezoe   June 1

*"...Can I bring him back again? I will go to him,
but he will not return to me."* 2 Samuel 12:23 NIV

King David fasted and prayed while his young son was
critically ill, but the child died. Despite his heartache and longing
for the boy, David accepted that his son would not return to him. In
his grief, he made a profound statement: "I will go to him."

Recently, a young man who attended our church died. Eric
was a sixteen-year-old Christian who loved life. He was involved in
band and other school activities and he had a loving relationship
with all members of his family.

Eric had battled a heart problem most of his life. It appeared he
was winning the battle but then he began to have more problems.
He died following surgery.

Understandably, the family was heartbroken and they struggled
with the pain of Eric's death. As Christians, his family realizes that
Eric cannot return. Like David, they live with the assurance that
one day they will go to be with Eric and have a beautiful reunion.

*Loving Father, thank You for the promise that Christians will be
reunited with their loved ones in heaven. Amen.*

UNDER CONSTRUCTION

Norma Mezoe   June 2

**And we know that in all things God works for the good of those who
love him, who have been called according to his purpose.**
Romans 8:28 NIV

A road I travel frequently was under reconstruction for a long
time. Often it seemed that the road builder was totally confused
about the work that was being carried out. Finally, the construction
has been completed. Now I can see that the contractor actually
had a plan and the results make traveling on that road much
smoother.

Sometimes I have looked at things happening in my life and

they seemed to be a total mess, just like the road. I knew God had a plan for my life but I couldn't imagine how He would fit all of the jumbled pieces together. Now from the vantage point of age and the passing of years, I look back and see clearly how He has smoothed my life and helped me through the construction periods.

God, Master Planner, thank You that You know the plans for my life. Please help me to fit into Your plans. Amen.

Previously published The Secret Place, and The Gem.

GOD'S CREATION

Gerald W. Bauer   June 3
In the beginning God created the heavens and the earth.
Genesis 1:1 RSV

In the beginning God speaks into a void,
invites a world into being.
By silent voice God speaks words that create
the design that He intends.
God plants a garden, a delight to view
and good to eat.
God puts in place a management team -- male and female --
to care for this world,
according to God's intent.
This world a sacred trust,
fresh each new day
from the mouth of God.

Lord Jesus, help us always to see this world as a gift from God and creation as God's act of love. Help us also to see our role as God's caretakers, serving Him in all we do. In Your holy name. Amen.

OCEAN FOOTPRINTS

Darlene Rose (Bustamante)   June 4
"...as He who called you is holy, you also be holy in all your conduct, because it is written, Be holy, for I am holy.'"
1 Peter 1:15-16 NKJV

A whale footprint is a circular area where the surface of the water is smoother than the surrounding water. The whale's tail creates a vortex as it moves through the water just below the surface, leaving behind its impression. I got to witness one first-hand one spring morning. It's a beautiful display as a whale comes up out of the water and glides back down beneath the surface. As the whale swam away, I could see the smooth spots on the surface. We were told these were its footprints and a way to tell where the whale has been.

Like the whale, our lives leave behind an impression too!

Do we leave a *smooth* image in a *rough* world? Would another who came from behind, want to follow in your footsteps—or them?

As children of God, let's strive to leave an impression on others so they will want to personally know the Jesus we love and whose footsteps we follow!

THE GAG ORDER IS LIFTED

Christi Brooks   June 5
Her parents were astonished, but he told them not to tell anyone what had happened. Luke 8:56 NIV

A dead child raised from death to life. Who wouldn't celebrate? The little girl's parents were ready to tell everyone about Jesus, the One who with a single command banished death and returned their precious daughter to life and health. But Jesus told them not to spread the word. He didn't want them to tell people who He was or what He had done.

Yet we read in Matthew 28:19 NIV, "Therefore go and make disciples of all nations, baptizing them in the name of the Father and of the Son and of the Holy Spirit."

Jesus has lifted the gag order. We are no longer to keep silent about Him. We are to tell people from one end of the globe to the other that He is the Christ, the Son of the Living God and that eternal life is available only through a relationship with Him.

Why, then are so many not speaking of Him?

Are you living as if the gag order were still in place?

FIRST THINGS FIRST

Leslie Winey   June 6
You shall have no other gods before me. Exodus 20:3 NIV

The Lord knows the bent of the human heart and our interest in chasing after things that give personal satisfaction. It's easy to read and dismiss the Bible verses that deal with idolatry when they refer to golden calves or carved figurines. Those don't apply today, but the definition of an idol is "an image used as an object of worship; one that is adored." That definition changes things.

I am a committed Christian, but given a choice between my favorite television program or Bible reading and prayer, I often choose television. Sometimes my idol is my own preference or agenda rather than someone else's interests or desires. Perhaps we purchase products on impulse and move beyond our budget. Rather than take time to write a note of encouragement or sending a card to someone, we choose to take a nap. Regardless of what our "idol" looks like, when we use a disproportionate amount of time, energy or affections that rightly belong to God , our choices become "other gods."

Read the definition again and ask the Lord to help you identify the idols in your life, put them in their proper place, and keep Him on the throne of your heart.

Dear children, keep yourselves from idols. 1 John 5:21 NIV

LISTEN FOR. . .

Marsha Hood   June 7

birdsong welcoming the dawn--
strident caw of crows
calling rooftop to rooftop,
mother jay's raucous cry
warning stalking cats from her nest,
whistles and throaty outbursts
of black-capped chickadees,
chattering house wrens,
trilling song sparrows,
God singing his love.

He. . .will rejoice over you with singing. Zephaniah 3:17b NIV

A WHISPERING GOD

Jana Carman   June 8

...a great and powerful wind ... an earthquake ... a fire, but the LORD
was not in [these]. And after the fire came a gentle whisper.
1 Kings 19:11,12 NIV

Our house is on a narrow country road, no neighbors closer
than half-a-mile. Visitors say, "It's so quiet here!" And I reply, "Yes.
Isn't it wonderful?" I am a "quiet freak." I love quiet sounds—birds,
the grandfather's clock ticking, the creaking of an old house. I have
tinnitus, an ever-present background noise in my head, but I can
ignore it to a certain extent.

This is a noisy world—traffic, radios, TVs, raised voices, ever-
present music—and many pipe it into their ears deliberately. Why
are we so addicted to noise? Is it so scary to be alone with our
racing thoughts that we need distraction?

Mother Teresa said, "God … cannot be found in noise and
restlessness. God is the friend of silence."

Elijah found that God is a whispering God. To hear what He
wants to tell us, we must turn off the noise. Most surrounding noise
can't be turned off, but haven't you learned that selective hearing
can be a blessing? Turn off what you can, tune in to God, and hear
Him whisper, "I love you. Listen for My voice. I am always with
you."

Listen to his voice, and hold fast to him. For the LORD is your life....
Deuteronomy 30:20 NIV

TRANSFORMED BY GOD

Ruth Stewart   June 9

Therefore, if anyone is in Christ, the new creation has come: The old
has gone, the new is here! 2 Corinthians 5:17 NIV

It looked like a bunch of matted leaves, but as I picked it up, I
realized it was a cocoon. I remembered that butterflies and moths
live in cocoons while the process of metamorphosis is taking place.
I took it home.

I placed the cocoon on the window sill above my kitchen
sink. After dinner I noticed it move, so I watched awhile. To
my amazement, I saw something trying to emerge from the

cocoon. When it had freed itself, it was no more than a mass of wings and body. After trembling for awhile on the window sill, the luna moth extended pale green wings and began flying in short bursts.

I was awestruck by the transformation taking place before my eyes. God performs this miracle every day for people who accept Him or renew a relationship with Him. As God freed the moth from the bondage of the cocoon to its newfound freedom, so God frees those who turn to Him for newness of life in His Spirit.

Opening the window, I watched the moth fly into the dusk of early evening. I breathed a prayer of thanksgiving for God's transforming power.

IS YOUR ANGER HELPING OR HURTING?

Laurel Shaler   June 10

Understand this, my dear brothers and sisters: You must all be quick to listen, slow to speak, and slow to get angry.
James 1:19 NLT

Some time ago, I was upset with my husband over who-knows-what. Before I knew it, I picked up a plastic cup from the bathroom counter and threw it across the room. Although the cup was lightweight, it still hit the floor with a thud. My action surprised us both. Yep, I was angry.

While not all anger is bad, the Bible tells us to be slow to anger. When I begin to get angry, I try to stop and ask myself, "Is this anger helping or hurting?" Almost always, the answer is a resounding "HURTING", ringing like an alarm in my head. When I do get angry unnecessarily, I remind myself that everyone falls short sometimes, so I ask for forgiveness from God and those I hurt. Then, I commit to try harder.

It's tempting (and easier) to just give in to anger. It often becomes a habit...our "go to" emotion. But, with God's help, we can ask ourselves, "Is this anger helping or hurting?" We can listen first and speak second. We can avoid those nasty consequences of anger. I plan to keep working on this area of my life. Will you join me?

CALM IN THE MIDST OF CHAOS

Brittany Mayak   June 11
But Jesus stooped down and wrote on the ground with His finger,
as though He did not hear. John 8:6 NKJV

The woman who was brought to Jesus after being caught
in adultery, must have felt ashamed. The rage and hatred her
accusers displayed towards her surely made her fearful. But
consider Jesus. He was filled with peace. He did not rush to the
woman's aid, nor join in with her accusers. He calmly stooped
down and began to write in the dirt.

Jesus chose to be calm and not react based on others'
reactions. In fact, the scripture stated, *"as though He did not
hear."* He responded in a way that did not fit the situation. We
can have the same calm response when faced with intense
circumstances. God created us in His image, and our identity rests
solely in who He is! He is calm in the midst of tense situations, and
we can be too.

Dear Father God, thank You for allowing us to see who we are
through Your Word. Please help us to continue to know our identity
by searching the scriptures for Your truths. Amen.

LOW, STEADY AND SURE

Robert Gutierrez   June 12
Little by little I will drive them out before you, until you have
increased enough to take possession of the land. Exodus 23:30 NIV

God doesn't bring us victory over our challenges and sins all
at once. If He slew all our "enemies" instantly we would have no
reason to depend on Him and our faith wouldn't grow. Instead, He
brings us along one step at a time. With His strength and help,
we conquer ground slowly but surely. God desires to drive out our
enemies as we rely on His promises and grace. As we do, our faith
and trust in God also grows.

If God brought us up against our giants all at once most of us
would crumble with the enormity of it all. Rather, He knows how
much we can handle. With each challenge and victory we learn
to trust God and rely on Him more for His sustaining grace. As

time goes by, God enables us to face bigger and greater enemies. Faith doesn't magically appear overnight. Instead, it is like a tree, growing gradually with each victory.

Lord, thank You for Your presence and promise to defeat my enemies. I pray that I will trust Your grace and strength for every battle I face. Amen

ARE YOU LISTENING?

Christi Brooks   June 13
But don't just listen to God's word. You must do what it says. Otherwise, you are only fooling yourselves. James 1:22 NLT

Wouldn't it be lovely if we only had to tell our children to do things once? We could avoid hearing questions like, "When did you tell me to clean my room?" or "I didn't know you told me to feed the dog!"

I imagine God feels much the same way about *our* listening skills. "When did you tell me to correct my sin before confronting someone else about theirs?" (Luke 6) or "I didn't know you wanted me to take care of the homeless!" (Matthew 25)

We sit in church week after week. We attend Bible studies and memorize scripture. We read passage after passage, but are we really listening to God? In the book of James we read that true listening means doing. We need to respond to what He tells us in His Word. That may be actively confronting our sin, sharing the gospel, helping the poor, expressing thanks, and encouraging fellow believers.

He is speaking, so let's actively listen and *do*. Is He speaking to you today?

PROUD YOUNG SAUL OF TARSUS

Read ACTS 9:1-9; 17-22

Evelyn Minshull   June 14

Proud young Pharisee of Tarsus
flaunts his credentials, his status in the synagogue....
(This century, his office might serenely shout success:
walnut-framed diplomas dominating walls; awards on polished

pedestals;
autographed copies of Gamaliel's latest treatises safe behind
glass.)

Saul's stride proclaims superiority, defines authority;
his zeal presumes Divine approval
as heretic Christians are routed from their midnight pallets,
then herded to merciless judgment.
(Saul's beliefs, the only valid rules,
Saul's code, the only righteous measure.
Any who claim a various vision
at worst are infidels—at best, misguided.)

Then—suddenly—a thunderclap splits Heaven,
Shekinah Glory strikes, a disciplining Voice reverberates…
And all that once was certain overturns,
and those once quarry have transformed to brothers in belief.

If there be any Pharisee in me,   I pray that God will strike
my ego blind,
that I—like Paul—might truly see. AMEN.

*Father's Day in the US is celebrated each year
on the third Sunday in June.*

JUST LIKE DADDY

Courtney Newbery   June 15
***See what great love the Father has lavished on us, that we should be
called children of God! And that is what we are!*** I John 3:1 NIV

After fixing a leak in our shower, my husband had to paint the
ceiling. He worked for hours, meticulously covering every crease
and corner; his hands and face wet with paint. My two-year-old son
woke from his nap and came downstairs. Wide-eyed and curious,
he watched as my husband, high on the ladder, ran the brush back
and forth. Then, with lightning speed, my son hopped up, grabbed
a clean brush, dipped his fingers in the paint, smeared it all over
his face, and yelled, "Me too!"

Just as my son wanted to be like his Daddy, our Heavenly
Father desires that we become like Him. He longs for us to spend

time with Him, follow His example, and join in His work.

Do you want to be just like your heavenly Daddy? What are you doing today to let Him transform you into His Image?

Dear Father, thank You that You have called me Your child. Help me to look more like You each day. Amen.

CELEBRATE

Janelle Moore June 16

Passing through the Valley of Baka
they make it a place of springs... Psalm 84:6 NIV

My Dad (Pop) unexpectedly passed away recently. What a terrible shock and very difficult time it was.

As our family gathered to plan the funeral, Mum's attitude was "I want this to be a time of celebrating him and his life. I don't want it to be a dreary, sad time." Pop was an avid farmer who loved and lived on the land his entire life. So at the service we read a humorous poem about farmers. People laughed. His eulogy contained stories about some of the funny things he had done. People laughed. Pop loved to listen to the cattle market report and the weather report, so as we left the church, we played the two reports instead of a hymn. People laughed amongst their tears. It was indeed a great celebration of who Pop was and what he loved. Because of my Mum's attitude, a sad and difficult day became a time of reflection, thanksgiving and even laughter. Pop would have loved it!!

Lord, we thank You that though we may weep in our Valleys of Baka, You are a trustworthy God who can bring joy amongst sadness. Amen.

ANGELS AMONG US

Michelle S. Lazurek June 17

I went to a local coffee shop to finish a writing assignment. As I collected my things to pay for my meal, the waitress said, "Your lunch has been paid for." Currently struggling with finances, this met my financial need in a tangible way. In that moment, I was reminded of the verse that says, *"Don't forget to show hospitality to strangers, for some who have done this have entertained angels without realizing it!"* (Hebrews 13:2 NIV).

Often, we think of hospitality as opening our homes to friends. What if we show hospitality in other ways? Perhaps we "entertain angels" when we:

- Pay a stranger's bill at a restaurant, or the toll for the car behind you
- Display random acts of kindness such as smiling at someone or holding a door open to brighten a stranger's ordinary day.
- Pray a silent prayer for each person you come in contact with for twenty- four hours.

In what way can we entertain angels today?

FOUR QUESTIONS ABOUT PRAYER

Joseph Hopkins   June 18

1. **WHEN** should we pray?
Then He spoke a parable to them that men always ought to pray and not lose heart. (Luke 18:1)
Praying always with all prayer and supplication in the Spirit. (Ephesians 6:18)
Pray without ceasing. (1 Thessalonians 5:17)

2. **WHERE** should we pray?
I desire therefore that the men pray everywhere, lifting up holy hands, without wrath and doubting. (1 Timothy 2:8)

3. **FOR WHOM** should we pray?
Therefore I exhort first of all that supplications, payers, intercessions, and giving of thanks be made for ALL MEN. For kings and all who are in authority, that we may lead a quiet and peaceable life in all godliness and reverence. (1Timothy 2:1-2)

4. **FOR WHAT** should we pray?
Be anxious for nothing, but in everything by prayer and supplication, with thanksgiving, let your requests be made known to God. (Philippians 4:6)
In everything give thanks, for this is the will of God in Christ Jesus for you. (1Thessalonians 5:18)
All scriptures are from the NKJV.

STUFF

Beth Hadley   June 19
Lay not up for yourselves treasures upon earth,
where moth and rust doth corrupt. Matthew 6:19 (KJV)

It attacks from above and below. My stuff has turned bad. Unruly stacks of outdated and unread magazines piled by my bed threaten an avalanche. "Conquer clutter in 30 days," their glossy covers taunt. My precious belongings bomb my head and ambush my vulnerable toes. I cram my treasures back into closets, cupboards and crannies and ask God for help.

The truth creeps up on me like mismatched socks that huddle in overstuffed drawers holding out for their sole-mates. I need to get rid of my stuff. I sort a box of papers and unearth a coupon for 50 cents off Cabbage Patch Doll© cereal. With no expiration date! So what if I've never seen this product on the grocer's shelf? Someday, I will be the only one who was wise enough to save this coupon, and I will auction it on e-bay for millions.

Then God reminds me that holding onto my stuff is like trying to stock up on manna. It goes bad. He promises to provide for all of my needs, day after day. I need to put my faith in Him.

Lord, please release the hold my belongings have on me
and help me hold onto my faith in You. Amen.

FOLLOWING INSTRUCTIONS

Sterling Dimmick   June 20
Your word is a lamp to my feet and a light on my path.
Psalm 119:105 NIV

If it weren't for a six-hour computer course I took, I wouldn't even know how to turn on a computer. Occasionally computer issues crop up that cause anxiety. When I've had a really BIG issue arise, I call a friend with a Master's Degree in computer science. Recently, if I had taken the time to read the instruction sheet that came with the computer, I would have saved myself a phone call and some time.

It is the same with the Christian life. How much time do we take to read the Bible, God's instruction book for us? Do we meditate and ponder on His principles for living the Christian life, or are we content to read a short devotion or Bible verse?

Most products come with instructions for assembly and use. We know that we should read the manuals if we want to get the most out of a product or appliance, or it could end in disaster. Let's take time to read the Bible and let the truths of scripture take root.

Lord Jesus, may I manage my time so that I can meditate on Your Word and may You open my understanding to truths that will guide me to live for You. Amen

WHAT DO YOU EXPECT?

Tricia Lathrop   June 21

Delight yourself in the Lord and He will give you the desires of your heart. Psalm 37:4 ESV

Are you surprised when God answers your prayer?

When the angel freed Peter and led him out of jail, he went to the house where Christ-followers were praying faithfully for his freedom.

Rhoda heard the knock and answered the door. Imagine her surprise when she heard Peter's voice. In her excitement, she left him outside as she ran to tell the others. They did not believe her. She persisted in her story, but no one went to open the door and check. Meanwhile Peter continued to knock as they debated the possibility of his release.

Did those praying believe that God would answer their prayer? Probably, but they didn't expect it to happen that night in that way. Even Peter thought he was dreaming as he followed the angel out the door and into the street.

It's hard to pray with expectation; our doubt, pride and fear of rejection get in the way. God hears our prayers and wants to bless us. He delights in giving us good things. And when we focus on God and delight in Him, we can be assured that He will answer our prayers in His best ways, often ways we never expected.

WANTING BUT LACKING NOTHING

Jana Carman   June 22
... those who seek the LORD lack no good thing. Psalm 34:10 NIV

Like many kids, I puzzled over Psalm 23:1. I understood (sort of) that The LORD is my shepherd, but ... I shall not want? Did that mean I should not want? But I did want—a bicycle, ice skates, to go to summer camp. It was years before I learned that "want" meant "to lack, be needy or destitute." Thankfully I can say that I was never destitute. God truly did—and does—supply all my needs.

Years later, I still struggle with "wanting." When those catalogs ("wish books") come in the mail, I leaf through them instead of automatically consigning them to the recycle pile. (My mother's admonition comes to mind: "What the eye doth not see, the heart doth not desire.") So much time wasted, looking at things I really don't need.

I'm sure I'm not the only one with this problem. So maybe this principle will help both of us: God supplies all I need, and if He doesn't supply something, could it be that I don't really need it?

Oh my, is that merchandizing heresy? But set that alongside Psalm 34:9 NIV: *Fear the LORD, you his saints, for those who fear him lack nothing.* Now there's a different perspective!

My Shepherd, my loving Father, You do indeed provide all I need.
Thank You!

HE SIGNS OUR PARDON

Leigh Powers   June 23
Therefore there is now no condemnation for those who are in Christ Jesus, because through Christ Jesus the law of the Spirit who gives life has set you free from the law of sin and death. Romans 8:1-2 NIV

It was our last day of Vacation Bible School and I was attempting to remind the children what we had learned that day: God is our provider.

"Okay everyone, God is our _____" I said. Blank looks. I tried and gave a hint: "God is our pro. . .pro_____"

A hand shot up in back. "Oooh! I know Miss, I know!" she said, bouncing up and down. "God is our probation officer!"

It was a funny moment, but sometimes we do view God as our

probation officer. We picture God as some cosmic cop, just waiting for us to slip up so he can get us. But God does not condemn us. He sets us free.

God is not our probation officer. Jesus lives as our advocate to intercede for us before the Father (Heb. 7:25). Be encouraged-- He does not condemn us; He stands to plead our case. If we are covered by the blood of Jesus, He does not hold the sins of our past against us. In Christ there is no condemnation. God signs our pardon: forgiven by the blood of the Lamb.

COMMITMENT

Sterling Dimmick   June 24
"..But as for me and my household, we will serve the Lord."
Joshua 24: 15b NIV

Commitment can be defined as loyalty or devotion to fulfilling an obligation to a person or activity. As Joshua was nearing the end of his life, he gathered the children of Israel together to reaffirm their obedience to God and His Law. While the Bible narrative is clear that humanity hadn't kept God's Law at first, after Joshua's death, the Israelites were faithful for a time. (Joshua 24).

Today, in a wedding ceremony a "pledge" is spoken as the couple stands before the officiating pastor, and then rings are exchanged. In other ways, we commit to follow through on obligations. We commit to legal documents and financial responsibilities.

Can we say as Joshua said…"we will serve the Lord"? No human is perfect, but let us strive to be committed--through the Perfect One--to what God would have us do for His glory and honor. (Hebrews 11).

Lord Jesus, may I be like Joshua and others before me to make the commitment to serve You in all I do. Amen

WHAT'S IN A NAME?

Adele Jones   June 25
But you are a chosen people, a royal priesthood, a holy nation,
God's special possession, that you may declare the praises of him
who called you out of darkness into his wonderful light.
1 Peter 2:9 NIV

In the Bible people's identities were defined by their name, or redefined by their renaming. Even today, I believe that our name is an important part of who we are. My name means "noble" or "of noble birth." In the natural I have neither claim to nobility nor do I convey a noble disposition at times. Yet, as a child of God, my birthright has been transferred from the ordinary to the extraordinary.

No matter what lineage our name suggests, by salvation through Christ, His identity is bestowed upon us and His robe of righteousness covers us like a precious royal garment. In Him, we are part of a royal priesthood and we are being transformed daily into the likeness of the King of Kings and Lord of Lords. Take joy today in the extraordinary name that you bear.

Lord Jesus, You offered Your life so that we could be called God's children. Thank You. May we bear Your name with dignity and gratitude as royal heirs of Your Heavenly Kingdom. Amen.

THE GIFT OF SIGHT

Evelyn Minshull   June 26
The eye is the lamp of the body. If your eyes are healthy, your whole body will be full of light. Matthew 6:22 NIV

LORD:
although I celebrate my vision so recently restored,
and praise You for it…
forgive me if I mini-mourn the loss of magic conjured by my cata-
racts—the nightly pyrotechnics:
when every light source gathered its own universe—
complete with galaxies
of light-chips, light-motes, light-flecks and shards.

Enchanting!—that my failing eyes should entertain such wonders!
(Only You, Lord, would defeat deformity with artistry!)
Amazing!—that all but a few of Your creatures
(earthworm to emperor; ant to astronaut; fly to philosopher)
are gifted with sight.

Astounding!—that You imagined, then purposely designed and
crafted

each creature's cornea, each lens, each iris
for its unique requirements and environment!
(May I sincerely thank you that my eyes differ from the
dragonfly's?)

Lord, Your creativity is limitless. Our capacity for wonder expands daily! How can we fail to praise You—each time we blink—for Your gifts, grace and goodness? Amen.

FOLLOW ME

Ruth Stewart   June 27
Whoever desires to come after Me, let him deny himself, and take up his cross, and follow Me. Mark 8:34b NKJV

Sheets of rain beat upon our windshield as we drove through the night. Lightning ripped the sky. Flooding was predicted in low lying roads. As we entered a city near our destination, we heard that the highway on which we were traveling was closed at the underpass.

We stopped at a service station to ask directions around the flooded road. One man who overheard the conversation said amiably, "Just follow me; I will lead you around the flooded roads back to the highway." Not wanting to inconvenience him, we protested. He insisted, so we followed him until we were back on the highway. We pulled up beside the man and thanked him.

This man's kindness is a miniature picture of what Jesus did for each of us. He not only pointed the way to the Father, He walked the way in love, obedience and sacrifice, even to the cross. When Jesus lived on earth, He said "Follow me." He is still leading the way through our storms and sunshine, obstacles and roadblocks of life. We only have to follow Him as He leads us safely back to the highway, toward the destination He intends for us.

KEYS TO THE KINGDOM

Donna Bond   June 28
But if from there you seek the LORD YOUR GOD, YOU WILL FIND HIM IF YOU SEEK HIM WITH ALL YOUR HEART AND WITH ALL YOUR SOUL.
Deuteronomy 4:29 NIV

There it lay, glinting in the June sunlight--mocking me, even: the blue stone in a key ring holding my desk key. I had been searching for it for two days--my purse, my tote bag, my desk drawers, the wastebasket and even the shred box--to no avail. Custodians and main office personnel were on the lookout for it. On the third day, there it was, lying on the pavement behind my car. I had been to and from my car five times in two days and had not seen it. *Why now?* Because I was looking in the right place!

I thanked God that we had not had wind, rain or snow; that no one had driven over it; that it had not been discarded or stolen. I wondered, though, *how often do I miss seeing God because I am not looking in the right place?*

GOD'S GUIDANCE

Lana James   June 29
But he was pierced for our transgressions, he was crushed for our iniquities; the punishment that brought us peace was upon him, and by his wounds we are healed. Isaiah 53:5 NIV

Sometimes God does something in your life that is unexpected but you really need it. When I was twenty God sent me on a mission trip to Tonga for three weeks. All expenses paid! But the greatest thing was my release from suffering Obsessive Compulsive Disorder. I had the disorder severely for about 10 years. After coming back from overseas, the team had a Debrief of their experience. During Debrief, on a campsite I laid my burden of anxiety at the foot of a large, wooden cross. I prayed heartily for my release. When I stood up from being on my knees there was no longer that immense suffering and fear which I had held so closely. Praise God!

God knew I had to go on that mission trip. It was just as much about me as it was about serving others. He knew there was no other way for me to release my distress. Be assured God will guide you to relieve you from your burdens, sometimes in unexpected ways.

THE GREATEST OF THESE

Jana Carman   June 30

Love is patient ... kind, does not envy ... boast, is not proud ... rude..
self-seeking ... easily angered ... keeps no record of wrongs;
1 Corinthians 13:4,5 NIV

The Love chapter is often read at Christian weddings. These qualities, characteristic of those who love God, also describe God. They are also the oil that greases the squeaking wheels of marriage as two learn the complicated procedure of blending two lives, two personalities, two backgrounds, into one entity. No easy task, it can take a lifetime. (In my case, it's been 58 years, and counting.)

Two other words, part of marriage ceremonies of the past, are essential for producing the desired oneness of marriage. These words, nourish and cherish, should be resurrected and reinserted in modern vows. Nourishing is the process of nurturing someone to maturity—mentally, physically, spiritually, and relationally. We often think of that in terms of growing children, but we all, no matter what age, fall short of maturity, and we need help. Nourishing helps someone to "be all they can be."

The other beautiful word, cherish, means to protect and hold dear. Like nourish, it expresses a deep, unselfish love that wants the best for the loved one. That sounds like a recipe for a successful marriage, and a remedy for a struggling one.

Dear friends, let us love one another, for love comes from God.
1 John 4:1 NIV

July

THE POWER OF GOD

Kathy Johnson   July 1

But we have this treasure in jars of clay, to show that the surpassing power belongs to God and not to us. 2 Corinthians 4:7 ESV

On our trip to Hoover Dam we were amazed by the vastness of the dam and the amount of water it controlled. There is astonishing power in the dam in the water, but the power of a man-made dam does not compare to the power of God.

He created the universe with His power. Salvation comes to us through the power of Jesus, in His cross and resurrection. By His power He will raise us up on the last day. And during the present age **". . . *He upholds the universe by the word of his power"*** (Hebrews 1: 3b ESV).

Jesus willingly gave up His power as God to come to earth. He lived and walked on earth. He was tempted, yet lived a perfect life in our stead. He suffered, died, and rose victorious, so we may have newness of life in Him.

Dear God, make us mindful of the many aspects of your power – from creation to salvation to resurrection. Thank You for Your power at work in us to live each day. In Jesus' name. Amen.

THIRSTY BIRDS

Marilyn Nutter   July 2

"Blessed are those who hunger and thirst for righteousness, for they will be filled." Matthew 5:6

It was an unusually warm day and I noticed that my beautiful hanging ferns needed water. I filled the watering can and watered one fern, then started on the next. The minute water hit the soil, I heard rustling. I thought the can hit against dry leaves. I moved back to check, but that wasn't the case. Though a few leaves were wilted, they weren't dry. I poured again and the same thing happened, only this time two tiny pink beaks appeared wide open catching the water. Mamma bird had built a nest and her babies were thirsty.

Their open mouths impressed me. Thirsty babies, ready to be filled with what they needed and what was good for them. As we seek to go deeper and learn what Jesus wants to teach us, He says that our hunger and thirst will be satisfied. Like baby birds with open mouths, we will be filled with His righteousness. Jesus guarantees it. In our pursuit, He will give us exactly what we need, it will be good for us, and we will be blessed.

A NEW THING

Sarah Lynn Phillips   July 3

Over. The wedding, lovely under blue skies amid flowers and smiles, was over. I treasured the memories, studied the photos, and prayed for our daughter and her husband as they settled into a new life together in another city. I couldn't have asked more for them. At the same time I felt a nagging loss. Life would change for the newlyweds—and for us.

As I tried to adjust to our new normal, I read Isaiah 43:18,19 (ESV): *"Remember not the former things, nor consider the things of old. Behold, I am doing a new thing; now it springs forth . . . . I will make a way in the wilderness and rivers in the desert."* A new thing . . . In His gentle way, God seemed to whisper, "Savor the memories, but don't cling to the past. Look! I am doing something new, now, in this place. Don't miss it! I will make a way for you."

A reassuring comfort washed over me. The promise originally made to the nation of Israel gave me hope. Through the lens of gratefulness, I began to watch for new opportunities and look for God's hand. He who began His work in all of us would continue to perform it (Philippians 1:6). New times, new things…all in God's good plan.

YANKEE DOODLE

Dr. K   July 4
But as for you, ye thought evil against me; but God meant it unto good, to bring to pass, as it is this day, to save much people alive.
Genesis 50:20 KJV

"Yankee Doodle" became a favorite American music hit, much

to the surprise of Dr. Stuckburgh, a British army surgeon, who wrote it as a derisive, mocking, parody poking fun at the patriots.

"Doodle" was a slang word for dummy, doofus or dunce-- what Americans were to Dr. Stuckburgh. He thought they didn't have a chance to win the war, and he and the British soldiers who sang "Yankee Doodle" were laughing *at* the disheveled, shoeless Americans.

Instead of letting it get under their skin, the patriots started singing it. After 300 years we still love it. It's the state song of Connecticut, and we smile when we sing it at a patriotic activity.

The principle in Genesis 50:20 concerning Joseph's captivity and elevation to the second most powerful position in Egypt also applies to us. Yes, Dr. Stuckburgh meant it for evil, but God meant it for good. Don't be overwhelmed by life difficulties or what others say. Believe all things work together for good to those who love God.

O Lord, help me laugh off the unkindness of others, and sing in my heart your kindness to me. Amen.

LISTEN TO INSTRUCTIONS

Helen Hoover   July 5
Do not merely listen to the word, and so deceive yourselves. Do what it says. James 1:22 NIV

"Well, I didn't listen to your instructions and now my head, ears, and face are burned," Wendell winced after spending a day in the mountains with my husband, Larry, and me. It had been cloudy and cool, so despite our warning, Wendell assumed he wouldn't get sunburned and didn't need a hat or sunblock lotion.

Our Montana home, located at a lower elevation, is usually warmer than the higher mountain altitudes. Our guests don't understand how quickly the weather changes as we travel through the mountain regions, so they often fail to take our advice to use sunblock. Unfortunately, they suffer consequences.

I've also regretted not listening to God's advice. At times, I thought I knew what was best for me. Not appropriately dealing with anger led to health problems and saying words I later regretted. Harboring unforgiveness led to broken relationships and poor choices. Worry replaced trusting God. Critical judgments produced no grace. Pride led to inconsideration of others.

God understands the "mountains" in our lives and knows the best way to safely travel through them. Listening to, and following His directions makes all our trips easier. His Word offers perfect protection.

WINDBLOWN WAVES AT SUNSET

Gerald W. Bauer   July 6
Jesus said, "Come to me, all you that are weary and are carrying heavy burdens, and I will give you rest." Matthew 11:28 NRSV

Setting sun
from outstretched clouds.
Fading rays
on white capped waves.
End of day
life's tumult rolls.
God's light invites,
says, "Come to me."
Outstretched clouds,
inviting arms.
"My peace I give,
come rest in Me."

MOURNING DOVE SONG

from Psalm 86

Pan Sankey   July 7

Early one July morning while I was sitting outdoors and reading Psalm 86, the birds began to serenade the day. Then a mourning dove began singing its mournful little song over and over. It seemed to fit right in with this psalm of David's lament and turning to trust.

Like a mourning dove at the break of dawn
So my soul cries out for You alone.
You abound in love unto all who call,
You're the God Who wants to be known.

So I'll sing Your praise throughout all of my days

For great is Your love to me.
Your compassion and grace and Your mercy and strength
Are the help and the comfort I need.

Yes, I'll sing Your song throughout all the day long
For great is Your love to me.
Let Your joy fill my soul as Your goodness I extol,
For I know You will hear and answer me.

Yes, I know You will hear and answer me.

*You are forgiving and good, O Lord, abounding in love to all who call
to you….*
In the day of my trouble I will call to you, for you will answer me.
Psalm 86: 5, 7 NIV

I SEE YOU, LORD

Frances Gregory Pasch   July 8

I see You in the flowers
I hear You in the trees.
I feel Your awesome presence
In the cool and gentle breeze.

I see You in the smile
Of a peaceful, joyful face.
I feel that You are with me,
As I bow my head for grace.

Help me, Lord, to rest in You
And treasure all my days,
For if I get too busy,
I'll miss Your choice bouquets.

CRY OUT TO GOD

Bronwyn Worthington   July 9
The Lord is near to all who call on him, to all who call on him in truth.
Psalm 145:18 NIV

One day at the lake, a young girl carelessly wandered out too far. Before long, she was in water over her head. Gasping for air, she caught sight of her mother along the shore. The child yelled the only word she could manage, "Mom!" When she let out what seemed to be her last breath, she felt her mother's arms reaching for her. The faithful parent heard her daughter's scream and spared no time rescuing her drowning child. Steadily, she carried the youngster to shore.

"Mommy," the child exclaimed, "Can you forgive me for going into the deep water?" Looking intently into her child's eyes, the mother's smile affirmed that forgiveness had been offered in full.

We often struggle to remain close to our Savior. Losing sight of the Master, we venture off. Before long, danger lurks on the horizon. All the while our Lord waits, longing to lift our heads above the swirling waters of life.

God, thank You for watching over us even when we walk away from You. Prepare our hearts to confess Your name and repent of our sins. We know You will always respond with love.

ENDURE TO THE END

Ruth Stewart   July 10
And you will be hated by all for My name's sake. But He who endures to the end will be saved. Matthew 10:22 NKJV

I enjoy watching my grandson Drew play basketball on his high school team. In one particular game, both teams were evenly matched and the game went into overtime. Players on both teams were tired. Each player pushed as hard as he could.

One team had more endurance than the other, and won. The losing team may not have been as physically prepared, so they lost the game, not due to lack of skill, but because they ran out of energy. As I watched the losing team tire and lag behind in scoring, I was reminded of the apostle Paul's words in 2 Timothy 4:7: *"I have fought the good fight. I have finished the race. I have kept the faith."*

Paul endured by preparing well for life's challenges, including physical abuse and personal disappointments. He persevered with total obedience to God and knowing God is faithful.
What an example Paul is for us! We too have challenges and disappointments, spiritually and physically. However, with God's

Word as our road map, the Holy Spirit as our guide, and Jesus as our Savior, we have the resources to prepare for the "overtimes" of life. We can have the strength to endure to the end.

A CUP OF COLD WATER

Debbie Carpenter   July 11

"And whoever gives one of these little ones even a cup of cold water because he is a disciple, truly, I say to you, he will by no means lose his reward." Matthew 10:42 ESV

My friend, Joanne, was discouraged. Her adult son was far from the Lord. I knew that Joanne liked to send and receive cards and always succeeded in finding "just the right card" for a friend.

So, I decided to find a card to comfort *her*. I found one I knew she would like and sent it. I did not know how much it had meant to her until seven years later.

Joanne took me aside one Sunday morning after church and said, "We never know how much a small kindness can bless a friend in need." She opened her Bible and there was the card I sent. She had kept it in her Bible for seven years in order to have it available to read when she needed encouragement. What a gracious God we have who delights to work through even the smallest charitable deed.

Father God, open our eyes to see opportunities each day to give a cup of cold water in your name. May we respond by offering words, deeds or prayers for others in ways that please You. Amen.

BEAUTIFUL FEET

Lanita Boyd   July 12

As a child, I always admired my mother's feet. They were thin and elegant and nicely arched. I felt sorry for mothers with short, stubby feet.

But after she developed rheumatoid arthritis in her 80s, her feet changed dramatically. They broadened and became very sore, with each toe rubbing on the next one. I found her little toe stockings to put on each individual toe to keep sores from developing. Yes, it's true—those stockings exist.

My mother could no longer wear the elegant sandals of her

youth, but had to wear heavy-soled black "clodhoppers." She deplored the situation, as did I, but we could do nothing about it. Only in those shoes could she stand to put her weight on her pain-filled feet. Paying over $200 a pair for such ugly shoes added insult to injury.

After she died, I was touched by all the shoes she'd kept, even though she could no longer wear them. I understand that—clinging to pleasant memories through physical items.

Even though her feet changed in her later years, they were still beautiful. Why? Because God says so. She never quit sharing the gospel with everyone she met. *"As it is written: 'How beautiful are the feet of those who bring good news!'"* (Romans 10:15, Isaiah 52:7, NIV) Her shoes may have changed, but her beautiful feet remained.

ARMS TOO SHORT?

Jana Carman   July 13
Surely the arm of the LORD is not too short to save. Isaiah 59:1 NIV

Ask me, "Is your arm too short?" and I answer, "Yes, unfortunately." Every blouse or sweater sleeve is two inches too long, and needs shortening. Being "vertically challenged," I am often forced to ask a taller shopper to reach an item on a top shelf. So when the "short arm question" shows up three times in scripture, I think maybe God is talking to me too.

In Numbers 11:21-23, Moses doubts that God can supply meat for 600,000 men for a whole month. God replies: *"Is the LORD's arm too short? You will now see whether or not what I say will come true for you."* (NIV) So—yes, He can.

Next, Isaiah 50:2b, God rebukes the unbelieving Israelites, *"Was my arm too short to ransom you? Do I lack the strength to rescue you?"* "Duh! Of course not."

In Isaiah 59:2 NIV, their prayers (maybe mine too) aren't answered because *"... your iniquities have separated you from your God; your sins have hidden his face from you, so that he will not hear."* He can, but my sin stands between "Can" and "Will."

Lord, I know You can. May I do my part of clearing the path between us, so You will.

MOVING SALES

Marilyn Nutter   July 14

The grass withers, the flower fades, but the word of our God will stand forever. Isaiah 40:8 ESV

As I prepared for my moving sale, I scanned the items on tables and on my garage floor. They represented part of my forty plus years of married life. Some "exotic" objects such as an onyx piece from Mexico and a woodcarving from Haiti were mingled with odds and ends—candles, baking pans and tools.

Neighbors of my same age stopped in and sat with me during a slow time and we reminisced about changes that have taken place.

"Younger couples really aren't interested in our stuff," Linda said. "Their tastes and interests are different."

"Ours have changed, too, though," I responded. "Remember the avocado and gold? Then we moved to mauve and blue. Let's not even get into fashion!" We laughed at the thought of what we liked at the time versus what we like now.

Whether it is home decorating or fashion and hairdos, personal tastes, interests and styles change. The seasons of our lives change too, but the word of God stands forever. Regardless of styles and season, it is reliable, true and always timely.

Jesus Christ is the same yesterday and today and forever.
Hebrews 13:8 ESV

MINING FOR TREASURE

Nola Passmore   July 15

They tunnel through the rock; their eyes see all its treasures.
Job 28:10 NIV

Read Job 28:1-10

Job paints a vivid picture of the work of miners in Biblical times. Deep in the earth, there were deposits of precious gems and metals such as gold, silver, iron, and sapphires. In order to obtain these treasures, however, miners had to take action. They searched for ore in desolate places, dug shafts in the earth, swung precariously on ropes, and tunneled through rock. It was lonely and dangerous work, but there was a great reward. After cutting through the rock and earth in darkness, the miner would eventually see the treasures hidden within.

When we're going through a dark or difficult period, it's often hard to see the treasures waiting for us. Sometimes God will take the initiative to speak to us and comfort us, but there are other times when we have to take action to unearth those gems. We might need to spend time in prayer, study the scriptures, listen to a worship CD, join a home Bible group, or seek out godly teachers or Christian counselors. Rest assured that any effort you take to dig deeper into your faith is time well spent. God has many treasures waiting for you.

THE SPITE FENCE

Jana Carman   July 16
For he himself is our peace, who has made the two [Jew and Gentile] one and has destroyed the barrier, the dividing wall of hostility, … thus making peace … to reconcile both of them to God through the cross, by which he put to death their hostility. Ephesians 2:14-16 NIV

My grandmother loved flowers, and in particular, her lovely tulip tree,. Unfortunately, as the tree grew, it grew harder for family drivers to leave her home without driving on the neighbor's grass. We tried to avoid encroaching, but at one visit, we found a ten-foot telephone pole installed on the very edge of the neighbor's property, directly opposite the tree. Thereafter we had to inch around, hoping to avoid tree branches on one side and pole on the other.

The tree could have been trimmed back or even cut down, but it wasn't. Neither would give an inch. As long as my grandmother lived, the spite fence remained, a constant reminder of unresolved hostility.

The verses above speak of another spite fence, between Jew and Gentile. Jesus died to reconcile the two hostile groups to God and to each other. The way is open; as always, the will to reconcile is needed for change to come.

Thank You, Jesus, for the peace You offer.
Help me to sow peace. Amen

TRAINING WHEELS

Kelly Lyman   July 17
Let perseverance finish its work so that you may be mature and
complete, not lacking anything. James 1:4 NIV

My son begged me to ride his bike without training wheels. He
seemed ready, so one afternoon, I removed them. He climbed up
on the bike, full of excitement, and took off down our driveway--
promptly falling off, and skinning his knee. Tears streamed down
his face. I brushed them off, gave him a hug and convinced him
to get back on. After falling three more times, he proclaimed
he was never going to ride a bike again. A bit later, after some
encouragement, he tried again. By the end of the day, he was
riding his bike--training wheels free.

There are many instances in life where we want to give up.
Each trial is unique. Perhaps it's a ministry, a certain relationship,
a job, school, a habit or learning a new skill. Whatever it is, there
will be many instances where we want to give up, but God calls us
to jump back on our bicycle and try again. When we persevere, we
grow and mature in our faith. It's in our weakness that we God's
strength is made perfect.

And He has said to me, "My grace is sufficient for you, for power is
perfected in weakness." 2 Corinthians 12:9a NASB

WORD CHOICE

Marietta Taylor   July 18
Anyone who hates a brother or sister is a murderer, and you know
that no murderer has eternal life residing in him. 1 John 3:15, NIV

I disliked her. She rubbed me the wrong way, like sandpaper.
She was a co-worker so there was no escaping her. I picked
at everything she said and did. Then one day while reading my
Bible, I saw that God called me a murderer. Yes, a slanderer is a
murderer!

Our words are sometimes like knives. They can cut and wound
others deeply. Their effects can kill a person's spirit or reputation.

In Ephesians 4:29 (NIV) we are told, "***Do not let any***
unwholesome talk come out of your mouths, but only what is
helpful for building others up according to their needs…" God

wants us to use our words to represent Him and His love for us. That doesn't happen when we tear others down.

If we ask Him to show us His heart for the difficult people in our lives, He will do it. God is willing to help us do what He asks us to do. He has asked us to build up others with our words. He will help us speak life-giving words to and about others. Doing so gives them a tiny glimpse into God's love for them. What a privilege!

HOLY HUG

Betty Spence
July 19

...Love your neighbor as yourself. Mark 12:31 NIV

Thank You, Lord, for the hug
my neighbor gave me today.
It was a tonic for us both.
Now send me to someone
who needs a healing touch
and hug them, Lord, through me.

WALKING WITH GOD

Betty Spence
July 20

And Enoch walked with God: and he was not;
for God took him. Genesis 5:24

In step
with God, Enoch
never knew when the road
ran out and the bridge of faith locked
in place.

HEART CHECK-UP

Linda Reppert
July 21

My cardiologist knows my heart. He has measured every chamber and the capabilities of each valve. Thick files report specific numbers regarding every detail of my heart. No one on earth knows my heart as well as he does. But, my cardiologist will never be the passion of my heart.

Jesus knows my heart. He has <u>complete</u> knowledge of every physical attribute of my heart. After all, He made it and He gives me every heartbeat that I have. Jesus also knows the real spiritual condition of my heart. He is the passion for which my heart beats. He is my Lord. My heart will beat for him forever, long after my physical heart stops beating. His Word delights me and it reveals to me His heart for me.

What is the condition of your heart? Is it as the cardiologist sees? Is it just knowledge based? I began with knowledge of Jesus and then it converted to passion for Him. Have you gone from knowledge to passion?

Jesus says: *"You are the ones who justify yourselves in the eyes of others, but God knows your hearts..."* Luke 16:15 NIV

Jesus knows your heart and He desires your passion. Who does your heart beat for?

BELIEVING IS A MUST

Frances Gregory Pasch   July 22
Now faith is confidence in what we hope for and assurance about what we do not see. Hebrews 11:1 NIV

Before I knew you, Jesus,
I would worry and I'd fret.
Each time bad news came my way,
I'd really get upset.

Now I try to analyze
The news that I receive;
I look beyond the surface
So I will not be deceived.

I have learned, dear Jesus,
At times I must bear pain.
I also know it won't be long
Before you will explain.

I'm learning to accept what comes…
In You, alone, I trust,
For if I'm to be faithful...
Believing is a must!

ARE YOU RICH?

Jana Carman   July 23

The wealth of the rich is their fortified city; they imagine it as an unscalable wall. Proverbs 18:11 NIV

Foolishly, I've wasted hours fretting about paying my bills, even though God always supplies all my needs. So it was probably God's leading when I was asked to teach a Sunday school lesson on James 5:1-6—God's warning about wealth being all-important.

To focus the lesson, I asked, "What would you grab if you had ten minutes to get it before your house washes away?" (As in Superstorm Sandy, or maybe in a house fire or tornado.) Research shows that people grab the oddest things. Quick…what would *you* grab?

My husband's answer was, "My file drawer of forty years of sermons." My answer: "My computer with all my writing files."

I should have said, "My Bible." Nothing could be more valuable since ***The grass withers and the flowers fall, but the word of our God stands forever*** (Isaiah 40:8 NIV). Riches, indeed!

When I list all my true wealth—God's Word, food, clothing, shelter, freedom to worship, my own Bible—it's obvious how unbelievably rich I am—richer than 90% of the world. *I am amply supplied …. **And my God will supply all your needs according to his glorious riches in Christ Jesus.*** Philippians 4:18,19 NIV

Thank You, loving Father

THE GIFT OF TIME

Joan Nathan   July 24

Each of you should use whatever gift you have received to serve others, as faithful stewards of God's grace in its various forms. 1 Peter 4:10 NIV

One evening six elderly friends gathered around a table in the waterfront beach bungalow to plan church activities. At one point, they took a break to watch the sunset. Waves played a rhythmic tune, as if to say "Hush…hush. The best gift is yet to come." A bright orange summer sun moved behind low lying clouds and disappeared. The setting sun would be hidden today, but no one was disappointed as they looked at the purple, pink, and orange hues decorating the clouds. It was a wrapped present. Then one woman exclaimed, "Look, God opened a present. The sun popped and it came back out!" Yes, the sun was back with brighter orange hues, and it appeared rounder than before. "Did you know that the sun sizzles when it hits the water?" she asked. "Shhh. Listen." Everyone smiled as they listened for the sizzle when the sun finally disappeared below the horizon.

It was as if they had a personal message from God. Yes, our gifts come in different hues and time is a gift like a brilliant sunset. Older folks can pop and sizzle too as they continue to use their gifts and time to serve others.

FREE GIFT, NO STRINGS ATTACHED

Dolores Fruth   July 25
So if the Son sets you free, you will be free indeed. John 8:36 NIV

There is nothing free in life, they say
But we know differently today.
God's gift is absolutely free,
Abundant grace for you and me.
There is no fine print mentioned here,
No background check that we must clear,
No strings attached to pull us in,
No stated limit on our sin.
We cannot earn this gift divine
Christ gave his life while saving mine.
The price was paid by God's own Son
Forgiveness granted!
We have won!

A ROCK AND THE RAIN

Marilyn Nutter   July 26
The LORD is my rock, my fortress, and my savior; my God is my rock, in whom I find protection. He is my shield, the power that saves me, and my place of safety. Psalm 18:2 NLT

It had rained overnight and it was a humid morning, but my neighbor and I were determined to walk our usual three miles. Midway, our custom is to stop and sit on a bench near our lake. Today the bench was wet so Lanette suggested we sit on one of the rocks near the shore.

We shared a large rock and sat comfortably. We admired the lake and talked for a few minutes, then completed our walk toward home.

Scripture tells us we have a comfortable rock available every minute of the day. Whether we need a refuge, protection or security, God is our constant and eternal rock. We have choices each day as to where we want to "sit". We can choose the wet bench or chose the wisdom and security of our Rock. Do we want to be messy and damp...or secure?

WHY BOTHER?

Judy Dippel   July 27
Then Peter said, "Silver and gold I do not have, but what I do have I give you..." Acts 3:6 NIV

I'm guilty.

We are guilty of saying, "Why bother?" We think, "Who am I to do this?" "Why would women care what I have to say?" "What do I know?" "Do my kids ever listen to me?" Do you say that, at least some of the time?

How and why can we bother? By sharing you; your personal experiences guide and encourage; spiritual gifting supplies. Your legacy, the treasure that lies within you, is shared day-after-day.

As I write, I realize I've left a piece of myself with every generation this week:

> ❖ My son, a new father, told his dad. "Mom's right. Seeing life through a child's eyes is an exciting adventure!"
>
> ❖ My conversation with the elderly folks, where my mom lives, connects them, bringing them greater purpose and smiles.
>
> ❖ My legacy is left with my friend, Debbie, a non-Christian, as I share my heart for Jesus.
>
> ❖ Time spent with my grandchild gave her a glimpse of that special something within me.

We honor God when we generously give something of ourselves to every generation. It may not be silver or gold, but what we offer is priceless. Isn't it time to bother?

ETHEL

Bonnie Rose Hudson   July 28
A cheerful heart is good medicine,
but a crushed spirit dries up the bones. Proverbs 17:22 NIV

I learned later that her name was Ethel—a small woman who left a big impression. I spotted her at the grocery store. Ethel stood several inches shy of five feet tall when standing straight up, which I never saw her do. When I first encountered her, she was standing bent over her cart with her head resting on the handlebar. When I saw her later in the checkout line, she was still bent over. A clerk from the store was standing by to help her out to her vehicle. I overheard the clerk confirm that Ethel's daughter would be picking her up. Ethel quietly confessed to the clerk that she was tired. She must have asked for help because the next thing I heard was the clerk answer, "You're tired? Me too. Of course I'll push your cart."

A few moments later, when it was my turn to stand opposite the cashier, I remarked what determination the woman must possess. The cashier replied, "Ethel? And you know, she's always happy."

We went on to discuss how little things so often weigh us down, but here was a living example of a woman who didn't let the problems of life crush her spirit: her spirit that stood tall and straight and proud, even when her body would not.

AND THEN JESUS

Kim Rhinewalt   July 29
I have come that they may have life,
and that they may have it more abundantly. John 10:10 NKJV

At times I think if I can close my eyes quickly enough; I will miss it: the reel-to-reel replay in my mind.
I never do.
The full feature tumbles through my brain. Colored bits of a lie, an argument. Hazy grays and soundless pictures so that I shake my head to scramble them. And all over again I'm angry, embarrassed,

shamed.

Forgetting is hard, even though our souls were bathed clean. Each of us is sure that our past, our sin is different. Too much, too big, too bad for anyone to fix. And so we inch forward, heavy, like Atlas bearing his world.

It came one night, in an e-mail from my dad. The refrain, simple: "And Jesus....and then Jesus." No sin is so great that those three words can't make it right, nothing too ugly that Jesus can't erase. Nothing so big, that He is not bigger.

I was lost AND THEN JESUS found me. I was hungry AND THEN JESUS fed me. I was a sinner AND THEN JESUS saved me.

And then Jesus..........

Lord, Thank You for Jesus, Your gift Who makes all things whole.

Amen.

SODA RESIDUE

Rebecca Mitchel   July 30

Finally, brothers, whatever is true ... noble ... right ... pure ... lovely ...admirable—if anything is excellent or praiseworthy—think about such things. Whatever you have learned or received or heard from me, or seen in me—put it into practice. And the God of peace will be with you. Philippians 4:8-9

Sssssssssssssssssssss. I quickly pulled over to see what was making such a horrible noise, and then I realized, as I turned the corner, an unopened 2-liter bottle of soda had rolled and been punctured by something under the seat. Foamy soda was spraying everywhere. My son quickly threw it out the window, but not before we were all sprayed with its sticky residue.

It was then that I realized how easy it was for me to become like that bottle of soda. I get angry and start spewing words. Words that were hurtful, unloving and unkind. Words that would stick in others' minds like the soda clinging to the car windows. I would say I was sorry, but the residue of what I had said remained.

The Lord revealed to me how important it was for me to follow the guidelines of what He set forth in Philippians 4:8-9. I needed to totally dwell on him with every thought and word. He would help me become more like Him and less like the bottle of exploding soda.

Lord, help me to guard my heart, mind and mouth, so that whatever I do or say will leave a lasting residue of Your love on everyone around me. Amen.

NOT ALL THAT GLITTERS IS GOLD

Robert Gutierrez   July 31

And Lot lifted his eyes and saw all of the plain of the Jordan, that it was well watered... Then Lot chose for himself all the plain of the Jordan, and Lot journeyed east. Genesis 13:10-11 NKJV

We can't escape life's forks in the road. When tough decisions confront us we tend to opt for what appears most attractive. However, looks can be deceiving--what you see isn't always what you gain. You may even get the opposite of what you wanted.

In Genesis 13, Lot arrived at his fork in the road. He and Abraham had to separate because the land could no longer sustain both families and herds. Abraham offered Lot first choice of the land. Lot chose the land that looked good to his eyes.

This didn't bring him what he anticipated. Lot hoped for prosperity; he got tragedy instead. His journey east took him to Sodom. God later destroyed Sodom in judgment for its wickedness, and three members of his family perished.

Things which appear good aren't always good, and quick decisions can have grave consequences. Prayer is the best tool when decisions must be made. Seeking God's counsel can be life's greatest time-saver and pain saver.

Lord, help me to not make quick, rash decisions based on what I see, but to seek your guidance in every decision. Amen.

August

REFRESHMENT

Doris Richardson   August 1

The grass was getting brown and brittle, the corn was reaching up for water, the birds were chirping for rain, the soil was cracking in places, the leaves on the roses began to dry--all thirsty for a refreshing drink of water from the heavens. Even though we water the flowers with well water, it's not the same as natural water from the clouds.

Our souls get dry and parched, thirsty for the living water from heaven. People try to refresh with time off, dinner out, favorite TV show, a game of golf, or vacation to the beach. But none of these can do what the Word of God does for the hungry, searching, dry, empty soul.

Jesus said, *"It is the spirit who gives life; the flesh profits nothing. The words that I speak to you, they are spirit, and they are life."* John 6:63 NKJV.

Thank You for the rain, gently penetrating the dry soil, refreshing the flowers, causing the corn to grow another two inches, and thank You Lord, for refreshing us with Your Word. Amen.

DYNAMIC KINDNESS

Tommie Lenox   August 2
Be kind and compassionate to one another, forgiving each other, just as in Christ God forgave you. Ephesians 4:32 NIV

My friend Bea is a dynamo, full of life, loving and generous. Her looks belie her age – 95! Bea recently had a pacemaker implant. She didn't want a full anesthetic saying, "The older we get, the more apt we are to come back loopy." The surgeon agreed. For this routine procedure, a local anesthetic works. Usually.

Not this time! One wire slipped from the surgeon's grasp and pierced Bea's heart. In her pain, Bea screamed to God, "Take me! Take me!" God had other plans.

After Bea's seven days in ICU, the surgeon came for a follow-up visit. "I am so sorry," she said. "I have been doing this procedure for 20 years. Nothing like this has ever happened before!"

Bea reached for the hands that had nearly taken her life. "Let me tell you a story," she said. "When I was a little girl I broke my mother's favorite vase. I felt terrible! I went to her crying, 'I'm sorry, I'm so sorry!'

"My mother said, 'Did you do it on purpose? '

"'Of course not,' I cried. Mama hugged me and said, 'Then don't worry about it.'"

Bea hugged the surgeon and said, "Don't worry about it."

Friendship Day
VALUE OF FRIENDS

Judy Webb   August 3
Carry each other's burdens, and in this way you will fulfill the law of Christ. Galatians 6:2 (NIV)

"I don't have any friends. I don't want any friends, especially women, they are too high maintenance." This was my mantra for many years until God opened my eyes and my heart to the wonder of girlfriends. For all of my childhood and many of my adult years I lived an isolated existence, never wanting a friend, always holding people at arm's length.

The struggles of life and daily living have taught me every woman needs a couple of really good friends to laugh with, to love with, and to cry with. Scripture teaches that we were made to be in community, to walk alongside each other and allow others to do the same for us. Experience says relationships can be messy, but God wants us in the trenches, up to our elbows, with arms linked.

Friends come and friends go, but a true friend sticks by you like family. Proverbs 18:24 (MSG)

God uses friends to minister to us, to comfort us, and pray for us. Friends are a valuable gift from God to cherish and enjoy. Once such a friend is found, hold on to your hat …it is going to be an amazing adventure.

FAITHFULNESS

Shirley S. Stevens   August 4
Noah did everything just as God commanded him. Genesis 6:22 NIV

My mother distributed a paper cup of dirt to each of the four and five-year-old children in her Sunday school class. She told them to take the dirt home, water it each day, and keep the cup on a windowsill. "If you do so, something may happen."

Each week the children came back and complained, "Nothing is happening."

"Are you watering?" she asked. Most of them nodded yes.

After four weeks, three children excitedly reported that they had two green leaves. When she asked the children what they had learned, they replied, "All it takes is water, teacher."

"No," she answered, "all it needs is your faithfulness."

She had given them their first lesson in the power of faithful service. Later when she taught them about Noah, she reminded the children what had happened when they were faithful in their watering.

Living in a society where human beings sinned and rebelled against God, Noah was the only man who pleased God. He showed unwavering faithfulness. Repeatedly in Genesis, we read, "Noah did everything just as God commanded him."

Lord, remind us to bless the life around us and within us by serving You faithfully. Amen.

CH RCH

Doris Richardson   August 5

When we drove by the church I noticed the U was missing from the sign: CH RCH.

U are important in church. U are missed when you aren't in church. Hebrews 10:25 tells us not to forsake *"the assembling of ourselves together, as the manner of some is, but exhorting one another, and so much the more, as you see the day approaching."* We need to gather with other Christians for worship and admonition. We encourage each other through prayer and fellowship.

Romans 10:17 points out that by hearing God's Word, we grow in our faith. *"All Scripture is given by inspiration of God, and is profitable for doctrine, for reproof, for correction, for instruction in righteousness, that the man of God may be perfect, thoroughly furnished unto all good works."* (2 Timothy 3:16-17 KJV)

Don't be like many others who are dropping out of church, or take a Sunday off. Be sure U are there. Invite someone else to join U.

LOVE IS IN THE DETAILS

Sherry Taylor Cummins   August 6
Read 1 Corinthians 13
Love is patient, love is kind. It does not envy, it does not boast, it is not proud. It is not rude. It is not self-seeking, it is not easily angered, it keeps no record of wrongs. Love does not delight in evil but rejoices with the truth. It always protects, always trusts, always hopes, always perseveres. Love never fails. 1 Cor. 13: 4:-8a

We associate 1 Corinthians with weddings and a charge from a pastor to a glowing couple. Looking closely, we don't see romance, but a detailed list of active love.

Do you love when it doesn't feel good? Do you secretly rejoice when one who has mistreated you finally gets what he deserves-- or doesn't? When your adult child makes decisions outside of your teachings, do you suffer long, do you bear it? Do you endure overwhelming circumstances with difficult people and cling to God's love and promises when no relief is in sight?

Love is more than a feeling or a verbal affirmation—love is an action. The beauty is that God loves you and His love is in all the details. As we learn to love like Him, we can love actively too.

A TIME TO LAUGH AND A TIME TO WEEP

Cherie Reilly   August 7
To every thing there is a season, A time to weep, and a time to laugh; a time to mourn, and a time to dance; Ecclesiastes 3: 1,4 KJV

After my father died, my mother lived in a cozy apartment at a Christian retirement home for eighteen years. Her many friends talked a little louder as her hearing diminished, and offered a helping hand as her eyesight faded. Her mind remained alert and her memory was much better than mine. In March, Mom fell several times and had to be moved to a nursing home.

My mother died today. She loved Jesus with all her heart, and often attended Bible studies to learn the details and depth of His Word.

The death of a loved one leaves us with feelings of ambivalence: our human loss--yet confidence in her presence with our Savior. We grieve—there is a time for tears-- but not as those who have no hope. (1Thessalonians 4:13) *For we believe that Jesus died and rose again, and so we believe that God will bring with Jesus those who have fallen asleep in him.* 1 Thessalonians 4:14 (NIV)

REFUGE

Diane Sillaman   August 8
But as for me, the nearness of God is my good;
I have made the Lord GOD my refuge,
That I may tell of all Your works. Psalm 73:28 NAS

Some may think that if God loved us, we would not have so many inconveniences, troubles and hardships. This past week we had numerous fires throughout the state of Colorado. A major one was just eleven miles from our home. The highway to our home was closed for days due to the fire danger.

When we left Tuesday morning, we didn't know that we would not be home again until Friday night. We didn't take extra clothes, toiletries, or pajamas. We had not planned meals away from home aside from lunch on Tuesday. Our refuge, however, was the home of a dear couple who not only provided shelter, but love and prayer.

When things go along as we wish, we feel no need for help. Yet God loves our fellowship and praise. Our discomfort in life can serve as a motivation to run to the shelter of our God who is always waiting for us with His open arms. Our need for help brings an intimacy between the Helper and the one helped.

The Lord longs to help us. He loves us. Run to Him *today*!

The eternal God is your refuge,
and underneath are the everlasting arms. Deuteronomy 33:27 NIV

THE KINDEST RESPONSE

Sandra Bartz   August 9
Read 1 Peter 4:7-11

An agitated lady blocked the cafeteria line, glaring at the servers and wrestling dishes from their hands. Her daughter, standing beside her, spoke patiently, "Now, Mother, you don't want to do that." Mother hardened her face, determined to remain in control, though she did not speak.

Catching up to them, I remarked to the daughter, "We'd better hope to be that independent when we reach her age so we can deal with the challenges." She slowly turned and responded, "At 92 she ought to learn to accept a little help, don't you think? I'm very grateful for any assistance I can get." Then I noticed that the daughter was holding her own tray with one hand as her other arm hung uselessly by her side.

That experience showed me the person I am when I look at people. Do I see their behavior superficially or through the eyes of Jesus? Do I respond with the same patience and grace that I have received from Him? When we view people through the eyes of Jesus, we are able to serve them better.

Lord, help me to see people as You do and respond
with Your loving kindness. Amen.

THE TATTERED SHIRT

Donna J. Howard   August 10
When pride comes, then comes disgrace,
but with humility comes wisdom. Proverbs 11:2, NIV

I cringed with embarrassment as my husband got out of the RV to secure a campsite for the night. That sloppy, tattered shirt! It looked so awful. Why does he have to wear that? What will she think of us?

I watched as he talked with the lady assigning lots. She asked him a few questions and they laughed together. She didn't even notice his torn shirt.

I had judged my husband's appearance, but soon cringed at the tattered condition of my heart. My awful, ugly pride. I talked to Jesus and repented of my sin. I felt His love and I sensed His forgiveness.

Father, by the power of Your Spirit, keep me from judging others.
By that same power, remind me of the condition of my heart,
that I may display Your love—not criticism. Amen.

ENGAGING YOUR CORE

Shirley S. Stevens   August 11
You will seek me and find me when you seek me with all your heart.
Jer. 29:13 NIV

"Engage your core." The first time the physical therapist said this to me, I responded, "Engage what?"

I eventually learned that Martha, my therapist, wanted me to draw my bellybutton up and back towards my spine. I had to train to maintain my core contractions and still be able to breathe. As my core became stronger, my back hurt less.

As I lay on the table with an ice pack on my knee after my workout, I thought how these principles might apply to restoring my spiritual core. Some mornings when I read scripture and devotions, I lack focus and am distracted. My mind strays to my "To Do" list for that day or to some worry I have. I need to concentrate on His word, center, and engage my spiritual core. Only then, will I find Him.

PULLING WEEDS

Sheri Neuhofer   August 12

One gorgeous summer day I spent time pulling weeds and cleaning flower beds in my back yard. This task can be daunting as these beds are the last ones to get cleaned and I'm tired. We typically focus on our front yard because people see it as they pass by.

I had just started the second flower bed when the Lord used "weed pulling" as an object lesson. I recalled these words: *God does not see the same way people see. People look at the outside of a person, but the Lord looks at the heart.* (1 Samuel 16:7b NCV) I wondered for a moment: How do people see me? What does my inside look like?

Since God is the only one who truly sees my heart, does the content match the way I "appear" on the outside? When people look at me, do they see a reflection of Jesus? Just like the flower beds each spring, there will always be "weeds to pull" in my life. I don't want to wear the image of a beautiful flower bed in front of my house, while "my back yard" is full of weeds.

Lord, help me be mindful of my heart's condition. Pull my weeds, Lord. I want to be a reflection of You. Amen

INTO THE THRONE ROOM

Nola Passmore   August 13

In Old Testament times, you could be killed for approaching the king without being summoned. However, there was a loophole. Your life would be spared if the king held out his royal sceptre to you (Esther 4:11). Queen Esther, a young Jewish woman, knew the risks when she pleaded with King Xerxes to save the Jews. The Jews were spared as a result of her courageous actions (Esther 5:1-2; 7:1-4; 8:3-8, 16-17).

It's rare to have access to royalty today. We can't knock on the door of Buckingham Palace and expect to meet Queen Elizabeth. We would have to go through official channels, wait weeks or months for an appointment, and then only have a limited time in which to bring our case, if at all.

When Jesus died on the cross, He made a way for us to have free access to God. We don't wonder if He'll let us in, or go through a third party to get an appointment. We are children of the King and can enter His presence any time. As the writer of Hebrews urges us, *"Let us then approach the throne of grace with confidence, so that we may receive mercy and find grace to help us in our time of need."* (Heb. 4:16, NIV). What a privilege to approach the King of Glory and freely worship at His feet.

A FAINT REFLECTION

J. Mark Spruill   August 14
And we, who with unveiled faces all reflect the Lord's glory, are being transformed into his likeness with ever-increasing glory, which comes from the Lord, who is the Spirit. 2 Corinthians 3:18 NIV

A few nights ago, I went out with a little telescope to look at the stars. Venus was visible as the brightest planet. I think it is about the brightest object in the sky other than the sun and moon. A little bit later, Jupiter rose in the southeastern sky. It was bright, reflecting the sun's glory from millions of miles away. As I peered through the telescope, I could even see its moons. I decided to try for a bigger challenge.

A little up and to the right should be Uranus. Would it even be possible to spot such a faraway planet? I searched. There were dots of light everywhere. But focusing in on one, in the right spot and about the right brightness, I noticed it was different. Stars appear as a pinprick of light, but this was a minuscule disk of blue-green color. I had found it.

What a wonderful creation! Almost 3,000 times less bright than Jupiter. Smaller and much farther away, it is a tiny disk of light far out in space. And yet, for those who take the time to look, it is still faithfully reflecting the glory of the Son.

BUT AS FOR ME

Diane Sillaman   August 15
But as for me, I am like a green olive tree in the house of God;
I trust in the lovingkindness of God forever and ever.
I will give You thanks forever, because You have done it,
And I will wait on Your name, for it is good, in the presence of Your
godly ones. Psalm 52: 8-9 NAS

It is not merely that we describe God as loving and kind, or that He is effective in His actions, but God wants us to take Him personally. The Psalmist *counts* on God to be who He is. He is leaning his whole weight, all his circumstance, all his pain and disappointments in life on Who God is to Him. He has determined to wait in hope, in expectancy on the God who he knows will never fail. He has taken personally the beauty, character and power of God.

Because he likens himself to a tree planted in the very house of God, it's as if he says, "I am not going anywhere else to find answers." He is in unity with all the other people who also count on God to be faithful to them.

What are you facing today? Learn from the Psalmist. God can be trusted. He is reliable. We can choose to believe that and be at peace. Take Him personally.

HEART TROUBLE—VISION TROUBLE

Adele Jones   August 16
Read: Jeremiah 17:5-8
Stop regarding man in whose nostrils is breath,
for of what account is he? Isaiah 2:22 NIV

Recent years have seen expansion of an industry that threatens the rural heritage and livelihood of family and friends in the region in which I was raised. Many communities feel sold out for the sake of profit. Upon hearing of these changes I was distressed. Yet as I prayed, I felt the Holy Spirit breathe the words, "Let not your heart be troubled" into my spirit.

Not troubled? How could I not be troubled?

These events seemed to unfold relentlessly. Then I remembered the words of Isaiah 2:22. Who was I trusting in? Man or God? By fearing these decisions, I was putting my confidence, even my faith, in the governing bodies overseeing this industry.

Time and again I determined to shift my eyes off circumstances and place my confidence in the Lord. Only then could I release my worry, allowing expectancy for the Lord's provision to grow.

And He has provided in a number of ways.

Are you facing impossible circumstances for which there appears to be no ready solution? Remember, nothing escapes our Lord's attention and no situation is beyond His intervention. Lay your anxiety at the feet of Christ. And let not your heart be troubled.

HANDPRINT OF GOD

Lana James   August 17

See, I have engraved you on the palms of my hands;
Isaiah 49:16 NIV

Child, you are anointed
By the living God.
How wondrous
It is to be in His hands.
Lift your face to Him
And see acceptance in His eyes.
Feel His forgiveness
Fall upon you.

Your search has not ended
But it continues.
Take heart,
Your Jesus is always present.

BIRDS AND BUTTERFLIES

Evelyn Heinz   August 18
Let the skies be filled with birds of every kind. Genesis 1:20 b NLT

Over the years I've been a bird watcher and a butterfly
watcher. My bird feeder drew many birds to the backyard. I had
planted bushes and flowers that attracted butterflies and brought
me hours of enjoyment from the wonders of God's winged
creatures.

I do not have a backyard now that I have moved to a
retirement complex. As a gift, my son put a hummingbird feeder on
my apartment window. Today a tiny female hummingbird came and
stayed a while, looking in the window as if to say, "Thank you." I
got tears in my eyes at the sight of seeing it up close to me.

God, thank You for the joy you have brought to my new home!

**Their trust should be in God,
who richly gives us all we need for our enjoyment.**
1 Timothy 6:17 NLT

IT'S A MATTER OF THE HEART

Tabitha Abel   August 19
**For the Lord does not see as man sees; for man looks at the
outward appearance, but the Lord looks at the heart.**
1 Samuel 16:7b NKJV

"Mike's not very nice," the off-going nurse said. "Tattoos. Kinda
rough. You know what I mean?" I did –and thanking her I set to
work, glad I had prayed on my long journey to work in anticipation
of today's problems. Nursing had changed as patients reflected the
chaotic lives they often live today.

In Old Testament times God spoke audibly to Samuel, whom
He later directed to anoint the first king of Israel. Jesse's sons lined
up, with Eliab, the handsome eldest son, first. Samuel was about
to anoint him when God intervened.

"Wait."

With none of the six sons chosen, they called David, the
youngest brother, in from guarding the sheep on the hillsides of
Bethlehem.

"He's the one," God told Samuel. "Anoint Him. I can see his

heart." Samuel obeyed, and David later became king.

At the end of a hectic 12-hour shift I reported off to the same nurse.

"I talked with Mike today. He's in less pain now," I said. "He really is a pretty nice guy."

Jesus said, *"Judge not that you be not judged"* (Matt.7:1 NKJV). How easy it is to fall into that trap.

Lord, help me never to judge people based on others' reports. May I always be guided by the Holy Spirit. Amen.

COME...FOLLOW ME

Dorsee Bernat   August 20
Then He said to them, "Follow Me,
and I will make you fishers of men." Matthew 4:19 NKJV

All those Jesus called to follow and serve with Him were called to change. Change can be scary, costly, even dangerous.

Peter, James and John were fishermen. Fishing was their livelihood, all they'd ever known until the day Jesus said, "Follow Me." Imagine Peter's attempt to explain his decision to his family. Picture Zebedee, alone on the shore with his boats, watching his sons James and John, walk away with Jesus. Matthew, a hated tax collector, who worked for the Roman government, risked everything to follow Jesus. Despite the future's uncertainty, something in Jesus, worth the risk and the price, drew each of them.

Others rejected His call. The rich young ruler walked away from Jesus, unwilling to give up his earthly wealth. His fear caused him to miss the greatest treasure of all time.

Jesus calls us to follow Him. He won't pry our hands and hearts from what we treasure, but if we are willing to trust Him with the journey of change, He'll use our lives in ways greater than we can imagine and walk with us every step of the way.

RAINBOW CONNECTION

Helen Dening   August 21
"Blessed are the eyes that see what you see." Luke 10:23 NIV

As I headed home, my eyes soaked in the most beautiful

rainbow, with each color vibrant and breathtaking. Red flowed to orange, orange to yellow, yellow to green, green to blue, with blue melting into purple. Awestruck, a prayer poured from my heart as I thanked God for His faithfulness, His promises, and for the hope found in His Son, Jesus.

I took off my sunglasses to see the rainbow in the day's brightness, but I couldn't. My eyes could no longer see the beauty before me. It was only with the filters of my polarized lenses that I could witness such splendor.

Sometimes God seems to disappear. In our busyness, our view is often obstructed by the "stuff" of life—family, jobs (or lack of), finances, illnesses, and attitudes. But when we put on glasses of grace and faith, we see that He never left us.

It's often hard to see what God has in store for us when we're pulled in so many directions. Rainbows are great reminders of God's promises. He is always with us, is always available, and is always waiting for us to ask for His help. Ask Him for new eyes to see—eyes to see His rainbows.

Lord, give me eyes of grace and faith to see You today. Amen.

I am...

Lisa evola   August 22

Who I am.
I am a beautiful child,
yet I feel a mess.
Cares reside in my heart,
cares that no one should ever carry;
yet my hope is in my creator to mold a new vessel--a new me--
to heal and carry those cares when I am too weak,
to reveal to me the true beauty that I am;
the beauty that resides within me;
beauty that is unmistakable and unshakeable;
beauty that is the very foundation of who I am--
a beautiful creation of the Master.
So I shall take those cares and place them carefully
into a package to lay at His feet.
A package much like me,
tattered and torn, yet strong and weak.
And I will place them at the feet of my Jesus

so that healing can take place in this beautiful yet broken heart.
Yes, I am a beautiful child--
a beautiful child of the Master Artist
who is, I Am

For you created my inmost being; you knit me together in my mother's womb.
I praise you because I am fearfully and wonderfully made; your works are wonderful, I know that full well.
Psalm 139: 13-14 NIV

MEASURING SUCCESS

Gerald Bauer   August 23
Indeed I count everything as loss because of the surpassing worth of knowing Christ Jesus my Lord. For His sake I have suffered the loss of all things, and count them as refuse, in order that I may gain Christ. Philippians 3:8 RSV

I can count success in my life in many ways. I can point to possessions I have accumulated, college degrees earned and many other achievements. I can be proud of myself. But one problem remains. The satisfaction I get from each accomplishment never lasts. So I add another goal, but I already know this will satisfy me only for a short time. I find myself asking if there can be more to life.

I read St. Paul's letter to the Philippians. He too could boast of success. His many accomplishments could not be beat. He could say he was better than anyone. But Paul came to realize that the only true measure of success is to know Jesus Christ as Lord and Savior. By comparison, he counted all his achievements as loss.

When we find ourselves looking for the one more thing that will finally satisfy us, we need only look to Jesus. In Him we can find success that lasts for eternity and that nothing can take away from us.

THE GIFT OF CHOICE

Tabitha Abel   August 24
...choose for yourselves this day whom you will serve,... But as for me and my house, we will serve the Lᴏʀᴅ." Joshua 24: 15 NKJV

I was a "wannabee". I dreamed of being a successful writer

but could not consistently find the time to write until I stopped asking God for extra time and got up at 5 am three days a week to study my Bible and write for the Lord. Then He blessed me. Just as physicians don't become neurosurgeons overnight and violinists don't immediately become first violin in a major symphony orchestra, success comes from wise choices followed by action.

Joshua had it right. He was committed and followed through in the power of God.

What choices are before you today? Is it spending more time with children and wise parenting in partnership with God in order to leave a rich, eternal legacy? Is it eating smart and exercising when the alternatives are so appealing and yet leave us tired and overweight?

God created us to make intelligent choices that have eternal consequences. When we choose to study His word and listen for His voice, we can expect His best for us.

Choice is God's gift to us. Making wise choices is our gift to Him.

OUR FATHER KNOWS BEST

Janet R. Sady   August 25
Read Romans 8:26-28

My employer struggled with finances, and as the accounts payable supervisor for eleven years, I was in the middle of the conflict. I finally decided the job was just too stressful and I began to check the job ads in our newspaper. A position was advertised for an office manager at a Christian school. I prayed and applied.

When I went for my initial interview, twenty-five other persons thought this was the job they wanted too, but I was called back for a second interview along with five others. Then it came down to just two of us, but the other person was chosen.

"Why did this happen, God? You know I'm miserable here."

A month later, it became clear to me why I wasn't chosen. Our doctor diagnosed my husband with two types of aggressive cancer. I missed many days of work during his surgeries and treatments. Despite financial problems, my employers were loyal to me and continued to pay me my regular wages. The company went bankrupt, and I was the employee who stayed behind to finish up the work.

Before we even ask, God already knows our needs and prepares the way. My Father knew what was best.

Thank You, Lord, for Your omnipotent care. I love You and bless Your holy name. Amen

A PRAYER: ONE DAY AT A TIME

Pat Collins   August 26

That is why I tell you not to worry about everyday life—whether you have enough food and drink, or enough clothes to wear. Isn't life more than food, and your body more than clothing?
Look at the birds. They don't plant or harvest or store food in barns, for your heavenly Father feeds them. And aren't you far more valuable to him than they are?
Can all your worries add a single moment to your life?
Matthew 6: 25-27 NLT

Lord, keep me from rushing around so.
Help me to slow down
So I may not miss the many blessings You send my way.
Help me not to worry about tomorrow, but to enjoy today,
To take one day at a time.

There is so much beauty to be seen in each day.
I don't want to miss it by worrying about tomorrow.
You will take care of tomorrow.
You always do.
Today, let me enjoy the sunshine, the birds singing,
the small flower that may not be there tomorrow.

There are so many things to be seen and shared.
Help me not to miss today by rushing about,
but to really look at what it holds
and to be ever thankful for what You give me.
One day at a time. Amen.

DOUBTS AND ALL

Nola Passmore   August 27

When John the Baptist was in prison, he sent his disciples to ask Jesus, "*Are you the one who is to come, or should we expect someone else?"* (Mt. 11:3, NIV). This is the same John whose preaching paved the way for Christ's message (Luke 3:15-18). This is the prophet who baptised Jesus and declared Him to be the Son of God (Mt. 3:13-17; Jn. 1:34). Now in a prison cell, John had doubts. Are You really who You say You are?

My husband and I recently said goodbye to a dream we had been praying about for 12 years, a dream we felt God had placed in our hearts. Did we wonder if we'd really heard from God? Yes. Did we wonder about His goodness? Definitely. But through it all, God walked beside us, comforting us and preparing us for something new.

Jesus answered John's disciples by pointing to His miracles and declaring, *"Blessed is the man who does not stumble on account of me"* (Mt. 11:6, NIV). John may have been in prison, but God was still God and He could help John hold on in the darkest of places.

Do you need a special measure of faith to hold onto God today? Reach out to Him and He'll meet you right where you are, doubts and all.

A MAN WITH A MESSAGE

Deborah Riall   August 28
To exiles...who have been chosen according to the foreknowledge of God the Father, through the sanctifying work of the Spirit, to be obedient to Jesus Christ and sprinkled with his blood: Grace and peace be yours in abundance. 1 Peter 1:2 NIV

Early Christians were often persecuted for their faith. When Nero blamed the fire of Rome on Christians, they were forced to flee the city; others were exiled by their families, simply for believing in Christ. They were spread across what is now modern-day Turkey and suffered loneliness, homesickness and persecution.

If anyone knew about trials, it was Peter. He accepted the responsibility of leadership of the early church. He suffered loneliness, imprisonment and execution for the privilege of preaching the gospel. Early church tradition says that he was crucified; legend says that he was crucified upside down by his own choice.

During those days, many Christians were persecuted and

exiled for their faith. Instead of preaching to them, Peter gave them words of encouragement based upon his own experience with the love and forgiveness of Christ. He gave them hope.

Father, there are times when life looks bleak and I find myself wanting to just give up. Thank You for sending messengers like Peter to point us back to the source of Hope in this world. Amen.

THE VOICE OF THE SHEPHERD

Nola Passmore   August 29

Muffy, our beautiful Pomeranian, used to stay in our backyard when we were at work. When I came home and flicked the latch on the gate to our carport, she would bark as if I were an intruder. As soon I said, "It's okay, Muffy, it's me," she'd be quiet. She couldn't see me yet because she was in the yard beyond the carport, but she knew my voice. She knew she was safe.

In John 10:2-5 (NIV), we're told that *"the one who enters by the gate is the shepherd of the sheep ... He calls his own sheep by name and leads them out ... and his sheep follow him because they know his voice. But they will never follow a stranger; in fact, they will run away from him because they do not recognize a stranger's voice."*

Jesus, our Shepherd calls each of us by name. We should know His voice, but do we always listen? Are we always open to His leading? Do we start following Him, but veer off track when a stranger's words sound more appealing? Following the Shepherd is not always an easy road, but Jesus knows the route we should take for an abundant life now and in eternity.

Will we follow Him today when He calls?

RESURRECTION DANCE

Annette M. Eckart   August 30
But when they looked up they saw that the stone, which was very large, had been rolled away. Mark 16:4 NIV

Ruth and I met at the soup kitchen where we volunteered. Normally, she greeted me with a smile and a hug. One day, I rushed into the church hall and Ruth turned her back. I was confused, I knew she saw me. When I approached her, she bit out a chilly greeting and spun away. Later, I heard that someone had told Ruth where I attended church and she did not like my denomination. Her continual rejection hurt deeply. I prayed about quitting the ministry, but they needed help. I decided to stay.

Ruth continued to ignore me. I worked to keep my heart soft, but I began to resent her. My thoughts became ugly. *And she calls herself a Christian? She's a hypocrite.*

One morning, the founder led a service for volunteers and praise music moved us into the aisle. I looked up and saw Ruth opposite me! She didn't look like my enemy; she looked like my sister in Christ. We took hold of each other and sashayed down the aisle laughing and crying with joy.

The Holy Spirit rolled the heavy stone away from our hearts. Light shone on our darkness. Love triumphant resurrected our friendship.

LUCK OR PROVIDENCE?

Joseph Hopkins   August 31
"And whatever things you ask in prayer, believing, you will receive." Matthew 21:22, NKJV

Returning from a Christian retreat, my sister reported a remarkable answer to prayer. She wrote, "A woman was sick one night and a nine-year-old boy lost his $300 hearing aid. The group of 285 people prayed for these two people at breakfast. The woman recovered that day and played tennis in the afternoon, then walked to the lake across the college campus. Enroute she dropped a nickel, picked it up, and right away dropped it again. This time, when she reached down to pick it up, she found the boy's hearing aid in the grass beside the nickel."

What do you think? Was it luck or providence? The longer I live, the stronger my faith in the providence of our almighty and loving heavenly Father, under whose direction *"All things work together for good to those who love God, to those who are the called according to His purpose."* (Romans 8:28, NKJV)

September

Labor Day is celebrated in the US on the first Monday in September.

BRIGHTNESS AFTER RAIN

Linda Bonney Olin   September 1

*'When one rules over people in righteousness, when he rules
in the fear of God he is like the light of morning at sunrise
on a cloudless morning, like the brightness after rain that brings
grass from the earth.'* 2 Samuel 23: 3b-4 NIV

I knew how to produce excellent work and lots of it. But how to make other people meet expectations for quality and productivity was a new challenge I faced as a newly promoted manager. Pep talks failed to impress my new team. I had no authority to reward the best performers with pay raises, promotions, or extra time off. Motivational gimmicks fell flat.

I saw senior managers who wielded fear and shame to wring more work out of their subordinates. Was that what it took to be a successful manager?

The Holy Spirit's counsel to King David in 2 Samuel taught me otherwise. A righteous ruler motivates with inspiration, not intimidation, and wields authority with respect and compassion as well as strength. A godly leader, whether in workplace, school, or home, stimulates growth the way sunshine brings forth green sprouts of grass after a rain.

Sure enough, when I followed God's management model my subordinates and their output flourished

Lord, as You deal justly but gently with me. help me always to deal righteously with those You've placed under my earthly authority, Amen.

A DIVINE CHOICE

Sherry Taylor Cummins   September 2

Therefore, whatever you want men to do to you, do also to them, for this is the Law and the Prophets. Matthew 7:12 NKJV

Natalie sent her son, Juan, to first grade, grateful for each day that went well. Soon though, his classmate Adam began harassing Juan. Natalie decided to share her concerns with Adam's mother, Courtney. As the conversation unfolded, Courtney cried, apologizing and admitting that she was working with Adam's behavior. Adam's behavior improved in the following weeks, and he and Juan became best friends as did Natalie and Courtney.

In June, Courtney's husband Sameer developed lung cancer. Natalie babysat, provided rides and scheduled meals brought in so Courtney could visit Sameer. In August, Courtney also developed lung cancer. Sameer died on a Friday, his wife Courtney died in the wee hours the following Tuesday. At the funeral, Juan and a handful of loving eight year old boys, attended Courtney's funeral.

A divine choice made months before by one mother to treat another mother as she would like to be treated made a difference. At the worst time in his young life, when he needed it most, Adam had a safety net of friends by his side.

THINK ON THESE THINGS

Douglas Raymond Rose   September 3
...whatsoever things are true, whatsoever things are honest, whatsoever things are just, whatsoever things are pure, whatsoever things are lovely, whatsoever things are of good report; if there be any virtue, and if there be any praise, think on these things.
Philippians. 4:8 KJV

I was blessed to attend a Christian college. What I remember most after 50 years, is the devotional song, using the words of Philippians 4:8, that my biology professor led at the start of each lecture session. Dr. Williams knew that one of our greatest challenges as teenagers entering young adulthood would be to keep our thought lives positive and pure.

Recently I was reminded of these thought-provoking facts:
   The word hate has 4 letters—so does the word love.
   The word enemies has 7 letters---so does friends.
   The word lying has 5 letters---so does truth.
   The word hurt has 4 letters, so does heal.

Just as the apostle Paul said in today's scripture, when we turn our minds to positive thoughts, it transforms the way we feel and act.

Thank You, God, for the positive-ness of Your Word. Amen.

PUZZLES

Rose Marie Goble   September 4

   Most kindergarteners can count to ten, so why with just nine numbers, are Sudoku puzzles so difficult for some of us? There must be a secret I don't know about Sudoku.

   Our Bibles are written in languages we read and understand, but it is sometimes hard to know God's will and direction. Is there a secret in understanding God's Word? We can read commentaries and listen to preachers, but Jesus gave us a helpful Person in John 14:16 (KJV): *"And I will pray the Father, and he shall give you another Comforter, that he may abide with you for ever; even the Spirit of truth."* Further, verse 26 reveals the secret, "*But the Helper, the Holy Spirit, whom the Father will send in My name, He will teach you all things, and bring to your remembrance all things that I said to you"* (NKJV).

   Maybe He will show me how to do those puzzles, but I'm more concerned with daily guidance and the meanings in the Bible. I'm thankful that He has provided a dependable teacher and trustworthy guide.

WHEN YOU'RE SMILING

Becky Toews   September 5
   A happy heart makes the face cheerful.... Proverbs 15:13 NIV

   People. All kinds of people: lonely people; displaced people; beautiful people. But there's one group that I think we should hear more of: friendly people. We too easily overlook the impact of friendliness. A man waves you to go in front of him in a line of traffic. You pass strangers on a sidewalk and they smile. Small incidents that won't alter the course of our existence, but they make life more pleasant and cost us NOTHING.

   Friendly people aren't necessarily church people. There is no 11th Commandment that says "Thou shalt be friendly," but verses that exhort us to be kind and compassionate flood the Scriptures. And the greatest commandment of all is to love. I think of friendliness as a second cousin to love.

   True friendliness distracts us from the stress of life, even if momentarily. It makes a brief connection. For some folks, a brief connection may be all they experience in a day.

Typically we think in terms of doing something "big" as making a difference in life. Why not develop a culture of kindness by practicing friendliness on the smallest level? Begin with a smile. Maybe when you're smiling, the whole world really will smile with you.

MISSION STATEMENT

Pollyanna Sedziol   September 6

A few years ago our church asked each ministry to create a mission statement and a policy procedure manual for their departments. As the group considered possibilities, we developed a statement based on scripture.

Give thanks unto the Lord, for He is good, His mercy endureth forever (Psalm 107:1)
to all who call upon him in truth (Psalm 145:18)
who are the called according to His purpose (Romans 8:28b)
to believe on Him whom He hath sent (John 6:29)
That at the name of Jesus every knee should bow, of things in heaven, and things in earth, and things under the earth; And that every tongue should confess that Jesus Christ is Lord, to the glory of God the Father. (Philippians 2:10,11)

Not only did we complete the mission statement for our ministry, but I have used it as a guiding theme for my life.

Heavenly Father, Lord Jesus Christ our Savior, Holy Spirit our Guide and Companion – thank You for the words from Scripture which bless my daily life. Amen.
(All scriptures from KJV)

A WILLING LEARNER

Barbara Gordon   September 7
Do not merely listen to the word, and so deceive yourselves. Do what it says. James 1: 22 NIV

"What would you do if your mom was very sick and needed to go to the hospital?" I asked Andrea, my middle school student with special needs.

"Call 911!" was her quick reply.

"Show me," I responded, handing her the phone we used for practice.

Confused, she put the cell phone to her ear and said, "Hello?" The puzzled look on her face stated the obvious—Andrea could say the right words, but putting them into action was another story.

I am ashamed to admit it, but that scenario often illustrates my life. I talk of possessing the Fruit of the Spirit, yet live like those fruit have rotted. I confess Jesus as my provider and sustainer, but act as if I am carrying the weight of the world. Both Andrea and I could use a lesson in application.

It took hours of practice, but Andrea learned to dial 911 and clearly request help. I am practicing, too. With the Lord's guidance I am learning the difference between merely saying the right thing and living by Jesus' example. He is teaching me to be a doer of the Word as I humbly call on Him for assistance.

Heavenly Father, You are the greatest teacher of all. I want to be a willing learner. Please help me. Amen.

SEPTEMBER SUN

Lanita Bradley Boyd   September 8
Satisfy us in the morning with your unfailing love, that we may sing for joy and be glad all our days. Psalm 90:14 NIV

Warmth without burning, light without glare--
September sun.
All the heartaches and joys of the passing months
nestle in the glow of the
September sun.
September is where I linger.
The winter lies ahead, but for now I enjoy
God's peace with faith and love and laughter.

I have friends who have reached December;
It's comforting to see that the white on their heads,
like winter's snow,
obscures landscape scars.
All my years' experiences coalesce
To sustain my peace
in the September sun.

Father, "teach us to number our days, that we may gain a heart of wisdom." (Psalm 90:12 NIV) Amen.

SWORD FIGHT

Crystal Hayduk   September 9
All Scripture is inspired by God and profitable for teaching, for reproof, for correction, for training in righteousness; so that the man of God may be adequate, equipped for every good work.
2 Timothy 3:16-17 NASB

He threw out the verbal challenge. She raised her weapon and the sparring began. Thrusting and parrying in mortal combat. After several minutes of imaginary play, the Sunday school teacher noticed the two pre-school students in her large class were fighting, using their Bibles as swords. "Stop that right now," the teacher commanded. "Your Bibles are not weapons."

Obeying their teacher, the children slowly lowered their Bibles and reluctantly sat down, quieting their voices as they did so.

Witnessing this exchange, I understood the teacher's intent to stop the children's inappropriate behavior in the classroom. But although their Bibles should not be misused as pretend swords, the Word of God truly is a priceless and indispensable weapon.

In Ephesians 6, Paul implores us to put on the whole armor of God so that we will be equipped to stand firm against the ploys of the devil. We are to take up *"...the sword of the Spirit, which is the word of God."* (v. 17) Let us honor God's Word by reading it and being prepared to use it as a sword in spiritual battle!

TWO SPECIAL CHILDREN

Lanita Bradley Boyd   September 10
"A little child shall lead them...." Isaiah 11:6 NIV

At lunchtime, Emma chose to sit with Michelle. Afterward they went outside for recess with the other kindergarteners where they began to play jump rope.

Michelle joined the line to wait her turn.

"You can't jump rope with us!" one girl said. "You're weird. Just go play somewhere else." The others agreed.

Emma stepped toward the bully. "We have to let Michelle play with us!" she said. "She's special and we have to treat her special."

With that, the others hesitatingly agreed to let Michelle jump rope with them.

The next day Michelle's mother tearfully called Emma's mother. "Michelle told me what happened on the playground yesterday. She's never had a friend before Emma, and I want to thank you. Being a Down Syndrome child in a public school is quite a challenge. Emma has made such a difference for Michelle. Michelle loves Emma!"

Emma's mother responded, "Emma mentioned sitting with Michelle at lunch, but she didn't say that she was different. You've really made my day!"

Lord, we try to teach our children and set good examples, but so many times we don't know if they are incorporating them in their lives. Help me live in such a way that others can see Jesus in me—and in my children. Amen.

LIVING BY FAITH

Jana Carman   September 11
**Faith is the assurance of things hoped for,
the conviction of things not seen.** Hebrews 11:1 NIV

To live without faith is impossible. We trust that the oncoming car will stay on its side of the road; that the bridge ahead will not collapse under our car's weight; that the light will come on when we flip the switch. Faith in things we can't know for sure spreads an emotional safety net beneath us. Without it we would all be fearful gibbering idiots.

Too often people think faith is something only the super-spiritual have, and say, "But I don't have faith like that." Oh? You don't expect the sun to rise tomorrow morning? Experience leads you to expect certain things to happen, and one definition of faith is confident expectation. You can have that without feeling you are a spiritual failure, can't you?

Faith is trust in something or someone. If a person is trustworthy, your faith is well grounded. So just find that most trustworthy Person, Jesus, and lean on His promises. If you still feel a bit shaky, just *ask* for a deeper faith, one of the spiritual fruits that God grows in those He loves. If you are His, that's part and parcel of being His child.

Faithful is He who calls you, and He also will bring it to pass.
1 Thessalonians 5:24 NASB

IN HIS TIME

Frances Gregory Pasch   September 12
And I am certain that God, who began the good work within you,
will continue his work until it is finally finished on the day when
Christ Jesus returns. Philippians 1:6 NLT

I know I'm where God wants me,
That's why I do believe
The plans He has in mind for me
I truly will achieve.

Because He is in charge of
All the things I have to do,
I know I have His promise
That He will see me through.

So when I face a mountain
That seems too high to climb,
With Jesus close beside me
I will scale it in His time.

AN OVERFLOWING BUCKET

Sheri Neuhofer   September 13
Jesus said, "Everyone who drinks this water will get thirsty again
and again. Anyone who drinks the water I give will never thirst—not
ever. The water I give will be an artesian spring within, gushing
fountains of endless life." John 4:13-14, The Message

I admit I have a sweet tooth and crave chocolate. For others,
their craving might be a bag of salty chips. Yet we often don't feel
satisfied after eating, and still want more. Perhaps you have gone
through life craving something *much* more, and in your quest to fill
the void you have fallen into alcohol, drug addiction, or unhealthy
relationships, trying to fill your deepest longing.

As humans, one of our basic needs is to be loved. In John
4:1-26, a Samaritan woman comes upon Jesus sitting next to a
well. She has come to fill her bucket with water, but Jesus offers
something *more*. In just minutes with Jesus, she became the

bucket that He filled with living water: unconditional love and eternal satisfaction.

Just like this woman, you and I are buckets that Jesus wants to fill to overflowing from His eternal wellspring of life. He can satisfy our innermost craving if we allow Him the opportunity. Will you choose to let Him fill you?

SUPERNATURAL VISION

Janelle Moore   September 14
...fixing our eyes on Jesus.... Hebrews 12:2 NIV

What a week! Dad was in hospital, Mum was ill with a potentially serious re-occurring health problem and a close friend's Mum passed away. While I was shopping with my daughter, Bronte, Mum rang to let me know that Dad had just had a stroke.

Forgetting the shopping, we donned our sunglasses and headed home. It was an overcast day, and this matched the mood I was taking on. Suddenly, Bronte exclaimed, "Mummy, look at the rainbow!" And there, amongst the dull grey clouds was a small opening with a beautiful rainbow shining through. When Bronte removed her sunglasses and could no longer see the small but beautiful display, we realised it was not visible to the naked eye.

We immediately felt encouraged--this was God's way of giving us hope in what seemed to be a very difficult week. We rejoiced in God's goodness and were reminded that if we look at life through our natural eye, it is very easy to become discouraged and disappointed; but if we look at life through eyes of faith, how different the view is!

Father, help us to have Your perspective, regardless of what is happening in our lives. Amen

FEAR OR TRUST?

Crystal Hayduk   September 15
When I am afraid, I will put my trust in You. Psalm 56:3 NASB

"You'll need surgery to correct this," the doctor said. I refused to consider it. After all, why would I submit myself to go under the knife if I could function?

A year later, I sought the opinion of another doctor. "Your

condition has deteriorated," he said. I recognized that he was telling the truth, yet I hesitated. What's wrong with waiting when I can still compensate for the problem?

I knew that surgery would be inevitable at some point. My stress level increased just thinking about it. One day during my prayer time, it became clear to me that my reluctance was based solely in fear. I was afraid of the surgery, the risks, and the recovery time. Yet, as a Christian, I claim that I trust God. If I really believe that He is in control of everything and that whatever happens serves a purpose, then how could I be so afraid of a surgery that I clearly need?

I can base my decisions in fear or in trust, but not in both. I phoned the doctor's office. Taking a deep breath, I said, "I'm ready to schedule my surgery."

Lord, increase my trust in You. Take away my fear. Amen.

YES LORD!!!

Janelle Moore   September 16

"For I know the plans I have for you", declares the Lord, "plans to prosper you and not to harm you, plans to give you a hope and a future." Jeremiah 29:11 NIV

My twelve year old daughter was recently appointed School and Missions Captain. Oh, the excitement! She was overjoyed to be able to serve her school and her Lord in this capacity! I was recently appointed Board Secretary at our school. Oh, the hesitancy! I was very reluctant to serve our school and our Lord in this capacity!

But long ago, I determined to say "Yes" to the Lord, regardless of what He asked of me. As I battled to surrender my will, I saw opportunity for growth and expansion in my life and began to feel excited and expectant. Having now been Board Secretary for seven months, I actually enjoy it! I have had to rely on the Lord to help me and give me wisdom, learned new computer skills, learned to operate a Smartpen, and accepted responsibility in new areas. The growth has been good for me. God does indeed have our best interests at heart!

Lord, we say "Yes", a resounding "Yes" to Your plan for our lives.

May we be obedient and willing to follow
wherever You lead. Amen.

DO CLOTHES MAKE THE MAN?

Jana Carman   September 17
...clothe yourself with compassion. Colossians 3:12 NIV
...clothe yourself with humility. 1 Peter 5:5 NIV

In our area, students in many public schools are now required to wear school uniforms. Before this, some students faced ridicule when they couldn't afford the latest clothing styles. Unfortunately, the idea that fancy, expensive clothing is important is nothing new. In Bible times—as in many third world countries today—clothing represents riches.

We remember that the battle of Jericho (Joshua 6, 7, 8) was followed by the defeat at Ai because Achan took "a beautiful robe from Babylon" along with other "devoted things" God had designated as off-limits. Later (2 Kings 5:22-24), Gehazi, Elisha's servant, followed Naaman, now healed of leprosy, to ask for two sets of clothing and a talent of silver—and lied, saying his master wanted them.

What a hold fine clothing has on some of us!

My problem with clothing is hoarding those outgrown items, thinking that someday I will lose enough weight to get back into them. While they are still wearable, Good Will or Salvation Army could use them. Far better clothing to focus on is our character-- being *clothed with compassion ... humility,* or in the words of Proverbs 31:25, being *clothed with strength and dignity.*

Lord, help me make the best things the most important. Amen.

GOD'S CANVAS

Frances Gregory Pasch   September 18
LORD, our Lord, how majestic is your name in all the earth!
Psalm 8:9 NIV

Each Fall God takes His paintbrush
and paints an autumn scene...
A dab of red, a touch of gold
And luscious shades of green.

Each day he adds another hue
For all the world to see.
Behold his awesome canvas!
Observe His majesty!

SCARY FACES

Judith B. Henry   September 19

God spoke to Jeremiah, a young prophet, assuring him that He had selected him to deliver an extremely unpopular message to the nation of Judah. God said, *"Before you were formed I knew you"*... *"I sanctified you"* ... *"I ordained you."* (Jeremiah 1:5 NKJV) When Jeremiah protested that he couldn't speak because he was too young, God said, *"Don't be afraid of their faces."* (Jeremiah 1:8 NKJV)

What "faces" do you fear? When we are faced with delivering an unpopular message such as setting a boundary, confronting a co-worker, facing an unhappy family member, sharing your testimony, or speaking in public, isn't it "their faces" that make the encounter frightening?

Just as God prepared and encouraged Jeremiah, the apostle Paul gave good advice to his protégé, Timothy: *"For God has not given us a spirit of fear, but of power and of love and of a sound mind."* (2 Timothy 1:7 NKJV). In Ephesians 4:15, Paul encourages us to *"speak the truth in love."*

When the words we speak are truth, based on God's direction we can be confident, not fearful. God told Jeremiah, *"Behold, I have put My words in your mouth"* (Jeremiah 1:9b), then summarized the message Jeremiah was to deliver. God will give us the right words, as well!

NEW PLACES—NEW KIDS

Marilyn Nutter   September 20
So whatever you wish that others would do to you, do also to them, for this is the Law and the Prophets. Matthew 7:12 ESV

"My daughter is doing great with the move," commented my new neighbor who recently moved here from Ohio. "She's made a new friend and they've spent time together, but my son Jake is lonely. He hasn't met anyone. It's hard to make friends in the summer if there aren't kids on the street who are the same age. I'm sure he'll make friends once school starts, but that won't happen for another six weeks."

Summer is hard and if kids don't reach out to the "new kid," the school year can be hard too. It's easy for children, and even adults to stay in their comfort zone of familiarity and their circle of friends.

Try to put yourself in a "new kid's" place. Is there someone you know who has moved to your neighborhood or school? Encourage your child to reach out and introduce himself. As a parent, be a face that becomes familiar to new parents. Offer to help them find their way around and learn the ropes of a school or community. It doesn't have to be hard. Are you the one who can make it easier?

A PRAYER FOR GOD'S WORK

Gerald W. Bauer   September 21
Let the favor of the Lord our God be upon us, and establish the work
of our hands upon us; yes, establish the work of our hands!
Psalm 90:17 ESV

Let the work we do be fruitful, Lord.
Let the work we do honor You, Lord.
You give us gifts, abilities to use;
to serve Your world, care for all You have made;
all people, all creatures, all plant life and waters.
Honorable work honors You, Lord.
The works of our hands rise up in praise.
For the future of Your world You establish our work.
Help us to see that using the abilities You give us
serves You in many ways. In Jesus' name, amen.

ME? DISAGREE WITH GOD? Part 1

Evelyn Minshull   September 22
God is exalted in his power. Who is a teacher like him? Who has
prescribed his ways for him, or said to him, 'You have done wrong'?"
Job 36:22-23 NIV

Disagree with God? What arrogance! and yet…
and yet when Achan ignored God's NO-PLUNDERING-
IN-JERICHO edict, Achan's family and all that he had—even
animals—were stoned, burned and buried. (Joshua7:24-26.)

Why were innocent children condemned for their father's transgressions?

unless… God presumed that the seeds of disobedience had already been planted.

Certainly God knew—and knows—what is essential in maintaining order in His Kingdom. and yet…

and yet when the oxen stumbled as the Ark of the Covenant was being moved, and Uzzah reached to steady the precious cargo, he was struck dead. (2 Samuel 6:6-7)

Why?

unless… God was communicating that we often take the Holy lightly—withholding the abject awe Holiness deserves.

then again…

women today applaud Queen Vashti for refusing to debase herself before the king's drunken, lascivious guests. (Esther: 10-12) We wonder: why her demotion?

unless perhaps her refusal was more willful than virtuous… and perhaps because a new queen, Esther, must be in place to save God's people from proposed extinction.

Lord, when Your decision runs so counter to expected justice, help us to understand and accept. AMEN.

DISAGREE WITH GOD? Part 2

Evelyn Minshull   September 23

For my thoughts are not your thoughts, neither are your ways my ways, declares the LORD. For as the heavens are higher than the earth, so are my ways higher than your ways and my thoughts than your thoughts. Isaiah 55:8-9 NIV

…and yet it really didn't seem fair—did it?—that the vineyard workers not receive equal pay for equal hours? (Matthew 20:1-16)

And the stay-at-home-and-work son had every right to be miffed at his prodigal brother's homecoming extravaganza. Didn't he? (Luke 15:11-32)

…unless…God is underscoring the point that we won't necessarily be admitted to Heaven on a seniority basis; that God's mercy extends to the final breath—which sounds like a great deal for latecomers!

…and yet…(Luke 10:38-42) Mary won the Good Conduct Award,

while Martha received demerits for slaving over meal preparations and serving. If she, like Mary, had opted to scuttle kitchen duty and simply sit at Jesus' feet, who would have quelled hunger pangs and preserved blood sugar levels?

…until… we remember that man does not live by bread alone. (Matthew 4:4)

Lord, we thank You that Your thoughts are not our thoughts—for our perceptions are so often skewed by the here, the now, and the "what about me?" AMEN.

NOT BY SIGHT

Nancy E. James   September 24
For we live by faith, not by sight. 2 Corinthians 5:7 NIV

A "Trust Walk" in our church:
We pair up; one leads the other.

I close my eyes, feel my guide's hand
under my elbow. I stumble . . . wonder,
Could I move more freely alone?

I relax, plant feet more surely . . .
trust my guide's eyes, voice,
touch. We veer, walk a new direction.
"Reach!" she says. "What do you find?"
The piano, so soon? I plunk a few keys.

She steers left, then left again . . . back
to the vestibule, sooner than I expected.
I open my eyes, gaze down the aisle,
see stained glass window, gleaming cross.

How short that distance seemed
walked in trust.

FLIGHT

Beth Hadley   September 25
But they that wait upon the Lord shall renew their strength;
they shall mount up with wings as eagles. Isaiah 40:31 KJV

Calm as the waters Christ walked on
Blue heron balances on one stick leg.
I creep close.
Will the wild thing take flight?
Unblinking courage looks me in the eye.
Wings unfold like oars.
Majestic, awkward, too-big bird rises above impossibility,
Rows skyward, carrying calm on unruffled wings
To another shore.
Ruffled as the storm He calmed,
I spin plates: laundry, poetry, children
I tread water.
Will I go under?
Eyes fixed on the Morning Star I wait, a wide-eyed Peter.
Strength arises like daybreak.
Faithful, timid, willful woman looks beyond difficulty
Stepping lightly over waves, my fledgling's feathers sprout.
I soar.

HELP ME, LORD

Frances Gregory Pasch   September 26
Not that we are competent in ourselves to claim anything
for ourselves, but our competence comes from God.
2 Corinthians 3:5 NIV

Lord, help me not to be intimidated
by the accomplishments of others.
I am tempted to say
"I'll never be that good."

Instead, help me to concentrate
on my abilities.
Let me use them
the best way I can.

Instead of envying others
let me pray for them.
Let me be happy that You
are using them for Your glory, too.

Help me to be satisfied
with small beginnings,
trusting you to open
bigger doors
in your perfect timing.

FINDING GOD'S WILL

Jana Carman   September 27

Have you ever said—or heard someone else say—that they don't know how to tell if something is God's will? Generally, it's no big secret. He wants all men to be saved and to come to the knowledge of the truth (1 Timothy 2:4). In addition, His will is that you live pure and holy lives (1 Thessalonians 4:3-7); be joyful, prayerful, and thankful (1 Thessalonians 5:16-18); and be the kind of person you would love to live next-door to (check out the prayer below).

So when it comes to specific things, these steps will help clear up the confusion:

1. Does it agree with what God's word says? If God's word forbids it, you know it's not in line with His will.

2. Consult a trusted Christian friend for advice.

3. Bathe the decision process in earnest, ongoing prayer. And ask others to pray about it.

4. Consider circumstances but don't let them weigh too heavily in your decision.

5. Wait for God's peace in the decision.

Father God, You said that it's Your will that I respect Christian leaders, live in peace, warn idlers, encourage the timid, help the weak, be patient with everyone, refuse to repay wrong with wrong, and be kind.(1 Thessalonians 5:12-15)
In other words, help me to be like Jesus. Amen.

A PEACEFUL MORNING WALK

Donna Howard   September 28
Read Matthew 4: 1-11, Ephesians 6: 10-18

Be sober, be vigilant; because your adversary the devil walks about like a roaring lion, seeking whom he may devour. 1 Peter 5:8 NKJV.

One day, my husband and I and our little dog Max went for our usual early morning walk. We take the same quiet route every morning, so we know it well. However, a few minutes into our walk, our peace was quickly disturbed. As we walked past our neighbor's house, their large dog was outside on her leash. This was not unusual, but what happened next was very unusual. The neighbor's dog lunged toward us, broke her chain, and attacked our little Max. It happened so fast we did not see it coming.

Max tried to fight off the big dog but she was much bigger and stronger than Max. He needed help. My husband grabbed her collar and pulled her off Max.

Sometimes Evil attacks and tempts us so quickly that we do not see it coming. We try to fight the temptations, but we need help. Jesus was tempted by Satan, too, and He gave us a good example to follow. He fought Satan off with Scripture, and so can we.

AN ALWAYS THANKFUL HEART

Linda Reppert   September 29
Rejoice always, pray without ceasing, give thanks in all circumstances; for this is the will of God in Christ Jesus for you."
1 Thessalonians 5:16-18 ESV

Medically, I have a heart failure diagnosis. I have been given heart medication to stabilize my deteriorating heart. My body tolerates only a small dosage of this medicine. After almost two years, my heart defied logic and showed huge signs of improvement. Surprisingly, my heart improved from operating at about 50% capacity to 80% capacity. Medical personnel kept asking if my medicines had changed. No, they had not. God brought healing into circumstances in which He alone could be given credit. I am rejoicing and thankful!

However, through this experience, my main prayer has

become that I can learn and grow in the Lord as much on the way up (healing) as I have done on the way down (sickness). God has taught me so much about structuring wise use of my time and total dependence on Him through my failing heart, I would not trade those lessons for a perfect heart. I am as thankful for the sickness as I am for the healing.

Is there a circumstance that you need to be thankful for? God is always teaching us. Let's listen, rejoice and be thankful, on the way down as much as on the way up.

SPIRITUAL CHECKUPS

Nola Passmore   September 30
Read 2 Corinthians 13:5-10

In my 20-plus years as a university academic, I have set many examinations. A good test doesn't just require students to regurgitate information, but asks them to apply what they have studied. For example, they might use their knowledge to suggest a solution to a social problem or show how a particular theory applies to a case study. These tasks help me to determine if students actually understand what they are learning.

The same principle applies to our knowledge of the Christian faith. We're not just meant to have a head full of scripture. God wants us to understand it, apply it, and live it. James 1:22 (NLT) tells us, "*Don't just listen to God's word. You must do what it says. Otherwise, you are only fooling yourselves.* Paul urged the Corinthian believers to *test themselves to see if they were in the faith* (2 Cor. 10:5). I love the way that verse is translated in the Message Bible:

"Test yourselves to make sure you are solid in the faith.
Don't drift along taking everything for granted. Give yourselves
regular checkups. You need firsthand evidence, not mere hearsay,
that Jesus Christ is in you. Test it out.
If you fail the test, do something about it."

Have you taken a test lately? Why not join me in a spiritual checkup today.

October

AUTUMN CHANGES

Elizabeth M. VanHook   October 1
*There is a time for everything, and a season for every activity
under the heavens.* Ecclesiastes 3:1 NIV

The most beautiful changes of autumn are the colors of the
foliage. Dark green leaves become magnificent rich red, rust,
orange and gold. The weather changes from hot and humid days
to warm afternoons and cool evenings. We set our clocks back
one hour. Birds make their annual journey southward. Squirrels
start retrieving the nuts and acorns they had buried throughout
the summer. Carefree summer days surrender to students pouring
over homework assignments. Organizations and churches start
new programs.

God graciously moves upon our lives, taking us from summer
to autumn. As we curl up to enjoy cooler evenings, we reflect
where we were and look at a new perspective for the season
ahead. How is God speaking to you? What rich colors does He
want to paint into your life?

*Father, continue to keep us focused on You as we start this fall
season. Amen.*

MIRACLE SHOES

Miriam Sarzotti   October 2
*But my God shall supply all your need according to his riches
in glory by Christ Jesus.* Philippians 4:19 KJV

I peered out the window at another rainy October day in
Cranborne, England. *What am I going to do? I only have summer
shoes with me since I left my luggage back in London.*

"Lord, I am trusting you for my finances while I travel as
a visiting missionary. I need a pair of warm boots for this cold
weather. My pocketbook is empty. Help!"
That afternoon I stopped at a shoe store on the way to speak at
a prayer group. A pair of brown leather boots for 50 pounds was
in the window. *Those would be perfect, Lord.* At the meeting, the

leader told me, "Miriam, we can support you with prayers but not financially, as we are all on a pension."

Two days later a check for 50 pounds arrived from a woman at the group. God had miraculously met my need. He cares about the little things, even keeping our toes warm. He increases our faith as we trust him to supply all of our needs.

Heavenly Father, I trust You to provide all I need, knowing every good and perfect gift comes from You.

CREATION

Pauline Beck   October 3
Read Psalm 65
You crown the year with Your bounty . . .
Psalm 65:11 NAB

Today I hung a poem I wrote
in a conspicuous place on a wall,
and people passed by without taking note.

They didn't see it at all.
Now I know exactly how God must feel
when we hurry past the trees in the fall.

SECOND FLOWERING

Evelyn Heinz   October 4
Read Psalm 23
The Lord is my Shepherd, I shall not want...He restoreth my soul...
Psalm 23:1, 3 KJV

The mum plant in my garden was cut down to the roots, transplanted, put out in the sun, watered, and renewed into a second growth. People marvel at the beauty of the second flowering in the fall.

It has been twenty years since my husband passed away of operable lung cancer at the age of fifty-four. His favorite Bible passage was Psalm 23. I miss him, sometimes am lonely, but am never alone. God is always with me.

Like the mum, I have found it is never too late to bloom again.

Other widows may relate; life is different, but we are not alone. We find love, peace of mind and new direction in the arms of the

Good Shepherd. We can have a beautiful second flowering. He restoreth my soul.

DOLLHOUSE LESSONS

Donna J. Howard   October 5
Read Proverbs 6:16-19

When I was in first grade, our school had a special project. We painted and furnished a large dollhouse that the father of one of the students had made. One day another girl and I had stayed inside at recess to paint part of the dollhouse and I accidentally spilled some paint. I tried to clean it up, but the teacher noticed the mess. When she asked who did it, I blurted out, "I think she did," blaming my classmate.

The teacher soon discovered the truth. I had lied. She took me to the cloak room (coat room) and gently paddled me, not for spilling the paint – that was an accident – but for lying.

Later in life I learned that just as I could not fool my teacher, I cannot fool God by denying my sins. He knows everything about me.

An honest witness tells the truth, but a false witness tells lies.
Proverbs 12:17NIV

Lord, help me to always speak truthfully. In Jesus' name. Amen.

IN GOD'S GOOD TIME

Tommie Lenox   October 6
He has made everything appropriate in its time.
Ecclesiastes 3:11 a NASB

Time and space are impossible to comprehend when I think of the children I have taught since 1955. Joshua, Steven, Penny… so many children! I have had the joy of watching some of my students grow through elementary school, yet regardless of the years that have passed, in my eyes they will always be six and seven-year-olds, innocent, unspoiled.

At a recent local symphony concert, the evening sparked with excitement during the West Coast premiere performance of a new work by an Israeli composer. Imagine my amazement when I glanced at the performers' names, and read a congratulatory note to first violinist, Sarah, on the birth of her second child. My little Sarah! A mother of two, a concert violinist!

We see those who pass through our lives frozen in time. They remain where and when we knew them as mere snapshots in our memory. Yet God sees each one of us, from womb to grave. He knows us by name! In God's eyes, time and space meld into one harmonious whole as His purposes are fulfilled in our lives--in God's good time.

FAITHFULLY

Frances Gregory Pasch   October 7
After they prayed, the place where they were meeting was shaken.
And they were all filled with the Holy Spirit and spoke the word of
God boldly. Acts 4:31 NIV

Lord, help me
to never compromise
the Gospel.
Remove my desire
to please everyone
at the expense
of displeasing You.
Imprint your Word
so deeply in my heart
that I will faithfully
proclaim the Good News
with Holy Ghost boldness.

A CHILD'S BEDTIME PRAYER

Tim Bond   October 8
Jesus said, "Let the little children come to me, and do not hinder
them, for the kingdom of heaven belongs to such as these."
Matthew 19:14 NIV

As I lie down to sleep, dear Lord,
Please calm my fears and dry my tears
Forgive my sin and bless my kin.
Please guide my dreams to godly themes
And help me see what I should be

When I grow up and fill my cup
With Christian truth and Christ adored. Amen.

BE PREPARED

Katy Johnson   October 9

Read Ephesians 6: 11-18
Put on the whole armor of God; that you may be able to stand against the schemes of the devil.
Ephesians 6: 11 ESV

I watched with curiosity as a woman two campsites over from us rode her bike up and down the hills of the campground. That's not an unusual sight, except she wore all of her gear and a backpack! I later found out that she was preparing for a bicycle race and wanted to adjust to the weight so she would feel what she would face on race day.

As Christians, we are to be prepared to stand against the schemes of the devil. Ephesians lists the "gear" we need to wear. If we know God's Word, we can use His sword against Satan's lies. We wear His righteousness – we are forgiven of the sins that Satan would accuse us of. The Gospel gives us peace. Our faith shields us from the flaming darts of the evil one. We protect our mind by wearing the helmet of salvation and tighten our clothing with the belt of truth. All we need has been given to us so that we are prepared for any race day. Finally, we read: "pray":

As we face challenges each day, dear Lord Jesus, keep me in Your Word so I am prepared at all times. Amen.

BEWARE OF COUNTING

Christy Fitzwater   October 10

Read 2 Samuel 24

We count to make ourselves feel successful. I do it as I check to see how many people visited my blog site. My preacher husband does it to see how many people were at church Sunday. Many of us count the "likes", "follows" and the number of birthday wishes in "comments" in our social networking.

In 2 Samuel 24, we read that David wants to take census of

how many fighting men he had available in Israel and Judah. But Joab replied to the king, *"May the LORD your God multiply the troops a hundred times over, and may the eyes of my lord the king see it. But why does my lord the king want to do such a thing?"* (2 Samuel 24:3 NIV)

It's a good question – why do we want to do such a thing as count? Isn't it enough to know God will multiply the troops, without having to take census? If we are guilty of the prideful act of counting, what can we do to humble ourselves and trust the Lord for our success?

Father, show me where I have been seeking the approval of men, but instead, let me follow Your agenda and seek your applause. Amen.

October is Breast Cancer Awareness Month
Perhaps you have had a breast cancer diagnosis, or know someone who does. May the following three devotions from a breast cancer survivor bring encouragement.

HIS LIGHT OF DELIVERANCE

Sherry L. Cummins   October 11
..who delivered us from so great a death, and does deliver us; in whom we trust that He will still deliver us... 2 Corinthians 1:10 NKJV

I was diagnosed with breast cancer at age 35 following a baseline mammogram. I was afraid, exacerbated by the fact that the future I *felt* I knew, became unknown. In the beginning, my prayers were natural, conversational. But when the slightly gray clouds of challenge grew darker, my prayers were more focused. The light at the end of the tunnel was still visible but so far away that it lacked warmth. Then, I found myself in the "dark place" where the light no longer could be seen. I was on the edge of losing faith in myself.

During my breast cancer journey I could no longer rely on human tools, and I couldn't see or feel my God, my light. My prayers were incessantly communicated and beyond words. I struggled, not day by day, but minute by minute. During a meditative moment, I realized that I do not have to *see* the light, for He *is* the light! I knew with certainty that God was with me; He would not disappoint.

Regardless of my future or the outcome of my illness, He would shine over me with guidance, peace and warmth. When I finally surrendered my all to Him, I saw a glimmer peeking through the darkness...and I followed it to deliverance.

MIRACULOUS MEDITATION: CHANGING MY MIND

Sherry L. Cummins   October 12

Your miracle is on its way. Your focus, choices and mindset may be keeping you from seeing the manifestation of the glory of God!

When I had breast cancer I felt helpless, but learned through experience that I have choices, and you do too. You can choose fear, and people will feel for you. You can choose anger and no one will blame you. You can be depressed and people will be concerned. *Or* you can choose to think on what is noble and lovely.

I learned that when I chose to strive to overcome negative emotions and embrace my journey, I could see and experience the miracles of God. "Praise" thinking attracts blessings. Yes, there are challenges and dark days. But even in your darkest moments, if you remember that your miracle may come at any moment, you will have hope to hang on!

Your miracle may be complete healing. It may also be heightened awareness of His presence—the One who never leaves you or forsakes you (Hebrews 13:5)—to walk with you. When you choose to practice '"praise" thoughts, you will be awe struck and breathless at how God works in you!

Finally, brethren, whatever things are true, whatever things are noble, whatever things are just, whatever things are pure, whatever things are lovely, whatever things are of good report, if there is any virtue and if there is anything praiseworthy— meditate on these things. Philippians 4:8 (NKJV)

TICKLED PINK

Sherry L Cummins   October 13
You will show me the path of life; in Your presence is fullness of joy; at your right hand are pleasures forevermore. Psalm 16:11 NKJV

My grandmother lived in the tiny southern town where she

and Pa raised my mother. I was Gram's shadow, and even as a teenager enjoyed our visits together. On one of our visits, we headed to worship. As Gram and I walked hand in hand crossing the street to the old church, I stopped in surprise! "Gram! Look!" There in the road was her prosthesis, bold and brazen! Though she was a southern belle where *proper* ruled, she smiled. With a little giggle, she said, "Well, there's my boob," and picking up her missing piece, she tucked it in her bra and walked into church. She handled everything with grace, dignity and a dash of humor.

She had too many real crises in her life that God had seen her through to be upset by the little ones. God's blessings of humor will carry us over the rough spots in life. If we allow ourselves to look for the joy we will be well prepared for the pleasures that await us in eternity!

RISE AND SHINE

Deanna Baird   October 14
Read Isaiah 60:1-2 NIV
This is the day the Lord has made; let us rejoice and be glad in it.
Psalm 118:24 NIV

"Wakey! Wakey!" written in yellow above Isaiah 60 in my Bible, reminds me of the weekend my girlfriends and I attended a women's retreat.

After the Friday evening opening, we returned to our rooms and were so caught up studying and sharing that we hadn't realized just how late it was. At 4 a.m, laughing and giddy, we figured it was too late to try and get any sleep. Determined to stay awake, we opened the drapes to a dark sky and decided to go to the diner across the street.

An hour later, filled with coffee, our bodies flagging, we paused to take in the sun's rays; explosive plumes of red and orange seemed to be just what we needed. Energized, we returned to our room and began searching through our Bibles for a fitting verse. Someone called out, "This is it! Isaiah 60, the first and second verses. Together we read aloud, "Arise, shine, for your light has come! ..." Those verses became our rallying cry that weekend.

Dear Lord, may we always stand in awesome wonder at Your creation and the light that Your Word gives to life, renewing hope within us each day. Amen.

MY AUTUMN CAT

Jewell Utt   October 15
You will seek me and find me when you seek me with all your heart.
Jeremiah 29:13 NIV

My plump and furry orange cat Garfield blended into the pile of leaves as if he belonged. He was a faithful companion, acting more like a dog than cat. He licked my face and greeted me at the door. When I walked outside, there he was, padding alongside. If a dog approached, Garfield would charge forward in Halloween cat style.

I'm thankful for his unconditional love. He soaked up my presence when I was home, instead of being angry that I was gone so long. He died in the fall, but my memories are sweet.

I learned valuable lessons from Garfield: enjoying the present rather than what I don't have; being thankful for the presence of friends and time spent together, unconditional love and a sweet welcome.

God extends unconditional love to us. Sometimes we don't spend the time in His presence, but when we return, He is quick to welcome us and enjoy each moment.

The orange of autumn, reminiscent of the Garfield I loved, reminds me to be thankful for the things Garfield taught me and how God places loving things in my life.

THE REVEALING LIGHT

Janet R. Sady   October 16
This is the verdict: Light has come into the world, but men loved darkness instead of light because their deeds were evil. Everyone who does evil hates the light and will not come into the light for fear that his deeds will be exposed. But whoever lives by the truth comes into the light, so that it may be seen plainly that what he has done has been done through God. John 3:19-21 NIV

Flood waters crept up to the house trailer near the creek. When the morning light revealed their dire circumstances, the couple knew they were trapped. Dirty brown water swirled around their home. Then a rescue crew in a motor boat arrived and assisted them to safety.

ndividual lives are like this. We become embroiled in sin; perhaps deception, immorality, covetousness, or idolatry. Only when the light of God's Spirit comes into our hearts are we able to see the devastation. As we recognize our inability to help ourselves and our need to call on our Lord, He will come into our lives and rescue us from destruction.

Lord, help me to allow the light of Your presence
to fill my heart and life, and reveal my sins.
Thank You for rescuing me from the darkness. Amen.

BLESSED TO BE A BLESSING

Pan Sankey   October 17
Blessed are those whose strength is in you,
who have set their hearts on pilgrimage. As they pass through the
Valley of Baca, they make it a place of springs; the autumn rains
also cover it with pools. They go from strength to strength, till each
appears before God in Zion. Psalm 84:5-7 NIV

"Blessed to be a blessing"
– is that my prayer?
Or do I only seek Your freely given blessings
for myself?

Has my self-centered vision
become so weak that I can't even see
the desperate thirsty people
all around me?

How can God's Kingdom grow
if I just settle down and revel in His love?
A pool that has no overflow
becomes a stagnant bog.

Lord, grant the vision and the means
to bless these arid souls
with daily freshened streams
of Living Water flowing from Your heart through mine.
Blessings to share, to spread abroad,
to honor and delight my God.

SIDEWALK CHALK

Helen Dening   October 18

*Let us draw near to God with a sincere heart and with the full
assurance that faith brings, having our hearts sprinkled to cleanse
us from a guilty conscience and having our bodies
washed with pure water.* Heb. 10:22 NIV

The sidewalk chalk lay clustered near the driveway—a variety
of pale colors, each indistinguishable in its chalky coating. Even
when used, the colors appeared faded, subdued, and lusterless.

It rained that night.

he chalk now announced its presence with vibrant colors of
red, green, and blue, inviting a child to come, pick it up, and make
something beautiful with it.

I want my life to be like the washed, vibrant colored chalk—
inviting and useful. Before knowing Christ, my true identity was
covered in sin, and my words and actions had little impact in
revealing Christ's love.

When we invite Christ into our hearts, our sin is washed away
and our true identity is that of Christ. He is revealed boldly and
vibrantly, like the colors in the washed chalk. Our walk in faith
invites others to come and let Christ wash away their sin coating,
and use them, too, to make something beautiful.

*Thank you, Lord, for loving me and wanting to use me to reveal
more of You. Thank You for the many ways You remind me of Your
presence, like the example of rain-washed chalk.*

THE PERSISTENT SPIDER

Doris Richardson   October 19

Kerry and I were about to get into the car when Kerry looked
in the side mirror. "Look at this," she said. There was a spider web
from the top of the car to the mirror, all very delicately made after
its own unique design. She brushed it away and we went on.

Two days later, as Lisa walked past the car, she spotted
another spider web in the same location, same design. This
happened a few days in a row. Talk about persistence!

Are we that persistent in our Christian lives? 1 Peter 3:15
NKJV says, "...*always be ready to give a defense to everyone who*

asks you..." Galatians 6:9 NKJV tells us, not to *"grow weary while doing good, for in due season we shall reap if we do not lose heart."* James tells us to be persistent in prayer. *"You do not have because you do not ask."* (James 4:2 NKJV) *The effectual fervent prayer of a righteous man availeth much.* (James 5:16 KJV)

Let's be persistent in our walk and prayer life.

HARVEST GIFTS

Jewell Utt   October 20

The LORD will indeed give what is good,
and our land will yield its harvest.
Psalm 85:12 NIV

Behold a splendid mountain range
With colors bright and true
It makes my heart feel glorious
Creation's vibrant hue

The seasons they pass swiftly but
To Fall we must pay heed
The jubilee of harvest will
Meet many a great need.

FINISHING WELL

Denise K. Loock   October 21

I have fought a good fight, I have finished my course,
I have kept the faith. 2 Timothy 4:7 NIV

Just moments after Dad breathed his final breath, Mom patted his hand and whispered, "Well done, thou good and faithful servant." Six years later, I had the privilege of murmuring the same phrase when my Mom finished her earthly sojourn.

My siblings and I grieve our parents' deaths, but our aching hearts are soothed by the assurance that Mom and Dad now dwell in the presence of God.

Sorting through the contents of Mom's desk drawers and end tables, my sister and I discovered journals, notebooks, and devotional books filled with sermon notes and personal comments on her spiritual journey. One of the things we discovered was the faded typed pages of a testimony she'd given to a group of

Christian women.

She wrote, "There are three musts that have been incorporated in my life—I must be prepared to meet my Savior (Matthew 16:26). I must invest my life in those things [that] last forever (Matthew 6:19-21). I must finish well (2 Timothy 4:7)."

Mom and Dad lived well and finished well. My challenge is to follow the clear, straight path to Glory that they forged.

What trail are you blazing for others to follow?

WISE ADVICE: REALLY?

Christy Fitzwater   October 22

I was on a social media site recently and read that one of my friends had posed a question about a relationship she was struggling with. She was looking for advice. As I read the string of responses, I was appalled at the comments. Only a few of the thirty comments came close to giving her godly, biblical counsel on how to handle the relationship.

I thought of the similarity when I read about Amnon's lust for his sister. ***Now Amnon had a friend named Jonadab...Jonadab was a very shrewd man."*** (2 Samuel 13:3 NIV)

Jonadab was a close friend who saw how miserable Amnon was in his infatuation for Tamar. Jonadab recommended a plan for Amnon: rape Tamar. If Jonadab thought this was the right way to handle his lust, I wonder what other things he had encouraged Amnon to do before this?

Let's ask the Lord to give us discernment in where we seek advice and show us if we have any close friends who are encouraging us to sin or take a foolish path. Then ask Him to give us the courage to break free from these toxic friendships.

Do not be misled: "Bad company corrupts good character."
1 Corinthians 15:33 NIV

MY FRIEND

Darla Lynn Ivaldi   October 23

I prayed to You, but I listened first.
My prayers, oh Lord, went unrehearsed,

I spoke the words that came to mind,
but sometimes they were hard to find.

I prayed to You with open ears.
I told you all my deepest fears,
I told you things that bothered me,
I prayed away my misery.

I prayed so that I might be heard,
And prayed that I would keep Your Word.
It was You who died, then rose to save;
And I praised You for the love You gave.

Then I thanked You for the things You'd done,
And for the day that had begun;
And I stopped and listened once again,
I heard you say, "You are My friend."

I no longer call you servants, because a servant does not know his master's business. Instead, I have called you friends, for everything that I learned from my Father I have made known to you.
John 15:15 NIV

GIVING IT FORWARD

Nancy E. James   October 24
Every generous act of giving, with every perfect gift, is from above.
James 1:17 NRSV

When I walk in the park, I carry an identification card, money (in case I decide to buy ice cream), and my apartment keys. One time I returned home to discover that my five dollar bill was missing. Perhaps it fell to the ground when I reached for a cough drop in my pocket. I prayed that the bill had been picked up by the right person—someone for whom five dollars made a difference.

At a conference later that summer, I bought earrings handmade by another attendee. When the artist saw me wearing them, she asked, "Did you find the plastic guards to hold the earrings on?" No, I had failed to see them. The next day I wore the lightweight earrings again—and lost one. I chose not to let the artist know.

When we talked on the last conference day, the artist told me she had made enough from her jewelry sales to pay her travel expenses. I was satisfied that I had played my part—just as I chose to believe that the five dollar bill had found the right home.

Father, everything I have is a gift from You, Lord. Help me to give it forward to others without counting the cost. Amen.

PLAIN AS THE NOSE ON YOUR FACE

Melanie Rigney   October 25
Open my eyes that I may see wonderful things in your law.
Psalm 119:18 NIV

Do you ever study the Old Testament readings and think, "How could those silly people have *not* understood what the Lord wanted or was saying?"

The people of Jesus' time may have felt the same way when they were reading the stories of what we know as the Old Testament… only to ignore the presence of God in their own lives. They may have seen and recognized the similarities in the story of Joseph and his brothers and jealousy within their own community, for example, and chosen to ignore the lesson, or justified their own conniving and evil character. Surely, they were conversant in the prophecies of Isaiah and the others… but as Jesus fulfilled them, those who knew Him so often failed to recognize what was happening. Why? Because this radical came with a message of love, rather than with an army of men to liberate them.

Listening is one thing. Comprehending and acting on what we hear can be quite another. May God grant us the strength to do all three.

Lord, You make Your desires as plain as the nose on my face. Help me to not rationalize the times my will is at odds with Yours… and to obey. Amen.

HIDING PLACES

Janet R. Sady   October 26
Read Psalm 91
Thou art my hiding place; thou shalt preserve me from trouble; thou shall compass me about with songs of deliverance. Selah."
Psalm 32:7 KJV

As children, many of us had hiding places where we went when we were distressed. It may have been in a closet, under a bed, or in our parents' bed. Mine was under a hemlock tree in the woods near our house.

I needed a hiding place as an adult when my husband had two different cancers at once, my daughter contracted meningitis, another daughter feared for her life in an abusive relationship, and my sister had a stroke. I really just wanted to run away.

Where could I turn for help? The only place of refuge that I found was my heavenly Father. No one else had the answers. I felt like Peter when Jesus asked him, "Will you also go away?" My reply, like Peter, was: *"Lord to whom shall I go? Thou hast the words of eternal life."* (John 6:68)

As believers in Christ, our hiding place is in Him during the storms of life.

Father, I know that You are a safe hiding place in time of trouble. I place my life in Your hands for help and safe keeping. Amen.

DUTY vs. DELIGHT

Patsy Sanders   October 27
*Delight yourself also in the LORD....*Psalm 37:4a NKJV

Ever surprised during mundane cleaning chores at home? Once in awhile I discover something I felt was in "safekeeping" only to realize it had become misplaced and forgotten. This recently occurred when I came across a handwritten letter from my only brother.

Words resounded from his heart. He was a struggling college student but his needs were never mentioned – only his love for Christ, compassion for the lost, and expressions of complete surrender to kingdom work. However, he has been in heaven for 40 years!

As I read the letter, I saw how his delight led to please. I questioned *my* heart: Do I serve Christ because I love Him, or for what I can acquire from Him? Am I faithful to honor Him with every aspect of my life? Does my heart break over what breaks His?

Serving Christ and others should be done delightfully. We can be required to do many things. Obligation says *I have to,* delight says *I want to.* My brother understood this principle – do we? God is capable of replacing an obligated heart with one willing to please Him. *But we have to want to.* Just think what discoveries await you!!

POSITIONING MYSELF

Kimberly Henderson   October 28
O God, You are my God; Early will I seek You...
Psalm 63:1a, NKJV

I never expected the Lord to use the hound dogs next door to bless my life, but as I stared out my kitchen window one winter morning, I couldn't help but notice them huddled by my neighbor's back fence. The more I thought about it, I realized I had seen them by that fence for several mornings in a row-- curled up in the spot where the first warm rays of sun hit the yard.

I marveled at those silly, barky hounds. They knew exactly where to go for warmth. No one had to teach them. They just instinctively positioned themselves for survival first thing every morning.

The Lord reminded me of my need to position myself for survival. I know I can do nothing apart from Him, I know in His presence is the fullness of joy, and yet, how many mornings do I bulldoze forward into my day and my to-do list instead of sitting and soaking in time with the Lord?

I may not have noticed those dogs much before, but now they serve as a sweet reminder in my life--a reminder to be quick to bask in the warmth of time with the Son each and every day.

THE SON IS SHINING

Earl Kugle   October 29

Somewhere the sun is shining.
Sometimes it will just peek through,
For the clouds of doubt and darkness
Make it impossible to see its hue.
But look for the light of Heaven;
It will always be shining for you.
We have a God up in Heaven,
And His light is ever true.

Though darkness and doubt
May surround you,
No cloud can block your view,
For the light of God's love
And the presence of His Son
Will light a path for you.
So . . . look for the Son.
Don't worry about the rain,
For the Son in His Glory
Is coming again.

***And God will wipe away every
tear from their eyes.***"
Revelation 7:17c, NIV

A DIVINE PROTECTION

Deborah Riall   October 30
***...who through faith are shielded by God's power until the coming of
the salvation that is ready to be revealed in the last time.***
1 Peter 1:5 NIV

At first glance, this passage might suggest that God will shield Christians from calamity. As much as we wish that this were true, it isn't realistic.

Consider a parent and a child. For the first months of life, the parent holds the child close, but at some point the parent has to set the child down and let him learn to do things for himself. God does that with us, too. We enjoy periods of relative ease, but eventually challenges and trials start. Life gets hard, and then better, and then hard again. With each trial, faith and experience build and prepare us for the next trial.

God doesn't leave us without His help. Like a loving parent, God is always close by, watching in case the child falls. He will guide us through whatever life throws at us and His grace accompanies us.

Salvation doesn't mean that all problems will melt away. It means that we can get through them with God's help.

*Father, thank you for letting me learn life's little lessons. But better
still, thank You for always being near to guide and protect me when
I'm in over my head. Amen.*

Reformation Day, October 31
A Mighty Fortress Is Our God
Martin Luther, 1529
Taken from Psalm 46

Today is Reformation Day, commemorating the day that Martin
Luther nailed The 95 Theses on the door of the Castle Church in
Wittenberg, Germany on October 31, 1517. Luther composed one of
the most famous hymns of all time.
Read and meditate on the lyrics for today's devotion and go to your
Bible and do the same for Psalm 46.

A mighty fortress is our God, a bulwark never failing;
Our helper He, amid the flood of mortal ills prevailing:
For still our ancient foe doth seek to work us woe;
His craft and pow'r are great, and, armed with cruel hate,
On earth is not his equal.

Did we in our own strength confide, our striving would be
losing,
Were not the right Man on our side, the Man of God's own
choosing:
Dost ask who that may be? Christ Jesus, it is He;
Lord Sabaoth, His Name, from age to age the same,
And He must win the battle.

And though this world, with devils filled, should threaten to
undo us,
We will not fear, for God hath willed His truth to triumph
through us;
The Prince of Darkness grim, we tremble not for him;
His rage we can endure, for lo, his doom is sure,
One little word shall fell him.

That word above all earthly pow'rs, no thanks to them, abideth;
The Spirit and the gifts are ours through Him Who with us
sideth;
Let goods and kindred go, this mortal life also;
The body they may kill: God's truth abideth still,
His kingdom is forever.

(Public domain)

November

TREMBLE

David Young
November 1

Tremble, O earth, at the presence of the Lord,
at the presence of the God of Jacob. Psalm 114:7 ESV

Shudder O earth at the voice of God,
Every syllable lightning shod.
Stand in awe at His thunderous Word,
His truth in every language heard.

Stand in fear you listening Peoples
Trembling 'neath your earthly steeples
With straightening hair and tingling flesh
Disquieting hearts and souls afresh.

Empires crumble and the nations fall.
Parliaments enacting temporal laws
In your flimsy halls of steel and stone
Humble yourselves before His throne.

Humble your hearts before His glory,
Revealing the soul's enshrouded story,
Conceding truth like a flaming sword
In the presence of its rightful Lord.

TURNING OUR EYES UPWARD

Marilyn Nutter
November 2

Thomas Ken wrote the hymn *Awake, My Soul, and With the Sun,* but the last stanza has come into widespread use as the *Doxology.* It is perhaps the most frequently sung piece of music in public worship.

As we approach the season of Thanksgiving and Christmas, and with it, distractions and "noise," perhaps you would like to listen to recorded praise music available on the internet* to redirect your focus. Hymns of praise and Christmas carols carry rich meaning to turn our focus heavenward, yet too often their lyrics are lost in our repetition. The *Doxology* is presented today for your meditation.

Praise God, from Whom all blessings flow;
Praise Him, all creatures here below;
Praise Him above, ye heavenly host;
Praise Father, Son, and Holy Ghost.
* One resource is http://www.fln.org/one/?station=gentle

DEPENDABLE

Rose Marie Goble   November 3
***Now his parents went to Jerusalem every year at the feast
of the Passover.*** Luke 2:41, KJV

Employers, teachers, parents, and committee chairs love dependable people. "You can count on him/her. The job will be done."

Do you think that's why God chose Joseph and Mary? That He could count on them to obey the visions He gave them and raise the Christ child? His plan of redemption required the help of humanity. If people were to be saved, He needed the right couple, and they were His choice. He could trust this dependable couple with His only Son, the One who would die on the cross for the world's sins.

God is still looking for dependable people to fill the gap. My prayer and aim is to obey Him completely and fill some holes in the church and community with God's love. Will others describe you as dependable?

VISION CORRECTION

Jen Sloniger   November 4
Read 2 Kings 5-7

In reading the above passage, I'm struck by the difference between Elisha's perspective and those around him, especially the king of Israel. How was Elisha able to see God at work when others couldn't?

Most of us long to peek beyond the curtain into God's kingdom, to see chariots of fire, but the truth is we need spiritual eyes to see God at work in our ordinary days. Otherwise we'll be just as baffled as Israel's king, especially during trials.

Our vision quest begins by ditching every attempt to remake God in our image, and focusing on scripture instead. The Bible illuminates both God's sovereignty and goodness—how the two are inextricably linked—and provides two lenses through which we are to view Him. The king's responses revealed he had an eye for God's power, but lacked vision for God's goodness.

Using both lenses is the key to sharper spiritual vision and faith to overcome trials. Faith's firm trust in God's goodness and sovereignty allows us to peer through the temporal fray into the heart of God, where we see what doubters cannot: God working good for those He loves out of every situation. We may not witness angels driving fiery chariots, but if we use *both* lenses, we'll never fail to see Him at work.

I AM WITH YOU

Alan Ruffner   November 5
Do not be afraid, keep on speaking, do not be silent.
For I am with you, and no one is going to attack and harm you,
because I have many people in this city. Acts 18:9-10 NIV

Have you ever been called on to speak in front of a group? I was recently asked to preside over a funeral for a relative. Talk about being challenged!

The evening at the funeral home, after much prayer seeking God's guidance and direction, I was able to speak with boldness and loud enough for the folks to hear me. The next morning was the actual funeral service. Once again I pleaded with God to give me the words to share, and He did. I wanted to comfort, encourage, and challenge people to live the life that God has given them to make a difference in others' lives.

Perhaps you are asked to speak for a church gathering, speak at a conference, or even simply pray at a family dinner. Don't let fear get the best of you. Allow the Holy Spirit to use you to share your heart concerning our great God.

Heavenly Father, allow us to be bold enough to say "yes" when
You present opportunities to speak on Your behalf
because You promise to be with us. Amen.

"I will never leave you or forsake you." Hebrews 13:5 NKJV

NEVER ALONE

Dorsee Bernat   November 6

...then your righteousness will go before you, and the glory of the
Lord will be your rear guard. Isaiah 58: 8b NIV

My destination for a business trip was Milwaukee. I'd never
been there and had no idea of what to expect when I arrived. One
thing was certain: my friend and colleague, Mike, would be waiting
for me at the terminal. Knowing that he would be there to meet me
relieved my anxiety because I knew that I wouldn't be alone.

Life can be a lot like that trip, filled with the unknown,
uncertain, unpredictable, and yes, often uncontrollable. One thing
is certain. We don't have to make any part of the trip through life
alone, because we have a constant companion. Jesus will go each
step of the way with us, leading, guiding and protecting. When
we're not sure where the present path is taking us, we can have
confidence. He's already there and has promised to never leave or
forsake us (Hebrews 13:5). That's a promise we can count on!

Lord, thank You that no matter where life takes me,
You are already there. Amen.

WHY, GOD, WHY?

Jana Carman   November 7

When you are slogging through thorny ways, does your faith
sag? We all have high expectations: enough to eat and wear, a
secure, well-paying job; a decent car, home, possessions; a loving
family; good health; tranquil life; personal safety. These are all
reasonable expectations. But when God sees us leaning on these
things rather than on Him, He may decide to knock these props out
from under us.

What is God doing to us? How are His goals different from
ours? Our loving, all-knowing Father kicks away the crutches,
brings on the muscle-building trials, trains and molds us—all to
develop spiritual adults, not pampered children. Like a football
coach, He knows what we need to become the best we can be. He
gives us exercises to strengthen us where we are weak. He knows
our strengths and helps us to refine them by exercising them. So

Hebrews 5:7,10 encourages us: *Endure hardship as discipline; God is treating you as sons.... God disciplines us for our good, that we may share in his holiness* (NIV).

Thank You, dear Father, for Your individualized training program, and that You are right beside me through it all. Amen.

OUT OF KILTER

Helene C. Kuoni   November 8

He who covers his sins will not prosper,
But whoever confesses and forsakes them will have mercy.
Proverbs 28:13 NKJV

We hired an electrician to install a pair of sconces on our dining room wall, one on either side of the china closet. After he'd worked awhile, I checked his progress and noticed that the two lights were uneven.

"The left is higher than the right," I pointed out.

He put down his tools and came over to where I stood. Pondering his work from my perspective, he said, "Yeah, but no one will ever notice."

"No one will notice?" I responded, "I just did!"

Fortunately, he agreed to fix the problem.

How human it is to deny our wrongdoings, to cover up our faults! Are we like the electrician who needed to be confronted before correcting his error? Do we need to sense God's anger before we confess our failings?

I have learned that confession needs to be a part of my daily prayer. I work quickly to clear away all that hinders close fellowship with God, so that I can experience full joy in the Lord's presence, unhindered by unconfessed sin.

Lord, along with King David in Psalm 32, I confess my transgressions to you, knowing that You forgive the guilt of my sin. Thank You, in Jesus' name. Amen.

HOUSETOPS AND OTHER PERCEPTIONS

Marilyn Nutter   November 9

Do not bring hastily to court, for what will you do in the end if your neighbor puts you to shame? Proverbs 25:8 NIV

"Look Grandma! Only the top of that small house shows. The rest is underground."

Sheila quickly looked over to the side of the road, while maintaining her focus on driving. "No, honey, that's not a house. It's a small building to mark where underground utilities are."

"Well," said Gabby, convinced that she was right, "It still looks like part of a small house to me."

We all see things and proclaim what they look like *to us.* Our perceptions, though not always accurate, are our realities. We judge a rude person, later to find out she had just received bad news and had no time to talk to us. We look at someone who is overweight, and later learn she has a health condition that keeps her from exercising. We wonder why a beautiful young lady isn't married, only to hear that her fiancé broke off an engagement and she is still hurting. We perceive, and say it's real.

The Message paraphrase says, ***Don't jump to conclusions— there may be a perfectly good explanation for what you just saw.*** Give someone the benefit of the doubt before criticizing. You may be looking at a small utilities building but mistake it for a house.

FORGIVING PAINS

Darla Lynn Ivaldi   November 10

To forgive is to accept,
to put behind, and to let go.
And remember Him above
who shed His blood for those below.

Wrongfully accused,
although perfect in every way;
Still, He paid the price for sin
and gave His life away.

We are not deserving
of His pain and agony.
But He chose to forgive,
and to love, to set us free.

So when our hearts are in distress
remember what He did;

By death and resurrection,
He taught us to forgive.

Bear with each other and forgive one another if any of you has a grievance against someone. Forgive as the Lord forgave you.
Colossians 3:13 NIV

A GODLY REFLECTION

Denise Loock   November 11
Let your light shine before men, that they may see your good deeds and praise your Father in heaven. Matthew 5:16 NIV

The Queen of Sheba's skepticism about the vastness of Solomon's kingdom and his wisdom prompted her to visit him. She plied him with riddles and problems, perhaps hoping to expose a weakness. But she found only strengths. The soundness of Solomon's wisdom, the immensity of his wealth, and the well-being of his people impressed her. She stopped asking questions and began to seek his counsel, telling him *"all that was in her heart"* (2 Chronicles 9:1 NKJV).

Before she went home she said to Solomon, *"Praise be to the LORD your God, who has delighted in you and placed you on the throne as king to rule for the LORD your God"* (2 Chron. 9:8 NIV). Her curiosity about Solomon had been transformed into accolades for the God he served. God's truth had been planted in her heart through Solomon's wise advice.

As I reflected on the queen's words, I wondered about the people who observe me. What do they conclude about the God I serve? Do my actions prompt them to praise Him? Does my advice convey God's truth? Through Solomon's words and actions, the Queen of Sheba observed God's love, faithfulness, justice, and righteousness. Is that what other people see in me?

KEEP CLINGING

Rachel Kerr Schneider   November 12
Let love be without hypocrisy. Abhor what is evil. Cling to what is good. Romans 12:9 NASB

Have you ever felt that you were holding on for dear life?
I have.

For the past several years, I had been holding on for my husband's dear life, as he was slipping away with Lou Gehrig's disease. I found myself clinging to a good minute, a good mood, a good meal, a good friend, a good message.

Clinging is defined as "having a strong emotional attachment or dependence." That definition resonates with me, because that is exactly how I felt and still feel about my relationship with God. Our society tends to think of clinging as a negative. In this case, I beg to differ. Clinging to God, is in fact, clinging to good. A genuine relationship with Him will be evident in our relationships with others. God will use what was intended for evil, for our good, when we love Him and have answered His call on our lives.

So, keep clinging. When we cling to GOD, we are clinging to GOOD.

LIVES IN CONCERT

Marsha Hood   November 13

A harpist weaves
intricate patterns of praise,
her hands
duets of devotion,
creators of sacred strains--
soaring, unbounded joy of Bach,
soothing, dulcet tones of Pachelbel,
fashioning harmony
from single graceful notes.

Life's symphony
a blending
of the music of the moment
with airs of eternity.

WHAT'S IN MY CART?

Monica A. Andermann   November 14
*Butter and honey shall he eat, that he may know
to refuse the evil, and choose the good.* Isaiah 7:15 (KJV)

When I wait in the supermarket check-out line, I like to play a little game by taking a quick inventory of the cart ahead of me. Based upon the contents, I decide what that shopper's status might be. Gallons of milk, fruit snacks, and baby food call out "mother of small children" while frozen dinners, canned spaghetti, and boxes of dry cereal may suggest a single individual.

It's fun to peer at the purchases of others to pass the time on line, but I need to look more closely at what I have in my own "cart." What do I take with me when I walk out of my door each day? Do I push around hurts and resentments, or do I carry an encouraging heart, compassion, and forgiveness? Do I wear a frown, or do I smile regardless of how I may be feeling that day?

Just as I make assumptions about the contents of others' carts, so will people make assumptions by my actions, words and appearance. Each day, may I strive to make only good selections for what I keep in my "cart."

Dear Lord, please remind me to fill myself with Your loving kindness each day so that I may be an encouragement to those around me. Amen.

STEPS OF FAITH AND COURAGE

Sheri Neuhofer   November 15

Read Joshua 1:6-9
Have I not commanded you? Be strong and courageous.
Do not be afraid; do not be discouraged, for the Lᴏʀᴅ your God
will be with you wherever you go. Joshua 1: 9 NIV

"Jesus, I'm afraid." I clung to the edges of my comfort zone, petrified. "You want me to facilitate a small group study? I haven't had formal training. What if I don't know the answers to the questions they ask me?" I felt "safe" in my stillness. Yet remaining stagnant is not part of God's plan. God doesn't call us based on what we think we can do; He calls us based on what He wants to do through us.

Four verses in the first chapter of the book of Joshua are a reminder of the way God wants us to be in order to fulfill His purpose. In these four verses, God tells Joshua to be strong and courageous three times. Those words speak reassurance and strength into my soul.

I am certain God is leading the charge each week as I step out to lead women closer to Christ. When I am courageous and consistently seek guidance from His word, He prepares me to accomplish His purpose.

Perhaps God is calling you and, like me, you're "afraid to move." I encourage you to step out in faith with your strength and courage firmly planted in Jesus.

LET US GIVE THANKS

Debbie Carpenter   November 16

You crown the year with your bounty,
and your carts overflow with abundance. Psalm 65:11 NIV

There is a chill in the air. Leaves are falling from the trees. Pumpkin stands begin to pop up in vacant lots all over town. Here in Arizona, red chilies hang in bunches tied together by cords of raffia. Fall is here.

Many families begin to look forward to the coming of the Thanksgiving holiday. It's a time of aromas and sharing delicious food with friends and family members. It is a day set aside to say "thank You" to our God who is the giver of all good things. It is a day for thinking of loved ones, some near, and some far away, some no longer with us.

Occasionally I am tempted to focus on what I lack rather than all the blessings God so generously bestows. Thanksgiving, then, is also a time to bring our thoughts to God's faithfulness in providing what we need. He is indeed a God of abundance whose carts overflow.

LORD, thank You for providing me with everything I need. May I have a grateful heart each day of the year. Amen.

For great is your love, reaching to the heavens;
your faithfulness reaches to the skies. Psalm 57:10 NIV

LIVING AN ABUNDANT LIFE

Tommie Lenox   November 17

I have come that they may have life,
and that they may have it more abundantly. John 10:10 NKJV

To celebrate the 100th day of school, students at Fremont Elementary School collected 100's of objects: pennies, buttons,

leaves, toothpicks, and others. The highlight came when Maria Rojas, who is 100 years old spoke to the students. I listened as spellbound as the children, while she shared memories of working in a gold mine in Mexico and loading baskets of ore for the burros to take to town, washing clothes in a river and sewing her own clothes with "stitches smaller than a sewing machine could make.'"
 Maria Rojas' visit included tough questions. One timid kindergarten student raised her hand and said with awe, "How did you live to be 100?"

Without hesitation, in broken English, Maria fired back, "No drink, no smoke, work hard, eat good food, be good to your mother and father and go to the dances on special occasions!" She leaned forward in her wheel chair and said softly, "Here's best part. Mi padre make it when I little girl." She reached into her brightly colored woven bag and pulled out a rough hewn wooden cross. She held it high, so everyone could see. Her eyes sparkled. "This make you live long and happy too."

A CLOUDY DAY

Janet R. Sady   November 18
Now we see but a poor reflection as in a mirror, then we shall see face to face. Now I know in part; then I shall know fully even as I am fully known. 1 Corinthians 13:12 NIV

If we look into a mirror which has fogged over, it's difficult to see the details of our face. When we drive down the highway in fog, it is difficult to see what lies ahead.

In life, we may encounter job loss, sickness, divorce, and financial and social problems. Perhaps we feel confused and disoriented, wondering what God wants from us. What should we do, and which way should we go?

Although we can't see the details and the road ahead, God does. In prayer we know His presence and in His Word, we read His principles. God has also given us His Spirit as a light to guide us through our "fog." Someday we shall see Him face to face, and we will understand the purposes for which He allowed our circumstances in this life. For now, we walk by faith, not necessarily by sight. Since He knows our end from our beginnings, it is best to allow Him to be our guide.

Thank You, Lord, for Your guidance and direction in the midst of confusion and loss. Thank You for Your word which gives us enlightenment. Amen.

THE FORWARD LOOK

Joseph Hopkins   November 19

Do ghosts of past sins of both commission and omission come back to haunt you? They do me.

If only I had controlled my tongue when I spoke those hurtful words in anger. *If only* I had told my father how much I loved him before cancer took him away from me. *If only* I had befriended that lonely young man who committed suicide.

But once confessed and forgiven, our transgressions are **"removed from us as far as the east is from the west"** (Psalm 103:12, NKJV). If God remembers them no more (Jeremiah 31:34), why should we keep dredging them up?

When I am plagued with regrets over what I have done or not done, I've found it helpful to recite these words from Philippians: **"...forgetting those things which are behind and reaching forward to those things which are ahead, I press toward the goal for the prize of the upward call of God in Christ Jesus."** (Philippians 4:13-14, NKJV). I can close the door on troublesome memories and focus on God's will for the present and the future. **"Thanks be to God, who gives us the victory through our Lord Jesus Christ!"** (1 Corinthians 15:57, NKJV)

A THANKSGIVING SURPRISE

Miriam Sarzotti   November 20
Give thanks in all circumstances; for this is God's will for you in Christ Jesus. 1 Thessalonians 5:18 NIV

Although I love surprises, I didn't expect to find one in my Thanksgiving list of blessings this year. But I wrote, *Thank You, Lord, for my illness.* I planned to go on a retreat to spend a few days with Him soaking up His love. Instead, I got sick with bronchitis.

"Why, Lord, am I home sick?" He whispered to my heart, "You have been so busy lately not having any fun. I miss spending time with you." Spending time on the couch sick is fun? But He surprised me. I enjoyed myself watching old movies and sucking on a zillion popsicles. I felt the Lord's deep love and mercy surround me every day as He healed my body. He brought us closer together and I gave thanks.

What part of His will are you not accepting? As you give thanks in a situation, the Lord will reveal His power and give you a heart of gratitude as He blesses you.

Dear Jesus, I open my heart in obedience and give You thanks for my situation today. Show me Your power and love today as I place my trust in You.

A NEW LIFE

Frances Gregory Pasch   November 21
....the blood of Jesus, his Son, purifies us from all sin. 1 John 1:7 NIV

I reached across the chasm
Between my God and me…
The space was more expansive
Than the waters of the sea.
I could not touch God's outstretched arm
No matter how I tried.
There was no way to breach the gap
Because of sin and pride.

But then I learned that Jesus
Paid the price for all my sin…
If I would just believe in Him
A new life would begin.

So I repented of my sin
And stretched my arms out wide;
Not only did He breach the gap…
Within me He resides.

CHOICES THAT MATTER

Charles Earl Harrel   November 22
Read Joshua 24:1-15
*But if serving the Lᴏʀᴅ seems undesirable to you, then choose for yourselves this day whom you will serve...*Joshua 24:15a NIV

Laura and I pulled into the parking lot at Knotts Berry Farm.

We had been planning this date for months, ever since she graduated from high school. However, instead of rushing to the front gate of the amusement park, we stayed in the car to talk. During the past year of dating, we had talked about many things but never about spiritual matters.

We seldom attended church and knew little about God. That's why it surprised both of us when I blurted out, "If God really exists and we choose not to follow Him, then why finish this date tonight?"

Laura was silent for a moment; then we embraced and prayed our first prayer together. Obviously, my delivery was less than tactful, but my question seemed relevant, maybe even timely. We both committed our lives to God that night and pledged to serve Him. A few months later we were married. Two years later I became a youth pastor.

We all make decisions that affect our lives: some are easy, others more difficult. The most important ones, however, concern eternity. They are the only choices that really matter.

Dear Lord, may all my choices reflect Your will for my life. Amen.

PEPPERMINT MOUNTAIN

Helen Dening   November 23
But thanks be to God, who always leads us as captives in Christ's triumphal procession and uses us to spread the aroma of the knowledge of him everywhere. 2 Corinthians 2:14 NIV

Each time our grandchildren visit, they race to a favorite place, a small knoll covered in peppermint. As the children search the grass to see how far the peppermint has spread, they scuff their feet in the grass, releasing the peppermint scent. They climb to the top of "Peppermint Mountain" and roll to the bottom, filling the breezes with laughter and peppermint fragrance. Often the children roll down the hill together, to see who can get to the bottom first or who can roll into the thickest blanket of peppermint. Each roll brings squeals of delight and an eagerness for more.

My grandchildren's adventure is like our Christian walk. Just as the children delight spreading peppermint scent, we delight in Christ as we spread the fragrance of knowing Him. Just as the children want to find the abundant patches of peppermint, we too desire the abundant sweet fellowship of other believers, filling the breezes with Christ's love and grace.

Lord, may I be a pleasing fragrance of Christ
in the lives of others. Amen.

PRECIOUS FEET

Darlene Rose (Bustamante)   November 24
Read Luke 7:37-38 & Luke 7:44-50

Master, Teacher
Rest Your foot in my palm
I will moisten it with tears
And apply soothing balm

As I cradle Your foot
I weep and I cry
You've walked far and long
They're so worn and dry

Your precious feet
Mean so much to me
I wash them with love
Because of You, I can see

Oh Master, Teacher
Please remember me
As a servant who loves You
With the core of my being

BIT O'GRACE

Dr. K   November 25
The grace of the Lord Jesus be with you. 1 Corinthians 16:23 NIV

It was a great day to be alive, a beautiful spring day, warm, pleasant, sunshine bright, a day to delight in. That ol' groundhog must have felt the same way because there he was strolling across the highway, big as life. He had crossed the southbound lane, now stopping traffic on the other side. Good people halted rather than kill one of God's creatures on one of God's premier days.

All the groundhog had to do was keep going to be safe, but nooooo, our wandering groundhog, sensing there was extreme danger, turned and ran for home back across my lane. As it streaked for safety, God's grace was mediated by the good brakes on my car, and Mr. Groundhog disappeared into the field from whence he had surfaced in the first place. All of us in the cars smiled and felt good about the deliverance.

It occurred to me: if you and I knew the dangers around each day, we would understand we're a lot like that ground-hog. There are dangers we don't understand, dangers we don't even realize are there, yet God's hand of grace keeps us safe.

LORD, help me to be thankful for Your grace expressed in so many ways, some I don't even recognize. Amen.

MAKE ROOM

Jen Sloniger   November 26
In his pride the wicked man does not seek him;
in all his thoughts there is no room for God. Psalm 10:4 NIV

My grandfather died before I was born and my parents divorced early on, so the main influencers of my character were my mother and grandmother. Both women were self-motivated, reliable, and completely capable; ladies you could count on even when life fell apart.

I inherited many wonderful qualities from Mom and Grams. But as my mom would say, "Your virtue is your vice," and I also recognize a familial trait of fierce independence within me.

My natural inclination is to run wild with my own plans. But I've learned that if I don't leave plenty of room for God in my thoughts and plans I tend to dismiss Him when He shows up. I sometimes even resent His works as an obstacle to overcome on the way to achieving whatever I naively think is best.

How counterproductive to my Christian life! I don't want to miss God's real power because of my stubborn will-power. I desire His presence, not my fickle plans.

I want more of God, not less. So, let the purge begin.

What thoughts will I keep? Only those that leave plenty of room for the fullness of God and His sovereignty. Only those that seek Him first and foremost. What about you?

THE VOICE OF GOD

Darla Lynn Ivaldi   November 27

The voice of God is ever near
The heart that longs for Him to hear.

Words of wisdom from above
that speak to us in truth and love.

A language that is all His own,
And by the Spirit He makes it known.

To those who wait on bended knee,
The voice of God will speak to thee.

*Praise the L*ORD*. Give thanks to the L*ORD*, for he is good;
his love endures forever.* Psalm 106:1 NIV

SEEK AND FIND

Dixie Talbott   November 28
I love those who love me, and those who seek me find me.
Proverbs 8:17 NIV

Have you ever watched a toddler get down from his highchair? Turning around to face the back of the chair, he climbs down believing the floor is below him. Arms stretched to their limit, fingers clinging tightly to the chair arms, one foot held firmly on the footrest, the other reaching for that stable floor, he strains to reach that floor. Coming within inches of feeling its security, however, he whimpers, gives up and cries out for help. Sometimes mother rescues the baby from his dilemma; sometimes the baby falls and bumps his head.

The baby is like a person seeking God in many respects. A person gets all turned around trying to find peace and happiness. He may work for a good education, job status and financial stability. He hopes money and position will bring peace of mind and unlimited happiness. He believes God exists, but in the daily routine and upsets of life, he looses sight and hope of God's loving care. Crying out, he may seek professional assistance and find temporary relief from life's problems. Sooner or later, he is compelled to search for the true source of peace and happiness. If persistent, he will find that source; if repentant and believing, he will accept that source...Christ.

THE FIREPLACE

Rhonda Carroll   November 29
Seek the Lord while He may be found; call to Him while He is near.
Isaiah 55:6 HCSB

I love sitting by a warm fireplace on a cold winter's night. It's relaxing to watch the flames burn in beautiful red and orange colors. The warmth feels so good, but as the fire begins to die down the room quickly grows cold. To keep the fire burning, you have to give it attention by stoking the fire or by adding more wood to it.

Our spiritual life can become like the fire in a fireplace. If it is not given attention, it can grow cold. When we neglect time with God, our spiritual life can become like the fire that is left to die. God is continually pursuing a relationship with us, but it is up to us to accept His invitation. Just as we enjoy spending time with our friends, God wants to do the same with us. Spending time in prayer, reading God's Word, and fellowshipping with other believers will help us stay close to God and keep our spiritual life alive and well. Can you determine today, to keep your fire burning?

NIGHT PRAYER

Cindy Tuttle   November 30

Sleep with dreams of my love for you.
Sleep in the arms of gentleness and the hands of peace.
Oh sleep, my child, as I watch over you and smile
as I think of the love you will share.
Hear my lullaby as you slowly close your eyes.
Sleep, my child, for tomorrow is the dawn of a new day.

When you lie down, you will not be afraid;
when you lie down,
your sleep will be sweet.
Proverbs 3:24 NIV

December

A POEM FOR ADVENT

Delores (Dee) Hartman   December 1
Read Luke 1: 46-55

Advent means so many things, I know:
For some, it's stockings hung and mistletoe;
Bulbs and ribbons placed on Christmas trees;
Congested traffic caused by shopping sprees.

It's getting all our Christmas cookies baked;
Untangling Christmas lights to decorate;
Sending cards to friends, both old and new,
And saying that we have too much to do.

But more than these, the meaning that is best
Is it's the season when all earth is blessed
By a little baby boy in manger stall,
As He provides the greatest gifts of all.

His gifts of love, salvation, peace and mirth
Renew us as we celebrate His birth.
And each new Advent we become as one
Looking forward to God's blessed son!

*And the glory of the LORD will be revealed,
and all mankind together will see it...*Isaiah 40:5 NIV

TRUE CHRISTMAS

Lanita Bradley Boyd   December 2
*Religion that God our Father accepts as pure and faultless is this:
to look after orphans and widows in their distress and to keep
oneself from being polluted by the world.* James 1:27, NIV

Despair
Christmas
All tapped out
No food, no money
Meager Santa gifts hidden away

Urgent prayers ascend for my children
Christian friends arrive with gifts
Food, clothes, toys, money
All needs met
Jesus lives
Hope

GIFTS ON MY WISH LIST

Lydia E. Harris   December 3
*God so loved the world that he gave...*John 3:16 NIV

"What do you like about Christmas?" I asked my young
granddaughter.
"Presents!" she replied. I wasn't surprised. I would have answered
the same way at her age.
But now as a grandmother, I have a different perspective. The
years of accumulating possessions are waning, and I'd rather
downsize and re-gift what I have. But I still enjoy buying gifts for
my grandkids and others.
Although I'm not looking for packages labeled "To Lydia" under the
tree, there are other gifts I really want. They're the ones mentioned
in the book of Revelation. I don't completely understand them, but
I know they're beyond imagination. And they're reserved for those
who overcome. Four times Jesus says, *"To him who overcomes, I
will give"* (Revelation 2:7, 17, 26; 3:21).
What will Jesus give overcomers? The crown of life (Revelation
2:10); authority over nations (2:26); the morning star (2:28); their
names in the book of life (3:5); and the right to reign with Jesus on
His throne (3:21).
Jesus is the greatest example of overcoming. In John 16:33 (NIV)
Jesus says, *"In this world you will have trouble. But take heart! I
have overcome the world."* Through His power within us, we too
can overcome and look forward to incredible gifts.

*Lord, through Your power, help us live as victorious overcomers.
Amen.*

GIFT-GIVING

Sterling Dimmick   December 4
"And she shall bring forth a Son, and you shall call His name Jesus,
for He will save His people from their sins."
Matthew 1:21 NKJV

I like the Christmas season despite its ever-increasing commercialism. Ads everywhere seem to shout "buy this or "you must have that." It's easy to get caught up in the buying frenzy.

Yet the greatest gift ever given is free! It doesn't cost us a penny. The essence of Christmas is the gospel---the "Good News." John 3:16 (NKJV) says, *For God so loved the world that He gave His only begotten Son, that whoever believes in Him should not perish but have everlasting life.*

We enjoy giving something special or useful to friends and family. Take a *fresh look* at the gospel accounts in Matthew and Luke and ponder with Mary and Joseph the Gift God gave us. Perhaps sharing the greatest gift ever given with someone this season, could also make your Christmas, the most special ever.

COME FOR CHRISTMAS TEA

Debbie Carpenter   December 5
The Father has sent the Son to be the Savior of the world.
1 John 4:14b NIV

The Victorian tea room was warm and cozy, inviting us to temporarily put aside thoughts of shopping, wrapping, and baking as Christmas rapidly approached. The essence of oranges and cinnamon from the Winter Blend Tea steamed from the spout of the blue and white teapot, adding the aroma of relaxation.

A lovely ivory lace tablecloth graced our table with the centerpiece of a three-tiered server displaying finger sandwiches, scones, and small pastries to complete the picture. Lemon curd, Devonshire cream, and raspberry preserves provided tasty options for the scones.

As I looked around the table in the company of those I loved, my gaze fell on Nana Em, the family matriarch. With a heart of love, she had arranged this lovely treat for her daughters, granddaughters, and great-granddaughters, as she did every year the week before Christmas. What joy she had in giving this special gift to us.

What joy the Father must have had as He sent the gift of His Son to be the Savior of the world. In the moments that fill our Christmas celebrations, may we remember God's indescribable gift, His sweet gift of love, and may we be filled with joy.

CHRISTMAS GIFT

Donna Howard   December 6

**"For there is born to you this day in the city
of David a Savior, who is Christ the Lord."**
Luke 2:11 NKJV

Christ Jesus!
He was born in a stable,
Reared as a lowly carpenter, yet
Infinite, eternal. He
Submitted to the cross on our behalf and died
To save us from our sins. He was buried, then He
Moved the rock and
Arose from the grave, the triumphant
Savior of the world!

Give your life to Christ today.
Invite Him into your heart.
Faith is all you need
To live with Him throughout eternity.

Thanks be to God for his indescribable gift! 2 Corinthians 9:15 NIV

NICE TO REMEMBER

Evelyn Heinz   December 7

*But Mary treasured up all these things
and pondered them in her heart.* Luke 2:19 (NIV)

Beneath all the twinkling lights,
it is nice to remember
the bright star that shined
over Bethlehem a long time ago.

Opening our many Christmas gifts
it is nice to remember
the three wise men's gifts
given to the Christ child.

Gathering together with family and friends
it is nice to remember
the holy family in a simple stable
being visited by wise men and shepherds
oh, so long ago.

A WOMAN OF SAMARIA

Pollyanna Sedziol   December 8

Read John 4:1-42
"...I...am..." John 4:26

People hounded Jesus in the streets when he spoke the Truth – "I AM." The lengthy conversation Jesus has with this unnamed woman in the fourth chapter of John is beautiful! It emphasizes His love for us as individuals for whom He is open and available even before we know Him. Many years after their encounter, I imagine an aged and dying woman whispered, with a glowing light within, "Because He is, I am -- Because He is, I am!"

Lord Jesus, thank You for talking with this woman and recording this experience for us. Like the Samaritan woman, and regardless of our past or present, may we confidently know your love for us, and that because of I AM—we are. Amen.

THE TRAVELER

Pan Sankey   December 9

And the Word became flesh, and dwelt among us, and we saw His glory, glory as of the only begotten from the Father, full of grace and truth. John 1: 14 NAS

He left his home which was familiar, good, and beautiful,
entered a country where so much seemed so strange.
Even though He spoke their language,
they couldn't seem to understand Him,
and so, He talked it over with his Father.

He often joined the residents in everyday activities;
He did some carpentry, went to a wedding, broke up a funeral.
He even walked the shoreline,
doing His unconventional style of "fishing,"
 and all the while, He talked it over with His Father.

He, too, made some good friends, and shared with them
His Good News, knowing that His time with them was short.
Then when all He'd come to do was done,
He promised He would never leave them nor forsake them, until
that day He'd come to take them Home—
to Father.

> *"Father, I want those you have given me to be with me
> where I am, and to see my glory..." John 17: 24a NIV*

HIS MYSTERIOUS WAYS

Douglas Raymond Rose   December 10
According to your faith be it done to you." Matthew 9:29 ESV

"Where's that postman?" I wondered. It seemed so simple---that's what the magazine article said: "Remember your regular postman with a gift during the holidays."

But, alas, it wasn't that simple---for me, that is. I had carefully purchased a decorated box of Holiday Cookies wrapped in bright red wrap---now what should I do with it?

We live in a neighborhood with only small brick locked mail delivery boxes and I realized I didn't even know the postman's name. My chances of catching him on his motorized rounds were slim.

I went to main post office and around to the "mail hold" window. "I want to see that my mail carrier gets this gift. Could you tell me who it is?"

She looked at my home address and zip code number and grinned. "Why, yes", she answered. "Do you know what? It just happens to be me!"

Wow! I wished her a Merry Christmas and presented her with the box of holiday cookies. What were the chances of this ever happening again in our Texas town of well over l00,000 population?

Yes, God does work in mysterious ways---even in the United States government post office!

WHAT'S REALLY BROKEN?

Helene C. Kuoni   December 11
Ponder the path of thy feet, and let all thy ways be established.
Proverbs 4:26 KJV

I fell and broke my elbow and wrist. In a bulky cast, I was unable to wear my winter coat for six weeks and became homebound. Church friends came to visit or sent e-mail. I felt "connected" although I did not go to Sunday worship. After the cast was removed, I spent three weeks in a removable splint, but I continued to stay at home.

One day a box of flowers arrived– a gift from a gal who had been homebound with a bad back. She'd returned to church the previous Sunday and heard a prayer request for my recovery from surgery on both feet! I don't know how that rumor started, but I knew it was time for me to return to church. Not only had I been unaware of the needs of someone with an injured back, but the congregation was praying for the wrong part of my anatomy!

God was telling me to get up and let my healthy feet carry me back into the fellowship of believers.

*Gracious Lord and Savior, help me to not take lightly opportunities to worship You in the company of fellow believers. Thank You for those who **"share with God's people who are in need"**. (Romans 12:13 NIV) In Jesus' name. Amen.*

CHRISTMAS PREPARATIONS

Bonnie Rose Hudson   December 12
"For unto you is born this day ... a Savior, which is Christ the Lord."
Luke 2:11 KJV

I don't know how your usual Christmas season unfolds, but mine is usually hectic, filled with ever-growing lists of things that need attention, people I long to spend time with, and of course, decorating. I have a Christmas blanket I lay across my bed each year. It's a scene from Bethlehem with the words of Luke 2:11.

I confess the blanket does not always make it to where it

belongs each morning. Sometimes it lands in a pile on the floor. Sometimes it finds itself wrapped up in the bedspread. This morning, though, I smiled as I pulled it into its proper place! Then, I noticed it was slightly askew; I didn't have it straight.

I reached to straighten it and paused, the Christmas message on the blanket taking on fuller meaning than before. God had sent His perfect gift of a Savior to me just as I am. He wants to save me not only from sin but from worry, stress, and frustration. All He asks me to do is come to Him, just like the people came 2,000 years ago.

Lord, please help me come to You every day, no matter what parts of my life feel askew. Amen.

CHANGING OR CHASING?

Geanna Steinmetz   December 13

My husband is facing a transfer at work that would increase his commute to an hour. I have been praying that God will make it so that he doesn't have to drive that far. Yet as I pray, Jesus' words echo in my head, "*Your kingdom come, Your will be done, on earth as it is in heaven,*" (Matthew 6:10, NIV). *Your will be done...* I had to stop and think---*am I praying the right way? What if God's will is to send him there on a mission? Who am I to mess with that?* Yet, how often do we pray that *our will* is done?

In the garden we see Jesus begging and pleading with the Father, but He adds, *"Yet not as I will, but as You will,"* (Matthew 26:39, NIV). How much more effective would our prayers be if we started *chasing* the mind of God instead of trying to *change* the mind of God?

To chase the mind of God is to chase after God himself. Do we really want that which is outside of God's will? If we are not seeking God's agenda, then we are by default seeking the enemy's. There is no gray area here. Let's pray to be in God's will. There is no better place to be.

CHRISTMAS CONTRASTS

Marilyn Nutter   December 14

Christmas! We sing carols, gather with family and friends for celebrations, exchange gifts, and send cards giving our latest news. Yet, in our festivities, we may forget that...

While someone is laughing, someone is grieving.
While someone is busy planning, someone feels numb and lonely.
While someone sets a table for many, someone sets a table minus one.
While someone celebrates, someone is hurting.
While someone decorates with tinsel and lights, someone else's sparkle has been diminished.
While someone opens gifts, someone knows one of their most precious gifts is gone.
While someone writes a card or letter, someone has signed it with one less signature.

Circumstances such as death of a loved one, are irreversible, but could you be an instrument to offer strength and comfort to a grieving person by letting them know you remember? A call, visit or card can be a comfort. Consider filling in that person's name in the apostle Paul's prayer and pray for them today.

I pray that out of his glorious riches he may strengthen you with power through his Spirit in your inner being, so that Christ may dwell in your hearts through faith. And I pray that you, being rooted and established in love, may have power, together with all the Lord's holy people, to grasp how wide and long and high and deep is the love of Christ, and to know this love that surpasses knowledge—that you may be filled to the measure of all the fullness of God.
Ephesians 3: 16-19 NIV

LOOKING FOR DIRECTIONS?

Pan Sankey   December 15
Read Psalm 143:8-11 NIV

The LORD God revealed precise plans for building the temple to David, who passed them along to Solomon. ***"All this,"*** David said, *"I have in writing as a result of the LORD's hand on me, and he enabled me to understand all the details of the plan."* (I Chronicles 28:19 NIV)

The LORD has laid out detailed plans for our lives. David gives us a Six-Step-Program in Psalm 143:8-11 that helps us discover and implement them.

1. **When?** *"Let the morning bring me word of your unfailing love, for I have put my trust in you."* (vs. 8a)

2. **Where?** *"Show me the way I should go, for to you I lift up my soul."* (vs. 8b)

3. **What?** *"Rescue me from my enemies, O LORD, for I hide myself in you."* (vs. 9) Especially the enemies from within: fear, procrastination, pride, rebellion...

4. **How?** *"Teach me to do your will, for you are my God."* (vs. 10a) There is no greater Teacher!

5. **Who?** *"May your good Spirit lead me on level ground."* (vs. 10b) The terrain may appear bumpy, but His Spirit steadies us.

6. **Why?** *"For your name's sake, O LORD, preserve my life."* (vs. 11a) Our goal is to make Him famous!

As we close out a year and look forward to making "new plans," consider the words of Psalm 143 and listen for God's direction.

CHRISTMAS MUSINGS

Paul Collord   December 16

The babe of Christmas, the child, the man Jesus—has shown us the Father, and we are still learning to truly look and see and obey and become the people He intended us to be.

Our pastor said, "The first rule of discipleship is to show up," so we do.

God said, "Feed and clothe the poor and hungry," so we help at the food pantry.

Flowers are a gift of God's beauty, so we plant a small garden. Our family is a gift of the Father, so we spend time with them.

Marriage is God's plan, so we've celebrated 59 years.

Friends are God's blessing, and we touched base with dear ones this year.

Prayer is God's command, so we remember daily our family and friends and those who govern us.

A sermon series from years ago, "The Unexpected Jesus," continues to be our experience week by week. We thought we knew Him, but He amazes us again and again. The advent, His coming, reoccurs *daily*.

Christmas is a time to remember these things, so we do.

May the Lord Jesus Christ himself and God our Father,
who loved us and by his grace gave us eternal encouragement and
good hope, encourage your hearts and strengthen you,
in every good deed and word. 2 Thessalonians 2:16-17 NIIV

A MUSICAL CRESCENDO

Parise Arkelian   December 17
Shout for joy, you heavens; rejoice, you earth; burst into song,
you mountains! Isaiah 49:13a NIV

On the Plaza de Sant Roc de Sabadell, in Barcelona, Spain, a man with his bass fiddle is poised to start playing his instrument. A young girl approaches the man's hat on the ground and drops in a coin. As the man plays a few notes, a woman enters, sets up a chair, sits near the man and begins playing her cello. As she picks up the musical theme of "Ode to Joy" from Beethoven's 9th Symphony, other instrumentalists converge until there are violins, woodwinds, a brass ensemble, a kettle drum, a conductor, and singers. The music grows with a gradual intensity as each instrument and voice is added.

The reaction of the people gathering went from stillness to astonishment to elation of young and old alike. My response to this flash mob performance was an outpouring of joy as I began to rejoice by singing the hymn "Joyful, Joyful, We Adore Thee," penned by Henry Van Dyke to the music of Beethoven.

Starting with one man, the scene showed how worshipful

music has the ability to tear down barriers and soften our hearts to the unity of God's Spirit. Let us offer the fruit of our lips in praise and worship to experience the fullness of His joy.

LOOKING FOR PEACE?

Doris Richardson   December 18

In story after story, the nightly news speaks of unrest, not peace. We become discouraged, yet real peace is available to us.

First, we have peace *with* God that comes as we place our faith in Jesus' shed blood and resurrection. *"Therefore, being justified by faith, we have peace with God through our Lord Jesus Chris."* (Romans 5:1 KJV).

As we allow the Holy Spirit to control our minds and actions, we have peace *from* God. *"...to be spiritually minded is life and peace"* (Romans 8:6b KJV). *"The fruit of the Spirit is ...peace* (Galatians 5:22 KJV).

Thirdly, as we communicate with God in prayer, we have the peace *of* God. *"And the peace of God, which passeth all understanding, shall keep your hearts and minds through Christ Jesus"* (Philippians 4:7 KJV.) He forgives our sins, guards our hearts and minds, and gives us peace to replace our anxiety.

Many look for relief in many places that are temporary fixes. Only God gives true and lasting peace, and it is a free gift when we place our faith in His Son Jesus, and allow the Spirit to do His work.

BERTA'S BELLS

Tommie Lenox   December 19
*The memory of the righteous is blessed...*Prov. 10: 7a NASB

Three knitted bells, trimmed in white and tied with satin ribbon, have hung on the family room door for nearly forty years. Each time I open the door, tiny bells still ring out memories.

Berta and I became friends when our girls were young. We taught at the church preschool, exchanged mothering stories, and watched our girls grow. Our daughters were 8 years old when Berta was diagnosed with cancer. The congregation rallied around Berta's family, providing meals, transportation, and prayers.

Sometimes God's answers to prayers differ from ours. When it became apparent the cancer was terminal, Berta asked for needles and yarn – red, green and white. On each visit, I found her knitting. One day I asked what she was doing. Her eyes filled with tears, mingled with regret. "I am making Christmas bells for everyone I know. I don't want them to forget me when I am gone."

When the pain became overwhelming, she gave each of her friends a small package. Inside were Berta's Bells. My three bells are trimmed in white and joined together with satin ribbon. Others are green, the color of new life in Christ, and red, the blood of His Salvation. White is the pure light of Christ.

Berta, we will not forget.

STAR OF HOPE

Catherine J. Sercombe   December 20
And we have the word of the prophets made more certain,
and you will do well to pay attention to it, as to a light shining
in a dark place, until the day dawns and the morning star rises
in your hearts. 2 Pet 1:19 NIV

Magi -
Wise wandering sages?
Or fools who pressed through drought and desert
seeking that illusive Star of Hope?
Evening Star,
Morning Star,
Day Star,
Star of Hope arise within our hearts and
shine Your light throughout our night
You, a dark world's One True Light
who makes the foolish seeker wise with heavenly sight.

Lord, I do not always understand where You are leading me. My
will grows weary and faint. I am easily tempted to give up. Then
You gently remind me that Your Word is a lamp to my feet and a
light for my path (Psalm 119:105), and You will never leave me,
nor forsake me (Deut 31:6). Realising that You do know the terrain
ahead and that You will lead me and guide me, I find the courage
to walk on and take joy in the journey.

MORNING JOY

Margaret Provenzano   December 21
Read Genesis 1:29-31

He gives the joy of a morning, the sound of the sea.
He gives the magic of moonlight, the strength in a tree.

The blessings God gives me, His strength from above
are showered on mankind, expressions of love.

How can we count them, their numbers exceed
the waves in the ocean, the harvester's seed?

A look of awe at a butterfly's flight,
the twinkling of fireflies on warm summer nights,
the songs of the whales, the colors we see
all speak of His love for you and for me.

The gift that's for always and never will end
is the best that He gave us--this Gift that will mend
all the ills of the world, His Son He would send-
our Teacher, our Brother, Creator and Friend.

Father, may we cherish Your gifts every day of our lives. Amen.

**For God so loved the world that he gave his one and only Son,
that whoever believes in him shall not perish
but have eternal life.** John 3:16 NIV

GOD'S TOUCH

Charlotte H. Burkholder   December 22
Because your love is better than life, my lips will glorify you.
Psalm 63:3 NIV

I sat alone in the sanctuary, only candle flame punctuating
the darkness. Shivering in my damp jacket, I looked in vain for the
pastor who had promised to meet me following my private baptism.
Anxiety fluttered in my breast.

Suddenly a touch startled me. A little man stood behind me,
one hand on a vacuum cleaner handle, the other on my shoulder.
"Excuse me, Ma'm," he spoke gently, a bit of accent flavoring his

speech. "Do ya mind if I turn on the lights? I'm the janitor and I need to vacuum these here carpets."

"Oh, of course not," I moved quickly to leave the pew.

"Ach, but before you go," he smiled warmly, a strand of black hair straying down over one eye, the other twinkling at my dampness, "Can I get you a cup of hot chocolate? You seem to be rather cold."

Forty-five years later it still makes me cry. God's tender personal love for me shown through a complete stranger will resonate in my heart forever.

Loving God, thank You for Your loving-kindness found in unlikely places. Thank You for always being there with a touch for my deepest need. Amen.

SHEPHERD WATCHING

Pollyanna Sedzio   December 23

And there were in the same country shepherds abiding in the field, keeping watch over their flock by night. Luke 2:8 KJV
I am the good shepherd: the good shepherd giveth his life for the sheep. John 10:11 KJV

Thinking about
the reality of shepherds
watching their flock by night
by day ensuring safety
and well-being with no daily showers
no meals at home with family
rain-soaked, wind-blown
possession-less
other shepherds only peers

takes my breath away in wonder
that You are my Shepherd
keeping watch over
me, my daily life, my loves
til I am safe Home with You

graces my heart with joy
that you are both the Lamb
and the eternal Shepherd

at Whose knee all will bow
Whose Name all will praise.
        Selah....................Alleluia......................Amen!

CREATION

Shirley Stevens   December 24
He determines the number of the stars and calls them each by name.
Psalm 147:4 NIV

God cupped His hands
around this snow globe world,
blew His warm breath,
till galaxies unfurled.

God set the Star
of Bethlehem in place
then sent His Son
to grace the human race.

CHRISTMAS PROMISE

Margaret Adams Birth   December 25
For there is born to you this day in the city of David a Savior,
who is Christ the Lord. Luke 2:11 NKJV

We rejoice on Christmas day,
celebrate a Savior born a babe—
yet His Father up above
foretold a future sacrificial age.

While Earth-bound man hailed infant Christ,
God knew of Easter still to come:
sacred Son, cross, grave, victorious rising,
allowing His believing children to come home.

Centuries past the Three Kings' journey,
we fete Lord Jesus' birth—
share gifts that bear a pale reflection
of the gift that His life for us is worth.

He knew, though but a babe, He knew
what the future held in store:

that humble start in a star-lit manger
would triumph over fleshly death . . . forevermore!

THE CARPENTER'S ROOD

Shirley S. Stevens   December 26
But after he had considered this, an angel of the Lord appeared
to him in a dream and said, "Joseph son of David, do not be afraid
to take Mary home as your wife, because what is conceived in her
is from the Holy Spirit. Matthew 1:20 NIV

I dared deliver Him
His swaddling clothes
I warmed against my chest.
I touched Him first, I cut the cord.
Hurt I felt to hold this child
And know He was not mine.

Carpenter I am
Craftsman, not creator of the wood.
Midwife to chairs and tables
I chafe not.
Husband I am,
Why then so churlish a stepfather?
Returning to the manger,
I found Mary smiling.
"He is not mine either."

Under the rood star of Bethlehem
I knelt.
Not my will but Thine be done
I granted to my Father and my Son.

ABBA'S LULLABY

Sandy Mayle   December 27
He ...will rejoice over you with singing.
Zephaniah. 3:17 NIV

Sparrow common, Lily wild,
Shepherd's lamb and Abba's child,
in the rockabye of life

I sing over you.

When the night is drawing near,
see, your Comforter is here;
nestle underneath My love
as I sing over you.

When the storm is howling long,
close your eyes and sing along
with the never-ending song
I sing over you.

Sparrow common, Lily wild,
Shepherd's lamb and Abba's child,
in the rockabye of life,
I sing over you.

A WISE OLD LADY

Darlene Rose (Bustamante)   December 28

"There was also a prophetess, Anna, the daughter of Phanuel, of the tribe of Asher. She was very old; she had lived with her husband seven years after her marriage, and then was a widow until she was eighty-four. She never left the temple but worshiped night and day, fasting and praying.
Coming up to them at that very moment, she gave thanks to God and spoke about the child to all who were looking forward to the redemption of Jerusalem." Luke 2:36-38 NIV

I worship the Lord in this holy temple
And know no other way
To worship God Almighty
And serve Him both night and day –

My husband went on before me
But I was not left alone
For many years I've served here
This temple is my home –

I have fasted and I've prayed
"Oh Holy God – The Great I AM..."
And now, here amongst us
Is this child, this precious Lamb –

"I thank You, Lord, my Father
The Mighty One whom I revere
For You have provided Your Son, Jesus
Our Redemption is truly here!"

THEN AND NOW

Read Luke2:25-35

Evelyn Minshull   December 29

Then Simeon blessed them and said to Mary, his mother:
"This child is destined to cause the falling and rising of many
in Israel, and to be a sign that will be spoken against,
so that the thoughts of many hearts will be revealed.
And a sword will pierce your own soul too." Luke 2:34-35 NIV

In sanitized tableaux on Christmas Eve,
It seems we fail to recognize manure and mud—
much less acknowledge shedding of blood:
the blood of birth, that even then foreshadowed
the Blood of Calvary.

LORD, thwart our inclination to concentrate only on the "warm
and fuzzies:" the sweetness and angelic Glory of the Nativity;
the exhilaration of Palm Sunday; Christ blessing the children; the
excitement and triumph of Easter. Force us to face the totality of
Christ's life and ministry, including disappointment, betrayal, cruelty
and crucifixion-for us. AMEN.

ORDER MY DAY, LORD

Judith White   December 30

But everything should be done in a fitting and orderly way.
I Corinthians 14:40 NIV

As the year comes to a close, I begin to think about what I want to accomplish in the coming year. I furiously make lists and, anticipating an income tax return, decide how to budget for home and yard projects. After a few items are crossed off the list, I realize that my energy levels are no longer housed in a twenty year old body! I restructure and recalculate my projects.

Often I have to pray for God's guidance with my list of "to do's," ask Him to reorganize and restructure my day to fit His plans…

not mine. When I start with prayer, the day goes more smoothly and free of frustration. Because we serve an orderly Creator, He desires that everything should be done in a fitting and orderly way. "Everything" means -- our list of errands, our yard and house projects, our study time and private time with Him: *everything.* When we come before the King of Kings and Lord of Lords with open hearts, we hear the Master's voice. Jesus brings order to life and He does so in a fitting, perfect way.-

PRAYING FOR PEACE FOR THE NEW YEAR

Delores (Dee) Hartman   December 31

Another year is leaving us
The past has left our view.
A new year's coming on its way
To give us something new.

Let's pray this "new" is filled with joy,
With tenderness and care.
Let's hope that love shines round the world
With all that's good and fair.

Let's pray that we will learn to live
Our lives in grace, so fine,
That we will all be joined as one
In love and peace divine.

But the fruit of the Spirit is love, joy, peace, forbearance, kindness, goodness, faithfulness, gentleness and self-control...
Gal. 5: 22-23a NIV

Contributors to Volume 20

Our heartfelt thanks to the following contributors for sharing God's Word and their hearts of wisdom and encouragement. If a particular devotion has ministered to you, you are invited to contact the writer via the email or website provided.

Shirlee Abbott: lives in Sussex, NJ. Visit her blog at http://springtimesoul.word-press.com/ *Finding Shalom 3/2*

Tabitha Abel: Free-lancing, nursing and teaching on-line and volunteering in Chiloquin's Food Pantry which she and her husband Gary started 4 years ago, keep Tabitha busy. They are also active leaders in a Seventh-day Adventist congregation in Chiloquin, Oregon; tabithaabel@yahoo.com *Connected 3/28, It's a Matter of the Heart 8/19, The Gift of Choice 8/24*

Renae Adelsberger: lives in Jackson, TN with her husband. Though she works in commercial insurance, her true passion is her ministry, PedestrianGod. She has a heart to see middle and high school aged females embrace a love for scripture; renae@pedestriangod.com. *Idol Thoughts 1/20, Tired Ears 1/25*

Monica A. Andermann: lives and writes on Long Island where she shares her home with her husband Bill. She has been a contributor to *The Upper Room, The Secret Place*, and many editions of *The Cup of Comfort* and *Chicken Soup for the Soul* books. *Looking Forward 1/9, Careful Comments 1/27, Comfort Food 3/9, Peace I Give You 3/27, What's in My Cart? 11/14*

Connie Ansong: State College, PA. Sharing her faith, hope and love is her choice. She writes to encourage friends, loved ones. *A Fool's Legacy 4/1*

Parise Arakelian: is a retired Operating Room nurse who resides in Southern California. Her love for music has been demonstrated by her 15 year participation as a member of the Palm Desert Master Chorale. She is currently writes devotions for the *PresbyCan Daily Devotional*, monthly inspirational articles for the *Arcadia Gardens Newsletter* and has been featured in *The Sermon Illustrator.* parakelian@roadrunner.com, *Ministers of Light 5/12, A Musical Crescendo 12/17*

Deanna Baird: is enjoying this chapter of her life and has been published in *The Upper Room, Chicken Soup* series and has enjoyed being a part of *Penned From The Heart*. deanna.baird@gmail.com *Rise and Shine 10/14*

Anjanette Barr: is a wife and mom of three living in Juneau, Alaska. Her days are filled with silly antics and laughter, mountains of laundry, and more love than she could ever hope for or deserve. She blogs at www.raisingthebarrs.com. *Who Do You Think You Are? 1/26*

Bill Batcher: considers himself a poet under construction. A retired teacher, he leads a writers group in Riverhead, NY. His poetry has been published in magazines, anthologies and online collections, and has won several awards. A book of Easter poems, *Footsteps to the Resurrection,* was published in 2005. bbatcher@optonline.net *Sacrifice 1/11, Winter Prayer 2/9, Backyard Theophany 4/6, Bravo 5/3,*

Gerald Bauer: Huron, OH, Lutheran pastor, Associate Director for Mission Integration with Lutheran Homes Society (serves northwest Ohio and southeast Michigan), wide variety of publications. Bauergw@aol.com *God's Creation 6/3, Wind Blown Waves at Sunset 7/6, Measuring Success 8/23, Prayer for God's Work 9/21*

Pauline Beck: raised on a small farm and learned to see God in all creation. She believes that nature and all living beings are reflections of the Creator. She taught English in the Youngstown City School District for 25 years and discovered that poetry also reflects the Spirit of God and brings us closer to Him. Her first collection of published poems, *Spit and Spirit,* is scheduled for release in 2014. pencilvanian@verizon.net;. *My Soul is Magenta 3/30, Creation 10/3*

Dorsee Bernat: has been writing since junior high. Her greatest enjoyment is sharing spiritual lessons found in everyday life. She has been an RN and for the past 7 years, has shared her life with Phillip Kemp. She desires that her writing might be used by God to touch lives for His glory and at the end of her journey, wants to hear His "well done". dorseeb@yahoo.com. *Holy Ground 5/18, Our Savior's Arms 5/24, Come...Follow Me, 8/20, Never Alone 11/6*

Margaret Adams Birth: published or is soon to appear in journals as *Riverrun, Ship of Fools, The New Voices (Trinidad and Tobago), Aldebaran, Atlantic Pacific Press, The Poetry Peddler, Purple Patch (England), White Wall Review (Canada), Green's Magazine (Canada), Shawnee Silhouette, Mobius, Black River Review, Potpourri, Perceptions Blue Lake Review, The Wild Goose Poetry Revie and PFTH..* Writes fiction under the names Maggie Adams and Rhett Shepard; at her Facebook author page: www.facebook.com/MaggieAdamsRhettShepard *WHO Really Knows 5/29, Christmas Promise 12/25*

Virginia Blackburn: married for 57 years, has 4 children, 10 grandchildren, and several great grandchildren; home schooled 5 of her grandchildren for the last 13 years and has graduated three of them. Author of two books: *Formula for a Miracle*, and a children's book, *The Adventures of Roger and Penelope.* Contributor to *Penned* and *Secret Place.* blackburn.virginia687@gmail.com *Jars of Clay 1/16, Redeemed 4/19*

Donna Bond: active in music and women's ministries in two churches, married to Tim (also a writer for *PFTH)* for 39 years 2 grown children, 1 grandchild, school secretary. Former president of Seventh Day Baptist Women's Society (national level) Contributor to national magazine *The Sabbath Recorder.* In 2007, she worked on updating her father's 1992 book, *A Choosing People: The History of Seventh Day Baptists* (by Don A. Sanford). *Keys to the Kingdom 6/28*

Tim Bond: Married to Donna, (also a writer for *PFTH)* Tim administered a Christian drug rehab program for 12 years and has now been teaching the GED in a state prison for about 14 years. *A Child's Bedtime Prayer 10/8*

Joy Bradford: Christian, wife, mother, grandmother, Master Gardener, Volunteer teacher at Collin County Jail. Lives in McKinney, TX. joy_bradford_3@hotmail.com; *Glimmer of Light 4/11*

Kathleen Bradley: writes daily devotional posts at: www.fulfilledchristianlife.blogspot; has written nine Christian novels and loves sharing the Word of God.

kathleenbrdly@gmail.com, *God Waits 5/10*
Lanita Bradley Boyd: teacher, writer, and speaker in Fort Thomas, Kentucky. She especially enjoys mentoring young women, editing, and reading. Website: www.lanitaboyd.com; Lanita@lanitaboyd.com *Beautiful Feet 7/12, September Sun 9/8, Two Special Children 9/10, True Christmas 12/2,*
Jamie Britt: shares a message of hope and a desire to see women find their value in Christ. Blind from birth, she challenges us to see God's sovereignty and care in the midst of our trials. Through her blog, she encourages women to be transformed by the power of Christ, discovering we are never alone; Jamie is a graduate of the 2011 NCompass Writers Retreat and the 2012 and 2013 Writers Advance! Boot Camp. She's also a featured guest blogger on MorningGlory. blogspot.com and CindyRooy.com. Stop by Jamie's blog atwww.encouraging-women-strength.blogspot.com. *A Difference in Plans 1/17*
Christi Brooks is a wife, mother, writer, and Christian book publisher. She can be reached by email at christi@chaplainpublishing.com and her website is www. chaplainpublishing.com. *The Gag Order is Lifted 6/5, Are You Listening? 6/13*
Barbara Major Bryden: lives in Olympia, WA. with her husband. She enjoys her grandchildren, writing a small devotion that she sends out monthly, and taking photos of her garden, which become cards for family and friends. *Pack for Adventure 3/29*
Charlotte Burkholder: free lance writer from Harrisonburg, VA and enjoys writing devotionals and personal experience stories. Has been published in *The Secret Place, Celebrate Life, The Family Digest* and others. Married for 53 years and has four married children and eleven grandchildren. Email address is chburkholder11@gmail.com. *God's Touch 12/22*
Darlene Rose Bustamante: lives in Lake Elsinore, CA; inspired to write through life events and scripture. She enjoys the beauty of God's creation and thanks Him for her sons, family & friends and for granting her the desires of her heart. poemsbydrose@gmail.com *Eyes of Love 2/14. Ocean Footprints 6/4, A Wise Old Lady 12/28. Precious Feet11/24*
Debra L. Butterfield, is a freelance writer, writing coach and editor. Her most recent publication includes two stories in the compilation *The Benefit Package: 30 Days of God's Goodness from Psalm 103* (CrossRiver 2012). You can find her blog at www.DebraLButterfield.com. *Finch or Serpent? 4/23.*
Jana Carman: : pastor's wife, musician, former editor, writes poetry, devotions, monologues and plays, 2 books of performable poetry published by Lillenas Drama. ed4penned@aol.com *Choices 1/2, God's Track Record 2/24, Echoes of the Passion: Betrayal 4/17, Echoes of the Passion: Needs 4/18, Image Reputation or Integrity 5/19, A Whispering God 6/8, Wanting But Lacking Nothing 6/22, Greatest of These 6/30, The Spite Fence 7/16, Are You Rich? 7/23, Living by Faith 9/11, Do Clothes Make the Man? 9/17, Finding God's Will 9/27,Why, God Why? 11/7*
Debbie Carpenter: Retired from the Children's Ministries Staff at her church in Tucson AZ. Married to Bob and blessed with two daughters and their husbands, three granddaughters and one grandson light up our lives. Published in devotionals and anthologies. Cwrite2encourage@cox.net *Full of Surprises 1/15, The Faith*

of a Child 2/18, Each Deed a Sign 3/18, Dollhouse Lessons, 10/5, A Cup of Cold Water 7/11, Let Us Give Thanks 11/16, Come for Christmas Tea 12/5

Rhonda Carroll: pastor's wife and mom to two beautiful girls. She loves helping others grow in Christ through the study of God's word and by following God's design for healthy living. She enjoys writing and teaching healthy living cooking classes. www.fromthebibletothetable.com. rhonda.carroll@epbfi.com *The Fireplace 11/29*

Joan Clayton: retired educator, but her passion is writing. Religion Columnist in local newspaper, also published in many anthologies and in five of the *Chicken Soup* series. www.joanclayton.com; *joan@yucca.et The Love of My Lord 2/1, The Audience of One 3/16*

Carol Cleal: God's child, retired RN, recently widowed, 2 sons, 3 grandchildren, published yearly in *Penned*. clealbear@gmail.com *My Identity in Psalm 23 5/7*

Judith Clister: Bruceton Mills, WV is a retired elementary school counselor. She now works as a Spiritual Director companioning people in their spiritual walk and is director of Anam Cara Place, a residence set aside for retreat and renewal. jclister@frontiernet.net *Blind Robins 7/31*

Pat Collins: of Mercer PA. Writes stories for children. Her poems have been set to music, appear in church bulletins, published by Int. Library of Poetry. *Jesus Understands 4/4, A Prayer: One Day at a Time 8/26*

Dr. Paul Collord, retired university administrator, lives with his wife, Doreen, in Zionsville, Indiana. They continue to serve each week at a food pantry near Indianapolis. *Christmas Musings 12/16*

Jean L. Croyle has felt the Lord's calling on her writing ministry since elementary school days. She is the author of the novel *Encounters* and has been a photojournalist, editor and speaker. Jeannie and her husband enjoy fishing the rivers, camping, bird-watching, photography, and cooking. Being retired gives her time to volunteer and write when God's calling comes to visit. *Pruning the Heart 2/3*

Sherry L. Cummins: author of published devotional and hospitality books and articles. She serves in a leadership capacity within Meeting Professionals International and has Certification in Meeting Management. She has a BA in Human Resources. Sherry would love for you to share your thoughts with her at cummins.sherry@gmail.com and visit her Southern Yankee Hospitality website at www.sherrytaylorcummins.com. *The Mercy Rule 2/29, A Divine Choice 9/2, His Light of Deliverance 10/11, Miraculous Meditation: Changing My Mind 10/12, Tickled Pink 10/13,Love Is In the Details8/6*

Angela Davis began writing devotions in 2010 and has had several published in books, periodicals, and e-zines. She is currently writing a devotional book which will hopefully be in print later this year. She enjoys reading, walking, traveling (when time and money permit!), and spending time with family and friends. She lives in Columbus, Ohio. Contact: aldavis@columbus.rr.com *Therapy 2/2, How Does Your Garden Grow? 3/7*

Helen Dening: wife, mother of 4 sons and 5 grandchildren. Retired preschool educator and director. Creates, children books Silver Creek, NY, devotions, and curriculum. *Rainbow Connection 8/21, Sidewalk Chalk 10/18, Peppermint Moun-*

tain 11/23 h.dening.1@gmail.com

Sterling Dimmick: B.A. in Communication Studies, A.A.S. in Journalism. Likes outdoor activities, Bible study, Christian music as well as classical and some folk, many forms of literature, photography. sdimmick311@gmail.com; *Commitment 6/24, Following Instructions 6/20, Gift Giving 12/4*

Judy Dippel: is a speaker, freelance writer, and author of *Refreshing Hope* and *Friendship Interrupted.* She is a life long Oregonian and can be contacted at jld-writes@comcast.net *Ordinary Women-Or Not? 1/29, Why Bother? 7/27*

Gloria Doty: Fort Wayne, IN. She is a Christian author, writer, and speaker, writes two blogs about her adult autistic daughter and their life journey together, a regular contributor to devotionals and various magazines. Website and blogs at www.writingbygloria.com www.gettingitright gloriadotywrites@gmail.com ; blogspot.com, www.moms.fortwayne.com (blog tab: Not Different Enough) at *A Messy Cookbook 1/31, Drifting 3/4, Cleaning up Messes 5/17, Weed and Feed 5/30, My Last Option 5/31*

Annette M. Eckart: trains and leads international mission teams and preaches at worldwide conferences. Contact her at www.bridgeforpeace.org and visit her blog: http://annetteeckart.blogspot.com/ *Resurrection Dance 8/30*

Cindy Evans: enjoys living in the sunny south in Georgia, after relocating from Indianapolis. She is currently doing professional temp work, sometimes at Christian companies. She likes to do volunteer work at a local hospice office when she has a day free and also spending time with her husband and seeing inspirational movies. cindy.evans@usa.net. *Helping at Hospice 3/22*

Lisa Evola: is a writer who artfully crafts word pictures that speak to a woman's heart; a Bible study and ministry leader, who desires to touch lives, directing them to our Creator, the source of truth and life; www.abeatifullifeministry.com; www.facebook.com/abeatifullifeministry lsevola@yahoo.com *I am 8/22*

Christy Fitzwater: is a writer, pastor's wife, and Spanish teacher living in Kalispell, Montana. She is mom to a daughter in college and a soon in high school. She writes to help people know God better. Website: christyfitzwater.com, Pinterest: pinterest.com/fitzh2o. *Beware of Counting 10/10, Wise Advice: Really? 10/22, Valuable Life Experiences 5/27*

Dolores Fruth: resides in a faith based retirement community ; she loves writing poetry about her personal experiences and devotion to God. Her poems are published monthly and many have been adapted to music. dhf_15074@yahoo.com *Free Gift, No Strings Attached 7/25*

Elaine Given was born in the then Belgian Congo, the middle daughter of three children. Her parents were New Zealand missionaries there until the brutal death of her father, Elton Knauf, on 23 November 1960 just after independence was proclaimed for the Democratic Republic of Congo. Elaine and her husband Peter served in the same country after marrying, the birth of their two children in New Zealand, and theological studies in the United States. They are now retired and living in Hamilton, New Zealand. ehgiven@xtra.co.nz. *Service with a Smile 3/21*

Rose Marie Goble: writes devotionals, short stories, and self-publishes her novels on line. Go to Amazon.com or kindle to find *The Celery Patch* (Amish),

Hunky Dory Murder, Jailbird, Lakeside Lady Mayor, Dogger, and many more. She has also published the true story of her father-in-law, Bud Goble, who became prisoner of the Germans at the opening of the Battle of the Bulge in WWII--*Captured! Puzzles 9/4, Dependable 11/3*

Barbara Gordon: lives in west-central Missouri with her husband of 37 years. They have three married sons, and two grandchildren. Formerly a public school district administrator, her days are now filled with her grandchildren, reading, geocaching and jogging. barbgordon@hotmail.com *A Willing Learner 9/7*

Marion E. Gorman: lives in rural PA with her retired husband and they enjoy 20 grandchildren. Enjoys family events, gardening and scrap booking. Her writing goal is to encourage fellow believers with God's Word and His faithfulness. Has been published in magazines, anthologies, devotionals and take home papers. meggorman@gmail.com. *I Cannot, God Can 1/14, Life Edged with Gold 5/22*

Robert A. Gutierrez: a forklift operator and freelance writer. Loves history and enjoys watching baseball. He lives in southern California with his wife and four children. gutierrezr1980@gmail.com *Not All that Glitters is Gold 7/31, A Gradual Conquest 1/28, Slow Steady and Sure 6/12*

Beth Hadley: is the leader of the Write Circle, a writer's group at the local library in Sinclairville, NY where she is the Library Manager. She has formed a new Christian Writers group at her church. Contact her at bethwrites@hotmail.com. *Stuff 6/19, Flight 9/25*

Charles Earl Harrel: pastored for 30 years before pursuing writing. Has over 300 published works. His teachings, stories, and devotionals have appeared in 20 book compilations. Charles enjoys photography and playing 12-string guitar harrelCE@aol.com *Choices that Matter 11/22*

Lydia Harris: enjoys spending time with her five grandchildren ages preschool to teenage. Known as "Grandma Tea," she writes a tea column and is the author of the Bible study, *Preparing My Heart for Grandparenting.* Contact her at: LydiaHarris@Qwest.net. *Hold Me 3/19; Parades, Donkeys and Obedience 4/13; Gifts on My Wish List 12/3*

Delores (Dee) Hartman: is an elementary teacher, graphic artist, International winner for artwork, [placed on 2006 Peace Bonds], illustrator for book covers and books, copy-editor, published in *Altoona Mirror, Mature living, The Standard, Upper Case, Cross and Quill, The Path,* and *Writer Magazine.* deehartman@gmail.com *A Poem for Advent 12/1, Praying for Peace for the New Year 12/31*

Crystal Hayduk: lives in Chelsea, Michigan with her husband, where they are parents to three active daughters and one dog. She enjoys reading and music, but tolerates camping for the sake of the family. Crystal is a nursing instructor and a freelance writer; crystalhayduk.ag@gmail.com *Sword Fight 9/9, Fear or Trust? 9/15.*

Pamela Heemskerk: found writing took her by surprise when recuperating from an illness and it has become a major part of her life. Prefers writing non-fiction and has a passion for art, children, and telling people about hearing loss. She works as a physiotherapist with young children with a disability. Email: jheems@bigpond.com, *Welcoming the New Year 1/6, Secure in His Love 2/10;*

Evelyn Heinz: is a widow, seven grown children, eighteen grandchildren, two great-grandchildren.
When her children were grown she took her writing out into the community, giving poetry talks to
schools, libraries, retirement and nursing homes. She has had three books of poetry published, 18 small poetry books self-published. Taught Creative Poetry at a local Community College. Likes passing her love of God in inspiring ways through her writing. Contact: evelyn.heinz@yahoo.com
Always with Me 1/8, Special Security 4/21, Birds and Butterflies 8/18,Second Flowering 10/4, Nice to Remember 12/7
Kimberly Henderson: is a writer who lives in Upstate SC with her husband, three giggly girls, and one seriously spoiled Schnauzer. You can find this recovering perfectionist pressing through the toughest of days with humor, honesty, and the Word of God at her blog, www.aplantingofthelord.com. jkhenderson3@bellsouth.net *Positioning Myself 10/28*
Judith Henry: a follower of Jesus Christ since childhood. She and her husband, Mike, are active members of Bluegrass Baptist Church in Hendersonville, TN. She is involved in teaching, Worship Ministry and in mission exchanges with Japan. Following her retirement in 2001, Judy returned to her passion for creative expression in Fine Arts, primarily in oil painting. In April, 2013, Judy's chronological Bible study, *The Whole Truth* was published. It is a colorful, easy-to-read study based on the premise that lives will be changed if individuals immerse themselves in God's word. hmrjudy@aol.com *Scary Faces, 9/19*
Liwen Y. Ho: resides in the San Francisco bay area with her husband and two children. She is the author of her first picture book, *A Rainbow of Nine Colors* and blogs about life as a recovering perfectionist at http://2square2behip.blogspot.com *Our Eternal Glory 2/19, A Gentle Whisper 2/20*
Marsha Hood: retired teacher: busy writing, reading, and enjoying family and friends. Belongs to several writer's groups and especially loves learning from the amazing writers at Passavant Retirement Community in Zelienople, PA. Published in *Time of Singing, Penned From the Heart,* the *Pittsburgh Post-Gazette,* and *The Upper Case.* hood.marsha@gmail.com *Listen for...6/7, Lives in Concert 11/13*
Helen Hoover: Helen enjoys sewing, reading, knitting, and traveling. She and her husband are retired, live in Northwest Arkansas, and volunteer at a Christian college. Their four grandchildren and three great-grandchildren give them great joy. Helen's devotions and personal stories are published in books and Christian hand-out papers. *Listen to Instructions 7/5*
Joseph Hopkins: New Wilmington , PA; retired Presbyterian minister, devoted to sharing the Gospel world-wide; *A Blown Opportunity 3/17, Aftermath of a Landslide, 3/26, Four Questions About Prayer 6/18, Luck or Providence? 8/31, The Forward Look 11/19*
Donna Howard: of Orfordville, WI. She and Lynn (married 58 years) have 3 children, 5 grandsons and 4 great grandchildren. She enjoys family time, writing devotions and poetry, reading, crocheting, and Bible studies. This is her 6th year with Penned from the Heart. DHoward608@aol.com; *Amazing Love 2/7,*

Redeeming the Time 3/25, Jesus Prays for Us 4/15, God's Unchanging Love 5/4, The Tattered Shirt 8/10, A Peaceful Morning Walk 9/28, Dollhouse Lessons 10/5, Christmas Gift 12/6

Connie Huddleston: and her husband, Harry, begat two sons and five grandchildren. She would like her one sentence biography to say, "She prayed for all those she knew…and God heard." Contact: chuddles@embarqmail.com. Read her blog at http://cahuddleston.wordpress.com/. *Don't Skip the Begats 1/7*

Bonnie Rose Hudson: Writes for children and homeschoolers at www.writebonnierose.com and is an editorial assistant for *The Old Schoolhouse® Magazine* and SchoolhouseTeachers.com. She blogs for kids at *Exploring with Jake* at writebonnierose.wordpress.com and for parents and teachers at lookingoutthe1040window.wordpress.com. writebonnierose@gmail.com. *Old Age 3/11, Don't Throw Your Toys 3/12, If I Could, 4/16, Ethel 7/28, Christmas Preparations 12/12*

Elouise Hults: Country mom of five, grandmom of ten and her first great grandchild, Carter Joseph.
Has had many articles published, certified Christian Worker under the AIGA - Association of International Gospel Assemblies." *The Lord is My Helper 4/17, Forgotten 4/10*

Darla Lynn Ivaldi: *Forgiving Pains 11/10, The Voice of God 11/27, My Friend 10/23*

Lana James: is married with two children and leads a liturgical creative movement group at St Bartholomew's Anglican Church in Toowoomba, Queensland Australia. She enjoys sharing what God has done in her life and likes to write poems about her faith. Contact: lanamjames@gmail.com *God's Guidance 6/29, Handprint of God 8/17*

Nancy E. James: retired English teacher, leads workshops in creative writing and journaling. She is a member of the Squirrel Hill Poetry Workshop and the Pittsburgh Poetry Society and a past director of The Writing Academy, a Christian writers' organization (www.wams.org). Several of her devotions were published in The Writing Academy's *Daily Devotions for Writers*, 2008. Her chapbook of poetry, *Resilient Spirit: Poems for Lorraine*, was published by Finishing Line Press in 2013. *Not by Sight 9/24, Giving It Forward 10/24*

Kathy Johnson: lives in MN with her husband. They have 6 children scattered across the country, mother-in-law to 5, and grandmother to 5. Published in *Christmas in the Country, Lutheran Woman's Missionary League Quarterly, Woman's World, Portals of Prayer, My Devotions, Quiet Hour,* and *Love in the Lake of Lakes.* Also writes under the name Susan St. Clair. praisethelord277@hotmail.com *The Power of God 7/1, Be Prepared 10/9*

Adele Jones: lives in Queensland, Australia. Her writing is inspired by a passion for family, faith, friends, music and science – and her broad-ranging imagination. www.adelejonesauthor.com or contact@adelejonesauthor.com; *What's in a Name? 6/25, Listen 3/23, Heart Trouble-Vision Trouble 8/16*

Jennifer Kanode: is a part time ESL instructor and DJ for FM 90.3 WJTL, but more importantly is a mommy of three. She can be reached at jenniferlkanode@yahoo.com. *Generation to Generation 2/26*

Dr. K is Rev. Lewis W. Kisenwether, Jr.: retired January 1, 2013 after more than 38 years as pastor of First Baptist Church of Matawan, NJ. He is a kidney transplant recipient having received a kidney from his oldest daughter Elizabeth Lane. He lives in Ocean County, New Jersey and can be contacted at drlewk1@aol.com *Commitment 1/13, Be Happy for Others 3/24, Just Don't Do It 4/27, Be Spiritually Safe 5/9, Mother's Day 5/11, Yankee Doodle 7/4, Bit O' Grace 11/25*

Earl Kugle: an octogenarian still serving his Lord and others by writing and making available helpful poems to those who come for meals *Jesus 4/20, The Son is Shining 10/29*

Helene C. Kuoni: resides in PA's Lehigh Valley; writer of Christian devotions and short stories, co-authored the book *Her Pen for His Glory, the 1860s Verse of Isabella Stiles Mead* with her husband John.. Formerly employed by *The Secret Place* devotional magazine, Helene also enjoys coordinating annual Advent Devotional Guides for her church. Helene.Kuoni@hotmail.com *Out of Kilter 5/13, What's Really Broken? 12/11*

Tricia Lathrop: Became a Christian as a child and learned to love the Word of God, and has led Bible studies for over 30 years. My husband Norm and I raised three children who are now out on their own. We reside in upstate New York, but enjoy traveling throughout the US. *What Do You Expect? 6/21*

Michelle S. Lazurek: is the author of *Becoming the Disciple Whom Jesus Loved: Discover your Character in God's Love Story* www.michellelazurek.com www.mslazurek.wordpress.com
Fast Food Christianity 4/12 Do You Know Your Shepherd's Voice? 5/26, Angels Among Us 6/17

Carol J. Lee: is retired and lives with husband in rural Montana. She has 4 step-children (one deceased), 9 grandchildren, 2 great. Carol enjoys family, friends, writing, painting (water color), raising blueberries and raspberries, day trips with her husband, walks with Jesus. She is learning to live daily by the Spirit's power. *Pray and Believe 3/20, Memory Benefits 4/28, Not Remembering 5/5*

Tommie Lenox: tsdlenox@sbcglobal.net;, Living an Abundant Life, 11/17, *My Favorite Book 2/22, Service of Light 4/22, Dynamic Kindness 8/2, In God's Good Time 10/6, Berta's Bells 12/19*

Denise Loock: is a freelance writer, editor, and speaker. Sharing with others the joy of studying the Word of God is her passion. Her two collections of devotions, *Open Your Hymnal* and *Open Your Hymnal Again* encourage readers to open their hearts to the timeless biblical truths that classic hymns and gospel songs contain. Contact her via her website: info@digdeeperdevotions.com *Finishing Well 10/21,, A Godly Reflection 11/11*

Kelly Lyman: is a dreamer, a planner and a doer. Her favorite mantra is: "Go after a dream that is destined to fail without divine intervention." She is a former elementary school teacher who now stays home full time and loves every minute of it- even the hard ones. Kelly lives with her husband, 4 young children and their dog in Chester County, Pennsylvania. When not writing, Kelly performs with her community chorus. Visit her on her blog at www.kellylyman.blogspot.com or follow her on Twitter at @kellylyman. *Little by Little 2/27, Training Wheels 7/17*

Brittany Mayak: is a speaker and writer seeking to empower women to walk in their true identity. Please look for Brittany on FaceBook and Twitter (@brittmayak). mayakbd1@gmail.com *Calm in the Midst of Chaos 6/11*

Sandy Mayle: Contact: dasmayle@gmail.com; *Abba's Lullaby 12/27*

Linda C. McCutcheon: was born into and raised in a loving Christian home and accepted Christ at an early age. Along with a theology degree she has worked in various Christian and secular organizations in a variety of secretarial and administrative roles. For 12 years, she raised her daughters as a single mom but recently re-married and enjoys her new start with Bill and a blended family. Her passion is to help women to achieve all they can be amidst the pain and loss in life. She writes for *Power to Change* and is currently working on a book. lindamccutcheon24@gmail.com *From Where I Sit 1/21*

Norma C. Mezoe: lives in the small town of Sandborn, IN. (Pop. 400), is active in a church with a small congregation, but serves a big God. She believes the Lord led her to become a writer after a crisis in her life. Her first published article was in 1985. Her e-mail address is: normacm@tds.net *They Had a Plan 5/15, Family Reunion 6/1, Under Construction 6/2*

Evelyn   Minshull: Delighted grandmother and great-grandmother; lifelong teacher of writing and art; nature-lover; author of 26 published books and numerous shorter writings, eminshull@gmail.*com My Lost Coin 1/18, Pink—Source of My Teenage Bravado 4/3 Resurrection 4/25, Proud Young Saul of Tarsus 6/14 The Gift of Sight 6/26, Me? Disagree with God, Part 1-9/22; Disagree with God Part 2 -9/23, Then and Now 12/29*

Rebecca Mitchell*: homeschooling mother of 5. She writes, quilts, sews, plays piano, cooks, and is available to speak to youth & women's groups. Her passion is: "Know that even if you hit bottom, God can make you new again." *Soda Residue 7/30*

Rachelle Moon: runs on the rural roads of New Mexico, often with her husband Clyde or one of their 4 children. Read more at www.60miles.blogspot.com or contact at rachellemoon505@hotmail.com
Endurance 1/24

Janelle Moore: lives in Toowoomba, Australia where she enjoys being the homemaker for her husband and two children. She loves to write and is often inspired by her children. She also enjoys reading, scrapbooking and mosaicking. Contact her janellemoore2@bigpond.com; *Celebrate 6/16, Supernatural Vision 9/14,Yes Lord 9/16,*

Donna Morse: is a retired Registered Nurse and adjunct nursing instructor. She is a wife, mother of three, grandmother to eight, and great-grandma of one. Connecting life with Scripture is her passion. Writing and facilitating Bible studies; writing devotionals, profiles, and general articles for her church newsletter are regular writing pleasures. *Will You Love Jesus? 2/12, The Valuable Secret 2/25*

Joan Nathan: pastor's wife (37 years), mother of 6, grandmother of 7. Earned Doctorate in Nursing at Stony Brook University; is a clinical professor, Nurse practitioner in a private medical practice. Loves to travel with family, and to meet people. Medford, New York, Profjnathan@gmail.com *The Gift of Time 7/24*

Laura Neary Hervey: Akron, NY; 2 children, 2 grandchildren her love of teaching and teens. Writes Christian romance, Christian living, opinion pieces, and devotionals *Mercy 1/19*

Sheri Neuhofer lives in Chesapeake, VA with her husband and son. A freelance writer, Sheri has a deep passion to share the hope and healing she's found in Jesus Christ through short stories, dramatic skits, and devotions. In 2012, she was selected as one of the Top Ten runner-ups in Southern Writers Short Story Contest. You can find devotions on Sheri's Blogger page, http://atthehem.blogspot.com, Monday through Friday. slneuhofer@gmail.com. *An Overflowing Bucket 9/13, Pulling Weeds 8/12,, Steps of Faith and Courage 11/15*

Courtney Newbery: is a home manager who enjoys investing in the lives of her ever-entertaining husband and two children. She is a Licensed Mental Health Counselor in the State of Florida and holds a Masters in Biblical Counseling from Dallas Theological Seminary. Welike2write@gmail.com *Just Like Daddy 6/15*

Sharon Niggemeier: wife, and mother of 2 daughters, from Long Island. Enjoys spending time upstate in rural NY, being adventurous and reading. Her many roles include parish nurse, assistant professor of nursing, Bible study co- facilitator, and former Sunday School teacher. sharon1700@verizon.net, *Song of Ascent: A New Psalm Come Worship 3/31*

Marilyn Nutter: is the mother of three adult daughters and grandmother to six. She is the editor of *Penned from the Heart,* the author of three devotional books and a contributor to online sites and compilations, a Bible teacher and enjoys speaking to women's church and community groups. Contact: www.marilynnutter.com or marilynnutter@gmail.com *Fresh Starts for a New Day 1/1, President's Day 2/17, , Passion Week 4/14, Driving on Empty 4/30, Clear View 5/20, Thirsty Birds 7/2, Moving Sales 7/13, A Rock and the Rain, 7/26, New Places 9/20, Reformation Day 10/31, Turning Our Eyes Upward 11/2, Housetops and Other Perceptions 11/9, Christmas Contrasts 12/14*

Linda Bonney Olin: is a farm wife and Lay Speaker in the United Methodist Church. She writes Christian songs, dramas, fiction–whatever the Holy Spirit assigns. Her books Songs for the Lord and The Sacrifice Support Group are on Amazon.com. Visit her Faith Songs website www.LindaBonneyOlin.com. Contact: Linda@LindaBonneyOlin.com, *The Wrong Goal 1/23, Love to Die For 2/11, You Loved Me First 2/16, On Eagle's Wings 3/1, Brightness After Rain 9/1*

Frances Gregory Pasch: has had hundreds of devotions and poems published in devotional booklets, Sunday School papers, and book compilations. She has a weekly e-mail devotional ministry to over 300 people and has led her writers' group for the past 22 years. *Double Vision: Seeing God in Everyday Life Through Devotions and Poetry* will released in six months. Contact: paschf@comcast.net *I See You Lord, 7/8, A New Life 7/14, Believing is a Must 7/22, God's Canvas 9/18, Help Me, Lord 9/26, In His Time 9/12, Faithfully 10/7*

Nola Passmore is a psychology lecturer and freelance writer who has had a number of devotions, true stories and poems published. She lives in Queensland Australia with her husband Tim and enjoys being part of the Quirky Quills writing group. nola.passmore@westnet.com.au *I Lift My Eyes 3/13, Mining for Treasure,*

7/15, *Into the Throne Room* 8/13 *Doubts and All* 8/27, *The Voice of the Shepherd,* 8/29, *Spiritual Checkups* 9/30

Vanessa Perez: Has written devotions and short stories for various magazines. Currently, private English tutor, one of worship leaders in church. Plays piano, guitar, violin, volunteers for Christian ministries. Writing Christian fiction is her life passion. *Perceiving God 5/25*

Sarah Lynn Phillips: and her husband, Barry, live in northeastern PA. Their family has recently expanded to eight, including a grandson named Ty! Sarah is a freelance writer and editor of *The Women's LINK*, a seasonal women's newsletter. Her blog Penned without Ink, (www.sarahlynnphillips.com) reflects how God's ultimate story reaches our life stories. She is also working on a book with the same theme. Contact: pennedwithoutink@yahoo.com *Tug-of-Time 3/14, A New Thing 7/3*

Eunice Porter: is a retired state worker who is active in continued learning at Willamette University and community, church and philanthropic endeavors. A mother of three and grandmother of five, she enjoys sewing, tutoring and playing piano/organ. Contact: grandmaoe@basicisp.net. *Counting Our Days 1/4*

Leigh Powers: is a wife, mom, and writer from Winters, TX. She has a life-long love affair with the word of God and loves discovering how God is speaking through his Word. Blogs at www.leighpowers.com. *He Signs our Pardon 6/23*

Margaret Provenzano: *Morning Joy 12/21*

Cherie Brooks Reilly: is a retired teacher, wife, mother of four and grandmother of eight. Her book *Pumpkin Patch Proverbs and Pies* consists of stories about her life on a Pumpkin Farm. cheriereilly@verizon.net *Things That Go and Come Back 4/29, A Time to Laugh and A Time to Weep 8/7*

Linda Reppert: is the Ministry Mentor for *Real Life with Leslie Nease.* Fulfilling the call of being a Titus 2 mentoring women is at the core of all that she does. She loves to teach women's bible studies and speaks as God provides the opportunities. Linda has been happily married for 27 years and has been blessed with two sons. Contact: www.lindareppert.blogspot.com *Heart Check-up 7/21, An Always Thankful Heart 9/29*

Kim Rhinewalt: *And Then Jesus 3/6*

Deborah Riall: has taken several graduate courses at Luther Rice seminary and online writing courses. She has written several short stories, one of which won the Faithwriter's Weekly Challenge and has a small ministry on social media sharing devotions with others. Her goal in writing is to provide encouragement to others by pointing them toward Christ. *A Man with a Message 8/28, A Divine Protection10/30*

Carolyn Rice: is a graduate of Seattle Bible College. She serves as a prayer partner, a leader in women's ministry and teaches a class with her husband at their church in Everett, Washington. Her hobbies include reading, hiking, kayaking and sitting outside enjoying nature. She can be contacted through her website at treasuresofhispresence.com. *Remember 5/14*

Doris Richardson: of Sinclairville NY. Married 56 years, 4 children, 14 grandchildren, 6 greatgrands. Missionary 25 years. Worked in most church activities for women, youth and Sunday School, and Bible studies. Wrote devotionals for weekly hometown paper, plus various studies and articles. Looking for Peace? 12/18DorisRichrdson@aol.com; *Watch, Wait Wish 4/5, Refreshment 8/1,CU RCH 8/5, Looking for Peace? The Persistent Spider10/19*

Melanie Rigney: (www.melanierigney.com) is the author of *Sisterhood of Saints: Daily Inspiration and Guidance.* editorforyou@earthlink.net. *Yes, Lord 5/16, Plain as the Nose on Your Face 10/25*

Andrea Roe: has attended the School of Writing under the leadership of Jim and Janice Rogers. Contact: andreamroe@gmail.com; *The Pursuit of Happiness 2/6*

Beth Roose: is a member of the Hillsborough Baptist Church, Auckland, NZ. Now retired, she has seen missionary service. roose@maxnet.co.nz *Ever Near 3/10*

Douglas Raymond Rose: lives in Dallas metroplex; wife Esther and he have 2 adult children, 5 grandchildren. Journalist, freelance writer for Standard Publishing, Guideposts, Upper Room, EVANGEL, Dallas Morning News. Ordained Assemblies of God minister, Who's Who in Religion, member Academy of American Poets. dougrrose@juno.com *Think on These Things 9/3, His Mysterious Ways 12/10*

Elizabeth Rosian: is a freelance speaker, educator, and author of the series Books in a Nutshell, on writing for publication. She lives in Johnstown, PA, with her husband, and enjoys her many grandchildren, music, and crafts. *The Joy of Serving 3/3, Behind Closed Eyes 5/23*

Alan Ruffner: Writes stories about his family; enjoys writing devotions that encourage, inspire, and make one smile. Likes to write about biblical children from their perspective. theperfectlighthouse@yahoo.com *I am With You, 11/5*

Janet R. Sady: St. Davids Christian Writers Association board member. Certified lay speaker, teacher, storyteller. Awarded prizes in 2011 for poetry and prose. Published in *The Secret Place* and other periodicals. janfran@windstream.net, *Bringing Glory to God 2/28, The Revealing Light, A Cloudy Day 11/18,Hiding Places, Our Father Knows Best 8/25, The Revealing Light 10/16, Hiding Places 10/26*

Patsy Sanders: is Women's Ministry Assistant at Thomas Road Baptist Church, Lynchburg, VA. She holds a Bachelor of Leadership degree from American Leadership Institute and Seminary. She and her husband Jim, have been actively involved in fulltime ministry throughout their marriage serving various churches and ministries. They currently operate The Master's Inn, a youth camping ministry in Altavista, VA. Patsy is mother to two, "GG" to Chloe, Meredith and Dallas, a published writer, speaker, mentor, and Bible teacher. Patsy's passion is witnessing a life touched and transformed through Christ. Contact Patsy @ patsys@trbc.org *Appointments for a New Normal 2/21 Just Because 3/8, Life's Messes-God's Ministry 4/8, Duty or Delight 10/27*

Pan Sankey: Vienna, Ohio. She and husband Bob have three children and 10 grands. She's been writing since 1985, creates Bible study guides and skits, has mentored a women's group for 7 years, and proof-reads for Penned. She delights in writing poetry about God's creation, His Word, and His provision. Pfsankey@aol.com *Mourning Dove Song Poem from Psalm 86- 7/7, Blessed to be a Blessing*

10/17, The Traveler12/9, Looking for Directions? 12/15
Miriam Sarzotti: is a published author and artist who lives in the San Francisco Bay Area. She loves to share her faith in her art and writing. She is publishing her first book of her memoirs including her time as a Christian missionary in Israel. She loves to write devotions and greeting cards for the Christian market. See her art at www.giftsofhisglory.com and follow her blog at wwwlgiftsofhisglory. com/miriamsblog. *Miracle Shoes 10/2, Thanksgiving Surprise 11/20*
Rachel Kerr Schneider: rachel@rachelkschneider.com, www. RachelkerrSchneider.com.
Keep Clinging 11/12
Marcia Schwartz: Previous contributor to *PFTH* and a retired high school English teacher who has free-lanced poems, stories, and articles to a wide variety of Christian publications over the years. "Apples for the Soul," is a book of her devotions published by Outskirts Press released in 2012. *In the Twinkling of an Eye 2/5; The Silly Ostrich 3/5*
Polllyanna Sedziol: has had poetry published in over 60 religious and poetry magazines. Retired RN, widowed, 5 children, 3 daughters-in-law; 9 grandchildren, 4 great grands. Facilitates her church's Used Book Depository, a ministry which mails Bibles and Christian books overseas to Christians without access to such. Contact: rssps@fuse.net; *Bread into Stone 1/22, Joy! 2/13, Nathanel 4/9, Viewpoint 5/6, Mission Statement 9/6, A Woman of Samaria 12/8, Shepherd Watching 12/23*
Catherine Sercombe: Toowoomba, Queensland. Australia s a creative writing student, education business partner, manager, tutor and semi-retired mother (they've left home now). Described by others in publication as a 'creative and talented writer whose work reflects an infectious love of language', Catherine says this is the natural expression of God's infectious love. Her songs, drama sketches and poems have been performed in churches, schools and Indigenous Communities in Queensland, Northern Territory and Western Australia. She is a member of Toowoomba's Quirky Quills writing group. csercombe@stairwayed.com.au, *Star of Hope 12/20*
Laurel Shaler: Dr. Laurel Shaler is an Assistant Professor at Liberty University where she teaches in the Center for Counseling and Family Studies. She and her husband, Nick, live in Lynchburg, VA but spend as much time as possible in her hometown of Greenville, SC. Laurel is often found writing. Learn more on her website at www.drlaurelshaler.com. You can also "like" her on facebook (www. facebook.com/drlaurelshaler) or follow her on twitter (@DrLaurelShaler)." *A Bend in the Road 1/12, Is Your Anger Helping or Hurting? 6/10*
Diane Sillaman: mother of 4, grandmother of 2. High school math tutor. Loves camping, reading, writing. Lives in log home in mountains near Canon City, CO. Bible teacher, lover of God and people. Has lived in 6 states. Hiked the MD portion of the Appalachian trail with 2 girlfriends to celebrate her 50th birthday. *Instruments 1/30, No One Else 5/1, Refuge 8/8,* **But** *As for Me 8/15*
Jen Sloniger: lives a life filled with adventures—a good number of them beyond the realm of her stories. She writes fiction and devotionals from Arizona, where

she and her husband enjoy the thrill and chaos of parenting six children in a multi-ethnic family built through birth and international adoption. Visit her at www. jensloniger.com. *Make Room 11/26, Vision Correction 11/4*

Betty Spence: lives in West Mobile, AL with grown son. Retired newspaper journalist and columnist. Published credits: poetry and devotions, Sunday School curriculum & church programs. Passion is reading, writing poetry. bettyspence. blogspot.com, *Holy Hug 7/19, Walking with God 7/20*

J. Mark Spruill: Contact: mark@markspruill.com *A Faint Reflection 8/14*

Geanna Steinmetz: wife, mother, sister, daughter, and friend. Has a BA in Theology from Eastern University, St. David's, PA. I enjoy all kinds of cooking and crafts. In my spare time I write a blog called I Am Nacho Momma. Most of the content is Bible study or devotional in nature. You can visit me at IAmNacho-Momma.wordpress.com. *The Purpose of Life 2/15, Changing or Chasing? 12/13*

Margaret Steinacker: Winamac, IN has two books published, as well as writings in several devotionals. A retired GED teacher, her first book – *Fearless Teaching from a Grocery Cart* details her stories of teaching in a county jail with only a grocery cart as a desk. Her newest book, *Unending Praise: 90 Devotions with Ask and Ponder, Prayers, & Journaling in the Psalms*, was published in July 2013. Both books are available on Amazon in paperback or Kindle. steinmag@gmail. com; *How Do I Love You, Lord? 2/4, A Place of Refuge 3/15, My Cry Reached His Ears 5/2*

Shirley S. Stevens: retired English teacher, leads The First Word writers group in Sewickley, Pa, She is a board member of The St. David's Christian Writers Conference and a member of The Pittsburgh Poetry Society. Shirley has published poems in many anthologies including Poet Lore, Common Wealth, Along These Rivers, My Turn to Care, and The Christian Century. Her e-mail address is poet-cat@verizon.net.
Finding the Answer 4/26, Hope Grows 5/21, Faithfulness 8/4, Engaging Your Core 8/11, Creation 12/24, The Carpenter's Rood 12/26

Ruth Stewart: is a retired Library Media Specialist from Hanover County, VA. Author of *This Gentle Land*, and *Legend of the White Canoe*. Has also published articles, poems and devotionals in periodicals. Contact: d.r.stewart@comcast.net
Transformed by God 6/9, Endure to the End 7/10, Follow Me 6/27

Dixie Talbott: Dixie is married with three grown daughters and seven grandchildren. She is a speaker for Stonecroft Ministries, a sign language interpreter at her church and enjoys scrapbooking and photography. Dixie grew up in Ohio but has made Minnesota her home for almost 40 years. *Seek and Find 11/28*

Marietta Taylor: is an author and speaker. She is the author of *Surviving Unemployment:Devotions to Go* and currently serves as a monthly contributor to The Pearl Girls Blog at http://margaretmcsweeney.com/blog. Marietta has contributed to Writing on The Word and Granola Bar Devotions, has served as a monthly blogger at the Go ask Mom Blog at www.wral.com under the tagline Mom of Teens and was a contributing author to *PFTH* Vol XV. www.mariettataylor.net or www.marismorningroom.blogspot.com; maritay918@gmail.com. *Word Choice 7/18*

Keren Threlfall: may be contacted at threlfalls@gmail.com and writes at keren-threlfall.com *Beauty Speaks in Every Place 4/24*

Sonya Lee Thompson: is a freelance writer and speaker who resides in Virginia. When she's not writing, her time is devoted to raising her six children and loving her husband. For more inspiration or to have her speak to your women's group, visit her blog at: www.sonyaleethompson.com *The Sky Is Falling 5/8*

Becky Toews: has served in ministry for over thirty years, studied the Bible extensively, including tutelage under the late Dr. Francis Schaeffer in Switzerland in 1977. Pastor's wife and mother of two and serves as adjunct professor of English Composition and Public Speaking at Lancaster Bible College in Lancaster, PA., where she resides. Becky has a widespread speaking ministry that includes women's conferences, churches, retreats, and university fellowships. Author of *Virgin Snow: Leaving Your Mark in the World.* www.beckytoews.com, becky-toews@newcovcc.us; *When You're Smiling 9/5*

Kenda Turner: is a wife, mother, and grandmother who enjoys writing, walks in all seasons, and photography. Those interests spill over into her blog Words and Such at kendaturner.blogspot.com. Email: kendaturner@gmail.com. *Small Bird, Great Praise 4/2*

Cindy Tuttle: currently has three books available on Amazon: *Joining the Dance of Life*, *Prayers and Stories for the Soul*, *Cathy's Secret*. She writes and sings Christian music and has worked with people with mental illness for over 20 years. She is a full time caregiver for her mother who is 100 years old: "The best ministry I could have". Contact: cindytuttle08@comct.net *Night Prayer 11/30*

Jewell Utt: is the Director of a local food pantry and Women's ministry leader at her church. Her desire is to encourage women through writing, speaking and music. Married 34 years, she has three grown sons. jewellutt@yahoo.com www.jewellutt.com *My Autumn Cat 10/15, Harvest Gifts,10/20*

Elizabeth M. VanHook: photographs butterflies and flowers when not busy at church or doing historical research about her aunt's family and connections. *Autumn Changes 10/1*

Jo Ann Walczak: is from PA. A middle and high school teacher of English and journalism for over thirty years, in her retirement Jo Ann has turned to blogging, free lance writing, and editing. She has had a ministry to China since 2000, has taught spoken English in a public high school in China for a year, and she has returned to China six times to work in an orphanage. She broadcasts live on Blog Talk Radio into China every morning at 7:00 am. with "The Voice of Hope," and it is translated into Mandarin. She has enjoyed leading women's Bible studies in her church, Parker Hill Community, since 2003. . www.joannjoneswalczak.blogspot.com. *Loong Love 2/8*

Judy Webb: is the Director of Small Groups at her church and when not working is writing. She has been contributing to a blog, Daily Bible Blast for about 4 years. Judy lives in Hilliard, Ohio, is a widow, a mother and a grandmother. She would love to hear from anyone who wants to connect with me. judithannie.webb@gmail.com *Value of Friends 8/3*

Carol Weeks: Carol and her husband David have been married for 43 years and have 2 children and 4 grandchildren. Since retiring from the Marshall County Alabama Circuit Clerk's Office as a Court Specialist, she has started a speaking and writing career with her Speaking Hope Ministry at www.speakinghopeministry.blogspot.com. *Back and Forth Prayer Plan 5/28*

Judith White: is from McMurray, PA. Loves to teach and the Bible is her favorite subject. Author of *And I Heard God Whisper, Walk with Me and Being Led Beside Still Waters*. She is a speaker for women's retreats, and teaches an online Bible study at www.the soundingboardteaching ministries.com Contact redpony97@comcast.net, *When Sorrow is All We Feel 5/13Order My Day, Lord 12/30*

Martin Wiles: is a "preacher's kid," author and minister who understands the struggles believers face in their Christian journey. He can be followed on his blog, Love Lines From God (www.lovelinesfromgod.com). Dr. Wiles has authored *Morning By Morning, Morning Serenity, Grace Greater Than Sin, Authentic Christianity and Grits & Grace & God.* He is a regular contributor to Christian Devotions, PCC Web Daily, the Eagle Record, Common Ground Herald and the WOW blog. He and his wife Michelle currently reside in Greenwood, South Carolina. mandmwiles@gmail.com. *Living with Purpose 1/5*

Stacy Williams: lives in Central Ohio. She loves Jesus, traveling, the ocean, essential oils, seeing God answer prayer and encouraging others! She has a Bachelor's degree is sociology and a Master's degree in journalism and communications. She currently works as a writer and health coach specializing in natural healing options. Contact: www.findingpurposeinthepain.com *Trapped? 2/23*

Leslie Winey: lives in Indiana, works for a newspaper full time and writes in her spare time. She desires to present truth and glorify God through her writing. She is a wife, mother and proud grandmother of five and counting. Leslie enjoys worshipping and being active at her church, reading and taking walks. Contact: leslie.winey@gmail.com *First Things First 6/6*

Bronwyn Worthington: is a freelance writer living in Spokane Washington where she resides with her husband and children. Contact: bronwor@gmail.com. *Cry Out to God 7/9*

David Young: Pastor and writer for more than 40 years. Published articles, stories, poems, devotionals and plays in various periodicals. Has three books in print, a novel, *In the Wilderness* (Createspace 2013), a best seller for a time on Amazon, and two non-fiction books, *Joy* (Createspace 2012) also an Amazon best seller, and *In the Spirit,* (Createspace 2012); http://daveswatch.com/ Lives in the Pacific Northwest with his wife. bdavidyoung@gmail.com *Tremble 11/1*

Veronica Young: veonicianspires@yahoo.com *Serving Boldly 1/3*

Other books and tools from SON-RISE to make
"HIS SON RISE IN EVERY HEART"

From the Civil War by Florence W. Biros

Dog Jack - best seller	9.95
Christopher Fox - Confederate story	9.95
Love and Loyalty	
- Traits that Made Lincoln Great	14.95
Dog Jack Feature Film DVD	9.95

ALSO

Tangled Truths	9.95
-Magical mystery novel by Gloria Clover	
Singing Cowboy	7.95
- fun, intrigue novel by Karen Martin	
Penned from the Heart	9.95
- some copies of past issues available	

First Book $3.00 shipping and handling
    FREE postage on purchase of
    more than one item.

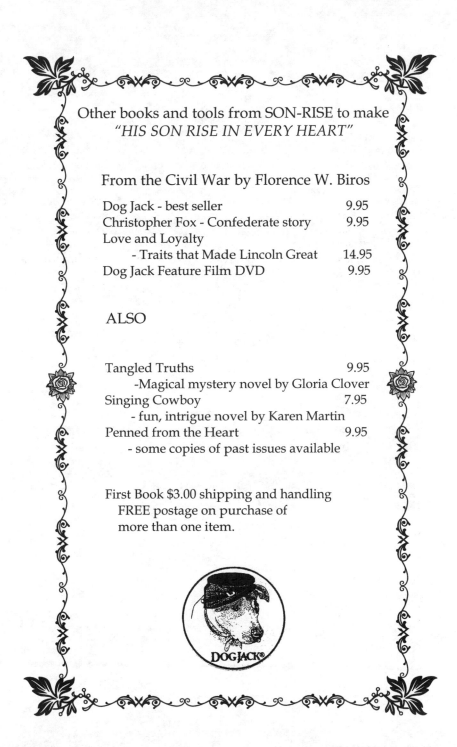

DOG JACK®

"Sin's Deception"

Pull back the curtain and what do you see. The maggot and the worm,
That eats all you dignity.

It rings and it worms, it tapes and it hooks, in every cranny and every nook.

Like the skin of an apple, that seems to shine. But, underneath the surface, the worm does dine.

An illusion and attraction, that draws you in. But, to bite this fruit, brings death in the end.

It can poison your system and shut your life down. It can destroy relationships and even put you in the ground.

This thing that I speak of, so alluring and vaunting, is the short season of sin, that leaves you wanting.

Duane Allen Short

*Don't be deceived: Sin can destroy your life! You may not think so, when you're being tempted by its pleasures. But, the end result may leave you regretting!

"Myself To Blame"

I am the master of my life. To decide is mine, whether wrong or right.

I'm given a choice in every situation, the master of each path, of each destination.

Choose wisely, choose wisely, wisdom cries, don't choose wrong! Because, the consequences of poor choosing, can last so long.

Now, I find myself sitting, in one heck of a mess! A life turned upside down, and full of stress.

I may blame it on the devil, and I may even curse at God. But, most likely it's because of the path I trod.

When I take a look in the mirror, there, I realize and see. All along I am to blame, my own worst enemy.

Duane Allen Short

"Clean Heart"

Be a man of the heart, and not of the flesh. Though the man of the flesh enjoys pleasure much more, the man of the heart is best.

To have a pure heart and express love, genuine. Is of more value than swift pleasure, that rots on the vine.

God says some of us are weaker vessels, and that we should never take advantage of such. This makes a man worth his "metal", yet inside, a heart with a pure and Christ-like touch.

To be strong in the midst of temptation, is certainly a hard thing to do. But, if you succeed and do overcome, it will certainly make you a better you.

It's so easy to fall in line with the weaker crowd, and not do the right thing. So easy to follow suit with a selfish heart, not caring about the trouble it may bring.

However pleasurable it can be, to allow our flesh to do what it wants to do. Please, let me tell you this: Unwise and hasty choices, sometimes have consequences that can break me and you.

Duane Allen Short

FOREVER
USA

Bank Swallow

Duane A. Short #A-525-858
C.C.I. / Death Row
P.O. Box 5500
Chillicothe, OH 45601

Florence W. Biros
51 Greenfield Rd.
New Wilmington, PA 16142

16142221551

Message from the Publisher…

For those of you who are computer buffs, you might understand the latest problem. When Jim Jackson's files of *Penned from the Heart* were translated they didn't become the same number of pages He figured 240, Faith Printing decided it would be best at 256. That left 5 blank pages (web presses do everything in increments of 16).

But the Lord was making provisions. Several men from Death Row have been faithful submitters for years, The day the bluelines were delivered we received three submissions from Duane Short that were straight from his heart, which filled three pages. We've also included his prison address because he certainly would enjoy hearing from you.

My other major concern is the "One Nation Under God". We'd like to think it is indivisible. We fought a tragic Civil War that nearly made us into two nations. That was 150 years ago, yet more and more divisions are springing up.

When I wrote Abe Lincoln's life story it became more and more evident to me that our freedom and liberty had been in such jeopardy then. It still is today.

We need to thank the Lord for our great nation and pray the Great Emancipator's own words, "That the nation shall have a new birth of freedom, and that the government of the people, by the people and for the people shall not perish from the earth."

The 16th President of the United States also declared, "The world will little note nor long remember what we say here." He was wrong! In the fifth grade we were required to memorize the Gettysburg Address.

A copy of "Lincoln Memorial Album of Immortalities" published in 1890 caused me to write Lincoln's "Love and Loyalty – the Traits that Made Lincoln Great" after I had written about the 102nd PA mascot, Dog Jack, with the dream of seeing him on the silver screen. Forty-four years that had been my vision. It finally came to fruition five years ago when the Premier of Dog Jack took place at the Soldiers and Sailors Home in Pittsburgh.

Have a dream of your own? Don't despair.-----Persevere!

The Lord's Blessings!
Florence

P.S. One of the most unusual books you'll ever read is by my musical friend – Judy Sherwood. She composed the music and wrote the words to all the songs in her book with the wild title – "Onions on Your Ice Cream." Next she wrote a story about how each song came about. If you're ecstatic about Jesus and music, you'll be thrilled to read the book and listen to the 2 CD's included. Great gift package for anyone. "Onions on Your Ice Cream & 2 CDs are only $20 post paid. Toll Free 1-800-358-0777.